BLOOD RELATION

BLOOD RELATION

ERIC KONIGSBERG

HarperCollins*Publishers*

HarperCollins books may be purchased for educational, business, or sales pro-motional use. For information, please write: Special Markets Department, HarperCollins Publishers, 10 East 53rd Street, New York, NY 10022.

A portion of this book was previously published, in somewhat different form, in *The New Yorker*.

FIRST EDITION

Designed by Elliott Beard

Illustrations: Page 1, Harold Konigsberg (*far right*), age twenty, at a family wed-ding, 1948 (*courtesy of Mrs. Leo Konigsberg*); page 89, Konigsberg restrained by Jersey City Police officers, 1958 (*courtesy of the* Jersey Journal); page 163, Konigsberg in court in Ulster County, New York, 1978 (© *Alan Carey/The Image Works*); page 223, Konigsberg (*on right*) at the U.S. Medical Center for Prisoners in Springfield, Missouri, 1971 (© *Art Shay/Getty Images*).

Printed on acid-free paper

Library of Congress Cataloging-in-Publication Data is available upon request.

ISBN-10: 0-06-009904-6
ISBN-13: 978-0-06-009904-6

05 06 07 08 09 ❖/RRD 10 9 8 7 6 5 4 3 2 1

For Ruth, my everything,
and for Alec, our everything

Contents

Part I

Family

ONE

Be Worthy of Your Heritage

THIS IS HOW MY FAMILY made its money. In May 1955, my grand-father Leo Konigsberg left the wholesale food business his uncle had started and struck out on his own, taking with him one delivery route, one driver, and two trucks. He added an afternoon route and drove it himself, dropping in on high-volume grocery stores and restaurants to see if anyone was running low and needed something on the spot. That was what Leo liked most about being a butter-and-egg man, getting out and seeing customers.

At first, Leo ran the business out of his home, in Bayonne, New Jersey. He made do that summer by storing nonperishables—pickles, mayonnaise, and shortening—in his garage. Perishables he had delivered to his house, and in the evenings he stored them on his trucks with blocks of ice, or ran them over to Jersey City, where he rented two walk-in coolers. In time, Leo was able to pay his father rent on a garage that he could convert into a warehouse and an office. As he frequently

3

reminded his children, the only free thing he ever accepted from his relatives was parking space in the driveway.

He built a successful outfit, and if you drove through Hudson County in the sixties or seventies, you probably saw the red trucks with their cream-colored cursive lettering: "Leo L. Konigsberg Foods. Bringing Fresh Hotel Bar Butter to the Stores." Leo was a big distributor for Hotel Bar, and in exchange for the mobile advertising the company had painted his trucks. He customized three of them with the names of his wife and daughters, which were stenciled above the grille: "Frieda," "Shelley," and "Barrie."

Leo's day began at four-thirty in the morning and usually went until ten at night, when he climbed the linoleum staircase to his family's second-floor apartment, sat down to a steak my grandmother had broiled for him, and fell asleep at the kitchen table. He made his first delivery by 7 A.M., then had eggs and bacon (he wasn't kosher outside the house) at one of the diners on his route. It was just a few blocks from one stop to the next, and he could make as many as four in an hour, thirty or forty a day. At its peak, his business had more than a hundred customers.

My grandfather was tall and, from the time of his marriage, in 1938, heavyset. On most workdays, he wore a sweatshirt over a short-sleeved dress shirt, and gray chinos with pockets he had reinforced at the tailor's because he always carried a lot of cash to make change. He was sweet mannered, but too preoccupied with the task of supporting a wife and children for anybody to describe him as happy. He was suspicious by nature. He wouldn't let employees load cargo unless he was watching. He smoked El Producto cigars because they were short enough that he could finish one in the time it took his men to fill up a truck.

Leo was fanatical about his reputation. For years, the sales reps from Kraft continued to thank him for the time he'd saved them $30,000 by alerting them to a misplaced decimal point on his bill. He once reprimanded an employee for not applying the bulk discount to a small independent grocer's order for a single ham. He figured that if a merchant was buying only one ham at a time he could use a break. "Tell him it was our mistake," he told his salesman, and sent him back with a refund. Another time, passing through customs on the way home from a family vacation in Canada, he declared a one-dollar doll he'd bought for one of his daughters.

One night in 1958, Leo returned from his delivery route and was met in his office by three men; two of them had stockings over their heads and one shoved a crowbar into his ribs. They made him open his safe, which had more than two thousand dollars inside, then bound his arms and legs with heavy rope. The police who arrived on the scene afterward gave Leo a hard time, "as though he was the one who'd done something wrong," my grandmother recalls. Leo had never once stayed home from work, but he spent the next day in bed, sick to his stomach. What upset him most was the headline in the *Bayonne Times:* "KONIGS-BERG'S BROTHER VICTIM OF SAFE ROBBERY."

Leo was and would forever be known as the brother of a criminal. Although the United States Department of Justice struggled to ascertain a precise count, internal memos allege that Leo's baby brother, Harold (Kayo) Konigsberg, committed at least ten homicides in the service of organized crime, and perhaps as many as twenty. Others who knew Harold, including two of his lawyers, put the total even higher.

Although as a Jew Harold was ineligible to be made by the Mafia, his independent-contractor status gave him latitude and autonomy. Unlike a typical hit man, who answers to a hierarchy of bosses, Harold was freelance, and would work for whatever family hired him—even simultaneously for more than one if he felt like it.

People who came into contact with Harold—prosecutors, detectives, defense lawyers, underworld associates—reach for superlatives: "toughest Jew" (this, a full generation after the Jews had got out of the business or, at least, like Meyer Lansky, limited their activities to the white-collar end) and "smartest hit man." The Justice Department considered him the king of all loan sharks. Conducting business out of a half dozen offices in Manhattan and New Jersey, he claimed to have a million dollars on the street at any given time. Although he'd quit school at sixteen, at which point he still hadn't completed eighth grade, he claimed to have taught himself to read as an adult, and he served as his own lawyer in two major trials. Later, he wrote many of his own appeals, and even managed to get a murder conviction against himself overturned.

"For years, police and federal agents considered the hulking Kayo the most dangerous uncaged criminal on the East Coast," *Life* magazine reported in August 1968. The article stated that Harold shot some of his victims but "throttled others with his bare hands." A federal official described him as "an animal on a leash" for the Mafia, and added, "All they had to do was unsnap the leash and he'd kill for the fun of it." An accompanying photograph showed three officers clutching at Harold's jacket, fighting to hold his head still for a booking. In the picture, he appears to weigh 250. He has wavy, dark blond hair and a face like a veal cutlet. He looks at peace.

The life of my granduncle is something my family went to considerable lengths to ignore and at times conceal. The first I heard of him was in 1985, when, for my boarding-school newspaper, I was interviewing a buildings-and-grounds worker who had once been a cop on the Mob beat in New York. "Does the name Kayo Konigsberg mean anything to you?" he asked me. "He was a legendary knock-around guy, a hit man. He came from Bayonne, New Jersey."

I told the groundskeeper that I was from Omaha, Nebraska, but that my father had grown up in Bayonne. The groundskeeper had a lazy eye and thick glasses, and in the corners of his mouth I saw a smile.

"Go figure," he said.

I didn't think to be embarrassed. I wasn't sure what I felt, but when I tried bragging about my discovery—if that's what it was—to my classmates, this received blank stares. Then I felt clumsy and foolish for expecting that anybody would be impressed. I was enough of a fish out of water as it was, far from home and extremely self-conscious. For a long time, I didn't mention the matter again.

Ten years later, I was working on a magazine story about a Mob murder when a former detective asked if I was related to "the famous Konigsberg." By then I'd forgotten about Kayo, and assumed he meant Woody Allen (who, though his real name is Allen Konigsberg, is no relation).

I telephoned my father. "That's my Uncle Heshy," he said. "Please tell me you said you weren't related. Why would you want your name—our family name—attached to someone like that?" He told me to drop the assignment and to never write about the Mafia. So I dropped the assignment. I was always close to my parents and had few qualms about heeding direction from them. Their guidance had served me well.

Still, I was surprised by my father's reaction. I had always considered us to be as generic as midwestern Jews come, and this was the only time I'd heard him use a grand-sounding expression like "our family name." When my younger brother, Beau, had gone off to boarding school himself, we all joked about the presumptuousness of the school motto, Be Worthy of Your Heritage. I used to close letters to him with the line. It seemed to me that you could take it a couple of different ways.

I felt a detached thrill to know that I had a notorious criminal in my family, to know we had a secret at all. But I didn't trust others to see it that way, and I did not tell most of my friends. For a time, my feelings alternated between perverse pride and something not quite its opposite.

One night in 1997, I received a voice mail:

Well, I'm not gonna give you a message. And I'll tell you what I'm gonna do. Tomorrow's another day. If you're home between 8 and 8:30, you'll get a surprise. I'll call you, we'll talk, we'll have a nice conversation, and you'll have something to talk to your father and your brother about. And I'm telling you it's a very, very interesting conversation, Mr. Konigsberg. That's your name, ain't it? . . . All right, kid. Take care and God bless.

I had a suspicion that it was Harold's voice—the accent came from some far point on the Kramden Shore—so I played the message for my father. "It's him, all right," he said. My granduncle had evidently seen my byline in a magazine and learned that he had a writer for a nephew. He was calling from Auburn Correctional Facility, in central New York State, where he is serving a life sentence for murder.

When he reached me a couple of nights later, he said that he wanted me to come and visit. I was transfixed and made an effort to keep him on the line, bringing up Grandpa Leo's name.

"Let me tell you something," Harold said. "Your grandfather was one of the hardest-working guys you knew in your life."

He asked if I was familiar with Leo's prized collection of Liberty nickels. I was. Stories of Leo's thrift and determination invariably featured those nickels, first issued by the U.S. Mint in 1883 and discontinued in 1912. He began saving them as a young boy and kept adding to the jar long after he'd gained financial stability. The nickels went wherever Leo did; they were a part of him.

"I was robbing those nickels from Leo since I'm ten years old," my granduncle said. "I kept them in a sock."

•   •   •

The existence of my granduncle was all the more intriguing because my parents seemed to have made a point of separating themselves from their ancestries. This had come about as an act of naturally occurring mitosis, as if their lives had begun only the day they got married, in 1966. They had fallen in love at a wedding on Long Island, where they spent the evening trading dares to run off to Puerto Rico together for the remainder of the weekend. Thus was the theme of lighting out for new territory imprinted on us from the start. My favorite picture of them was taken just after their own wedding. My mother, her hair in a bouffant, wears pearl earrings and a bridal dress she'd bought at Lord & Taylor on her day off from work (on the pink-collar pages at *Look* magazine) without using up the entirety of a $150 gift certificate. My father is in a white dinner jacket and bears a resemblance to Dustin Hoffman in *The Graduate*, sheepish and insouciant. He holds his bride aloft in the classic over-the-threshold pose. She is winking.

We left New York for Omaha in the summer of 1975, when my father completed his urology residency and went into private practice. It was the four of us in our Estate Wagon—Dad, Mother, Beau, and me—plus the spastic standard poodle we'd kept illegally in our cramped apartment for the previous year. That first winter, when I turned seven, we saw a movie about a family that quits the city to live in the wilderness. At the moment their car begins to roar up the freeway, the skyline in retreat and one of them yelling, "We're getting out of here!" my mother leaned toward me and whispered, "That's what we did."

My mother had grown up in Forest Hills, the neighborhood that inspired Saul Bellow to call Queens "the colossal dingy borough," and a place whose population she described as "people who spend their entire lives waiting for a train to take them into the city." Her father, a jack-of-all-trades who'd fled the pogroms in Russia, had wanted sons but got two daughters. Her mother had recently died of Alzheimer's. Even with her bridge-and-tunnel past safely behind her, my mother couldn't stand to overhear my brother and me watching the sitcom *Taxi*. "Boys, find something else to watch," she would call out from the study, where she and my father sat reading *Film Comment* and *Medical Economics*. "That anemic little theme song, those sad accents!"

Everyone in my father's family remained on the East Coast, and both of his sisters built their lives closely around my grandparents. One even returned to Bayonne after she was married, to raise her children in the apartment upstairs from where she grew up. The other seems to have modeled her marriage on her parents', managing to have her children in May, for instance, just as my grandmother did, because it was her own birth month.

Grandma Frieda, Leo's widow (he died in 1991), has always had a regal personality, and to remain a close presence in her life would be to forever have supporting-character status. Frieda has terrific posture, possibly the world's largest collection of sweaters with her name on them, and burnished brown tresses that bring to mind the *Peanuts* character, also named Frieda, who is constantly boasting about her naturally curly hair. My cousins on that side of the family could be so cultish in their adulation of Leo and Frieda that, around them, my brother and I felt like sticks in the mud.

Even in Omaha, where my parents were highly sociable and my mother had a sister whose marriage to a local man made us distant in-laws of nearly all the city's three thousand Jews, my parents avoided any fully realized membership in institutions larger than our house. Beau and I were raised to be different from our Omaha cousins. They were devout and rooted in the community—to which they were expected to return as adults. Their upbringing followed a well-worn path: Sweetheart dances held by their American Zionist Association lodge, the racially mixed and high-scoring Central High School, a summer on kibbutz, to the Big Ten for college.

And though Omaha's Jewish bourgeoisie formed the core of their social set, my parents resisted joining its twin outposts, Highland Country Club and the Reform Temple Israel. ("*Goyische* Jews," my father said of them. "The kind of Jews who go into their father's business and get sports cars the day they turn sixteen. My boys aren't like that. You're going to struggle a bit.") They opted instead for my aunt's Conservative synagogue, though we rarely attended ("so uptight, so old-fashioned"), and my brother and I were allowed to skip Hebrew school so often that our uncle, the executive director of the shul, had to pull rank to keep the rabbi from canceling our bar mitzvahs. Contradictions were everywhere in the choices my parents made for us. Before Beau and I were sent back east for boarding school, they transferred us from public school ("not challenging enough") to a mediocre country-day with Episcopal leanings way across town, then fought with the headmaster over prayer in school.

My brother and I were born a year apart, and when we were young, we did everything together. Ours was a privileged Nebraskan childhood. We learned to ride English style at Ponca Hills and Western style at Bortell's horse camp; to fish at Trouthaven, a pond so heavily stocked that we sought out bait that *wouldn't* catch a fish; to ski at Crescent Hills, the low-grade slopes in Iowa; to ice-skate at Ak-Sar-Ben rink (spell it backwards), and to drive in the rink's parking lot. We played eight-man tackle football (because the schools in our conference were so small) against teams from the Indian reservations. We played Husker-Raider soccer. We were coerced by our mother to model shetland sweaters from Krug's Men and Boys in the Clarkson Hospital Style Show. We saw the Replacements play at the Peony Park ballroom, where, several years later, against our will, we were escorts at the Omaha Symphony Debutante Ball.

The happiest days of my youth involved tennis. By the time Beau and I were eleven and twelve, we were playing every day on the court in our backyard and traveling throughout the summers on the Missouri Valley tournament circuit. Tennis parents—sometimes our mother, usually somebody else's—drove us from one Holiday Inn to another, with stops home for laundry, and if either of us got deep enough into a draw to make it worth our father's time, he would rejigger his O.R. schedule for a day and hurry out to Wichita or Des Moines or Lincoln to watch us play. At best, we were moderately successful. Not enough fire in our bellies, our coach said. "Sometimes you just have to say the other boy needed it more," my mother would say when one of us got beaten.

That Beau and I came first in the family was not lost on us. Once, on the way to Kansas City, we stopped in St. Joseph, Missouri, where Dad bought Mother a mink coat at Einbender's. She had the furrier stitch the words "For Eric" and "For Beau" into the lining. It did not occur to me until many years later, when I mentioned it in a toast at my own wedding and everybody laughed, that this was a strange thing for a mother to do.

I have always taken for granted that I come from a family of honest and principled people. My father is a surgeon. He serves on staff at a half-dozen hospitals in town and on the faculties of two university medical schools. He often doesn't charge patients who can't pay their bills. My mother helped start a charitable organization dedicated to the advancement of fetal- and stem-cell research. My brother and his wife are both doctors. A needlepoint sampler that has hung in my parents' bathroom for thirty years reads:

LET ME LIVE IN A HOUSE
BY THE SIDE OF THE ROAD
AND BE A FRIEND TO MAN

•   •   •

Heshy was Harold's Yiddish name. When I took it upon myself to find out more about him, I learned that he'd got the nickname Kayo—as in K.O., for knockout—from a stint as a semipro boxer in the Hudson County smokers' leagues. The bouts lasted six rounds and were held on the old stage at Assumption Church hall, on Twenty-third Street in Bayonne, or at the Elks' Club. He was still a teenager, and his style was undisciplined, all potatoes and no meat. "He was a big slugger, but he couldn't really box unless he got in the first punch," Anthony Cortellessa, a childhood contemporary who saw him fight, recalled. Otherwise, Harold stood still in the center of the ring, thumbing his nose and spitting on his gloves, daring his opponent to come at him. "The way he got to be Kayo was, after he lost, he would wait for his opponent in the alley and beat the shit out of him," said Raymond A. Brown, one of his lawyers, who grew up in the area and still practices in Newark. Harold was also known as Boom Boom, the Bayonne Bomber, and Hershey—the last of these a Gentile's corruption of Heshy. The name stuck, and he took to passing out Hershey bars when he introduced himself.

By the time he was thirty, in 1958, he had become his own franchise—"KAYO, CRIME AFFILIATED," as the *Newark Evening News* put it in a headline. That was the year he became a family man. He married an Italian woman and they quickly had two daughters, both of whom have stayed in contact with him and speak to him on the telephone every week.

Kayo Konigsberg was the model for two fictional characters. He appeared in 1973 as Morris (Cagney) Cohn in "Bar Tales," a short story that Sidney Zion published in *The Antioch Review*, and in 1979 as Albert (King Kong) Karpstein, the antagonist of *Made in America*, a novel by Peter Maas. Both portrayals give us a Jewish gangster out of Jersey, a hit man of the first tier and a loan shark of last resort. Karpstein's humanizing vice is a Milky Way habit, and a hoodlum in his employ calls him Milky. "Kayo was too good a character not to make use of," Maas told me.

Maas pointed out that the part of the book in which Karpstein is introduced had been excerpted in *New York* magazine, under the headline "PORTRAIT OF A LOAN SHARK." I happened to be working as a writer for *New York* at the time, some twenty-five years after the story's publication, so I went to the stacks and dug out the issue. An artist's rendition of King Kong Karpstein, trunk-necked and bursting from his sports jacket, glared at me from the cover. When a coworker saw the old magazine sitting on my desk and asked why I was interested in it, I felt exposed, and told him I wasn't sure.

Cagney Cohn, Sidney Zion's version of Harold, is "a guy whose very existence could turn you into an atheist, since if there is a God then why is there a Cagney Cohn." Even so, the narrator declares at the outset that while Ben Hecht loved Jews without reason, "I love Jewish outlaws without reason." The narrator, a prosecutor, tells the tale of a friend whose gambling debt has gotten so delinquent that Cagney Cohn is dispatched by the Mob to kill him. All is resolved when the prosecutor takes ethical leave from his government badge and arranges a meeting with Cagney Cohn's lawyer, who, as a personal favor, persuades Cag to forgo the contract. The story was based on real-life events. Zion, who covered Harold's criminal doings as a reporter for the *Times,* did in fact enlist Ray Brown's interference when his cousin, a gambler, found himself in financial debt to Harold and fearing for his life.

"There's something about Harold I just fucking love," Zion reminisced not long ago at the Yale Club, where he introduced me to his friends as "Kayo's nephew." "He says '*Olev ha sholem*' every time he talks about one of the guys he killed. He never thought he was doing wrong. And he liked killing people. He was a very bad boy, by the way." Zion, who, even in old age and J. Press tweeds, comports himself as a Nathan Detroit of the newsroom, squinted at me appraisingly. "He could scare the hell out of someone just by looking at him. I don't think you could do that."

It wasn't unusual to find myself pressured to share people's affection for Harold, as if he were some kind of pet monster, his exploits leavened into black comedy. "Once you're involved with Harold, you get to know a lot of *Haroldkeit,*" Ivan Fisher, another of his lawyers, said. "You know, like *Yiddishkeit?* This was a guy who could, on command, froth at the mouth. He was my first true sociopath, and brilliant, brilliant, brilliant. But he could be just adorable.

"He'd remember any detail about you—where you'd gone to school, how you met your wife, where you shopped," Fisher went on. "He was cherubic, almost like a precocious child who wants your approval. You wanted to tell him, 'Good for you! You make me so proud!' I had a young woman who worked for me, and Harold saw it as his duty to take a sort of avuncular interest in her, calling her and her husband at home to try to help them work out their marital problems. He'd get them both on the phone separately—'Now, Herman, apologize to Barbara.'"

Anybody who spent time around Harold marveled at how he could be at once extremely brutal and extremely seductive. "I would not want to underestimate the breadth of his intelligence, but connecting with someone's psychic pressure points and finding a person's insecurities, that was his great genius," Fisher said. "He could break down people who had complete control over him—dispensing deputy marshals to get him fried chicken and orange juice—'Didn't I tell you I only drink Tropicana?' 'I'm sorry, Harold.' And, by God, they would go back and do it." Fisher, who was very young when he first defended Harold in court, said that Harold instantly divined his hopes of making a name for himself with one extraordinarily chthonic client. "He came to me as a legend, a defendant whom only a great lawyer could get acquitted, and he knew how much was riding for me on his case. I tell you, he could make his way into your sinews."

He had, according to myth, survived seventeen gun battles. He could run his thumb along a roll of twenties and tell if a bill was missing. He always ordered two steaks at once. Collecting on a loan in Newark, he ripped a metal leg off a bar stool and beat the daylights out of the half-dozen thugs in the club. When two detectives who arrived on the scene tried to break one of the legs off, they found that, even together, they couldn't so much as bend it.

"Hershey was my favorite client ever," Ray Brown said. "He made Frank Sinatra sing for my wife at a club of his." In defending Harold, Brown lost only once, a federal hijacking case in 1963. Many nights during that trial, the government later discovered, Harold had been out late shaking down his debtors; during the day, he nodded off in the courtroom. Brown, a star orator, played the room like a Pentecostal. "I work up to my summation," he recalled. "I say the case is so unjust I'm amazed that eagle on top of the flagpole in the courtroom hasn't screamed in protest. Right at my magnificent pause, Harold farted. The whole place turned, and there he was, off to sleep, wiping his mouth with his hand."

No less an arbiter of rogue decency than Murray Kempton was captivated, at least initially; he attended one of Harold's trials and wrote three columns for the *New York Post* about the fits he was giving the government. "The image of Harold (Kayo) Konigsberg has sat intactly enormous in the mind through years while the legends of Robert McNamara and Adam Clayton Powell have withered away," Kempton wrote in March 1967. He warned, however, "There are few worse mistakes than the close-up inspection of one's heroes."

•   •   •

Just after I began to get phone calls from Harold, my father and his two sisters, in a rare all-sibling effort, organized a trip to Las Vegas to celebrate my grandmother's eightieth birthday. Grandma Frieda's two favorite things in the world are birthdays and casinos. We stayed at the Treasure Island, because she'd heard reports of good slot payouts from the ladies on her weekly bus to Atlantic City.

Each of us in my immediate family fell into our traditional roles within the context of the larger clan. My father went out of his way to appear a good sport, picking up checks for meals and pretending not to be embarrassed when his brother-in-law had singing waiters bring a birthday cake to our table on three consecutive nights. My mother smiled her way through the weekend, intent on serving as my father's support system but issuing sarcastic asides whenever my grandmother led the way to the gambling pit. ("Come on, Lady Luck, baby needs a new pair of shoes!") My brother taught all the cousins how to play craps. I hovered behind a video camera, foolishly optimistic that the occasion had the makings of a documentary film.

When we were all having dinner the first night, I asked about Harold and was rebuffed by a chorus of innocuous recollections. My aunt Shelley volunteered a recurring memory of Harold as a young man, who would still be in bed whenever she and my father visited their grandparents on Sunday afternoons. "One time, your father was talking loudly and woke him up," she told me. "Heshy threw a shoe at him and went back to sleep." My father, of course, remembered no such incident.

"When Heshy was little and Grandpa and I were first married, he used to come over and I'd make him tomato sandwiches," my grandmother said. "He ate so fast the butter ran down his wrists and he stopped to lick it up." She remembered passing him on the street one day when he was about eight years old, playing hooky. "Don't tell my parents you saw me," he'd told her. She described Harold as "a *goniff*"—a crook—and likened him to a distant in-law of ours who'd once been convicted of cheating on his taxes.

I waited until after she'd blown out the candles on her cake before I brought up Heshy's name again. Everybody groaned. "Oh, you're back with this business," Grandma Frieda said. "There's no story there. Don't be impressed by him. He thinks he's some kind of big shot, but he's really just . . ."—she waited for the right word to come, but it didn't— ". . . *a big shit*!"

"You won't learn anything about your family from him," Aunt Shelley said. "What does he have to do with us?"

Frieda threw a beseeching look at my father. He had recently, and halfheartedly, accepted the fact that I intended to learn what I could about his uncle. This was not because he agreed that my simple curiosity warranted the exploration of a history that had been purposefully forgotten, but because he didn't want to stand in my way. "I'm not the sort of father who tells his son what to do," he'd said. "You're a big boy." I had told an editor at *The New Yorker* about my granduncle and had been assigned to write about him. The assignment actually made my father more cooperative. It was as if my quest, even if it took place in the public domain of a magazine, was justified now that it fell under the banner of gainful employment.

"I just don't get it," Grandma Frieda said to my dad. "You were the one who was always most embarrassed when Heshy was in the news."

"I was?"

My aunt Barrie said to him, "I think it's strange that your children know so little about who their grandfather's brother was. All my kids grew up knowing." She remembered it as "an unavoidable fact" of her own childhood.

I told them that I wished my writing about Harold didn't upset them, but that they couldn't talk me out of it.

Frieda rooted around in her piña colada with a straw. "Eric, Heshy will never leave you alone," she said. "Just a couple of years ago, he kept trying to call me. He wanted to borrow fifty thousand dollars so he could hire a lawyer for an appeal. He said if it worked and he got out, he could pay me back. *If it worked and he got out!* Why are you interested in somebody like him? What good could possibly come of it?"

My grandmother stiffened in her baronial chair. Across the table, my uncle and cousins stared down at the pirate show in the hotel's courtyard, which was built to resemble the deck of a galleon. Buccaneers were storming the ship.

My mother recalled coming across Harold in the *Times* when she and my father were courting. She had mailed the article to him, up in Boston for medical school, with a note that read, "Any relation?" My father phoned her that night, told her that it was indeed, and she quickly sensed that she should change the subject.

My father said that when he was young his parents had always instructed him, "If anybody asks, you just tell them, 'Yes, that's my uncle.'" He did that his entire life, except for one time, when a patient at New York Hospital posed the question. "I just didn't want to own up," he said. That was around the time when he began to get phone calls from his long-lost uncle Heshy, who was in prison and looking for medical advice. My father told him that there was nothing he could do and stopped taking his calls.

"I didn't want my family to be stuck with him," he said.

Baby Heshy is said to have weighed an astonishing thirteen pounds at his birth, in 1927. My great-grandparents, Fannie and Mendel Konigsberg, both of whom had emigrated from eastern Galicia (which is now in Ukraine), were nearing the limits of their procreative window by the time the youngest of their five children came along. Their first, Edith (Edie), had arrived fifteen years earlier, followed by my grandpa Leo, two years after her. They had two more daughters—Beatrice (Beattie, pronounced to rhyme with Edie) and Ruthie—and endured a stillbirth before they had Harold. Fannie was forty-two years old when Harold was born; according to family lore, his conception was the fruition, at long last, of Mendel's increasingly unlikely campaign for a second son. They named him after Mendel's father, Heschel Konigsberg, for whom my dad, Harvey, was also named, following the Jewish custom of building on the initial letter of a deceased relative's name.

Edie, who died in 1999, was an angelic soul. She worked all her life at a department-store cosmetics counter. She'd matriculated at Columbia as a commuter student, but quit after one semester, when Mendel's tuition check bounced. "She was sure everybody in the place knew what had happened," Beattie said. "She couldn't bear the thought of showing up on campus."

Beattie, eccentric and poky, with permed red corkscrews that she still has touched up every Saturday evening at her hairdresser's house, has always been my favorite among the aunts. She does her grocery shopping at 11 P.M., selecting string beans one at a time, then stays up nights, fixing herself a steak and reading celebrity magazines.

Ruthie, the aunt most dear to my father, was a nurse at Bayonne Hospital and died in 2001. She was squat, blond, and doting, and a fount of obscene jokes.

My father's aunts remembered Harold as an unusually good-looking child, with "gorgeous skin, pink and rosy like a little girl's," Aunt Beattie said. He had platinum ringlets, which Fannie did not cut until he was three years old, and then saved in a canvas bag in their living room, where, because Aunt Beattie still lives downstairs and has never been able to do away with her parents' belongings, they sit today.

"It was like Samson," Aunt Ruthie recalled. "Except the minute they cut the hair, he became the Devil." Indeed, while his sisters claimed to have become inured long ago, trying to laugh Harold off as "our infamous brother," the recollections they did share suggested that everyone's reticence stemmed not merely from embarrassment, but real trauma they'd lived through. It began early. "He was always getting jammed up at school—emptying the fire extinguisher all down the hallway, picking fights over hubcaps," Ruthie said. "He was a bull. He could eat twelve hot dogs from Petridis's in a single sitting. There were always tantrums where he banged his head. He could never read, but he could bite the other children."

"He'd eat Mama's food and he didn't care if anything was left over for anybody else," Aunt Beattie said. "He'd go out of the house with one piece of chicken in one hand and another piece of chicken in the other hand. Mama was embarrassed, but she let him do it. He was the baby."

Aunt Ruthie said, "Our father would take off his belt and Heshy would hide under the furniture. You couldn't count how many strokes he would give him with that strap."

"What else was Papa supposed to do with him?" This was Beattie again. "It was obvious that this was somebody that couldn't be controlled. Have you ever seen a grown man cry? Do you know what it was like for me to see our papa cry?"

Harold was a destabilizing force, an illiterate amid a family of studious children, a malevolently wild creature in a house full of Sabbath-keepers. His oldest sister, Edie, made class valedictorian at Bayonne High—the first of three of Mendel's progeny to earn this distinction, and another was salutatorian. Harold stole the medal from her bureau drawer and hocked it at a pawn shop.

He was well into his hoodlum stage, his cousin Ruthie Greenfield said, by the time he was five years old: "His mother brought him out to Rockaway Beach once when she was visiting us. She always had bad legs; the salt air was good for that. Heshy disappeared for a little while. And then two fathers came to my mother's door looking for him and they were furious. We found him hiding in the outdoor shower. They said he'd he'd attacked another child pretty severely."

A family friend, Faye Berlin, told of the time a handyman came to paint the Konigsberg house, and, seeing him at work, Harold ran to his ladder and began to shake it vigorously. The man yelled down asking Harold to stop, because otherwise he'd fall. "I want you to fall," Harold said.

When he returned to firm ground, the painter let Mendel know what he could look forward to from his son, who couldn't have been more than seven or eight: "*Konigsberg, dortn vakst a gangster*"—there grows a gangster.

TWO

Murder at the Farmhouse

SEVERAL MONTHS after our trip to Las Vegas, I drove to the Hudson River Valley town of Kingston, New York, the seat of Ulster County, where I knew Harold had once faced murder charges. At the county records department, I asked a clerk to pull the case file. He said he needed a docket number from me, or, at least, the year of the indictment. All I knew, I told him, was the defendant's name.

The clerk wrinkled his nose. It was a Friday and the office was about to close for the weekend. "I'm on my way out of here. But just for fun, what was it?"

I told him.

"Oh-ho-ho yeah," the clerk said. "The one where they never found the body."

I followed him into the stacks and watched as he pulled the appropriate ledger from a wall of clothbound volumes. There had been more than 150 court sessions between the indictment and the final verdict, many of them sealed. He offered to put in my request to view the public record of the proceedings, which alone took up 10,000 pages.

"What's your name?"

"K-O-N-I-G-S-B-E-R-G."

"No, no, *your* name," the clerk said.

I said they were the same name. He took this in placidly.

"Not sure if I see any resemblance," he said.

Although it was only one of dozens of crimes Harold had committed, the case in Ulster County was the murder that eventually set in motion his undoing. In the winter of 1961, a power struggle within the Local 560 chapter of the International Brotherhood of Teamsters pitted a reform-minded faction called the Green Ticket against the chapter's president, Anthony (Tony Pro) Provenzano, who had been extorting money from member trucking companies, misusing dues, and issuing sweetheart contracts. Tony Pro was a charmer with a heart of stone; a political magazine wrote at the time that "his face, unless graced by a smile, can be a masterpiece of malevolence." When he began to suspect that the Green Ticket was promoting the chapter's popular secretary-treasurer, Anthony Castellito, to run against him for president in the union's 1962 election, he decided to have Castellito killed.

Tony Pro had a lot at stake. With thirteen thousand members (most of whom were in "freight," or trucking), Local 560—headquartered, appropriately enough, in Union City, New Jersey—was one of the most influential chapters of the largest labor union in the country. His official yearly income of around $100,000 made him one of the nation's highest-paid union officials, putting him up there with his mentor, Jimmy Hoffa, the Teamsters' international president. And, according to the F.B.I., he had designs to skim another $250,000 from the union treasury if reelected.

In his spare time, Tony Pro trained racing pigeons, which he housed in a vast coop on the roof of the Local 560 building. He was also a *caporegime,* a Mafia lieutenant, in the Genovese crime family. Assembling a team to carry out the murder was easy. Harold—whose shylocking operation Tony Pro had bankrolled and whose brute force, in return, had been instrumental to Tony Pro's rise to power—came first. He, in turn, brought in Salvatore (Sally Bugs) Briguglio, a Genovese member who worked for him as a loan collector. Sally Bugs was trim and wore glasses, had black hair in a crew cut, had served two hitches in the army, and was into counterfeiting.

According to F.B.I. records and agents' interviews with informants, Tony Pro offered Harold fifteen thousand dollars for the Castellito murder, plus some of Tony Pro's take from the union. Sally Bugs, for his payment, was to be employed as a business agent of Local 560—a guaranteed position on the Teamsters' gravy train.

For a hundred dollars a month, Tony Pro leased Harold a two-room office on the fourth floor of the Local 560 building, from which he could monitor Castellito's movements and daily routine. Harold waited patiently, using the office for his loan-sharking business all the while, until, one day, Tony Pro came to him with orders that he and Sally Bugs drop in on Castellito's house in New Milford, New Jersey. Castellito would be at a union delegates' meeting, Tony Pro explained, and the only person who might be home was his twenty-seven-year-old son, Anthony Jr., himself a driver affiliated with Local 560. Tony Pro outfitted Harold and Sally Bugs with two fake F.B.I. badges and said they should gain entry by introducing themselves to Castellito's son as agents. Once inside, they were to kill Anthony Jr., wait for Castellito to return home, and kill him, too.

•   •   •

Harold and Sally Bugs rode to Castellito's house one day in late spring, when there was an unseasonable layer of snow on the ground. They flashed their badges to Anthony Jr., then found themselves in the living room with a problem: the elder Castellito's wife and teenage daughter were also home. La Cosa Nostra's preoccupation with the appearance of honor forbade the murder of women and young children, and, anyway, this wasn't part of the plan.

"These two guys say they're looking for my father and they sit down," Anthony Jr. told me recently. "The fat guy"—this was Harold— "is in a chair by himself. The other guy is on the sofa right across from me. My mother's on the opposite end of the sofa, wondering what's going on. I tell her, whatever it is, Dad can handle it. The big guy wore a chocolate-brown topcoat with a fedora style of hat. It was dug in all around, not crooked, so that it leaned to the front. The small guy had a little face and he was dressed nice; he was wearing little loafers and argyle socks.

"All of a sudden, our German shepherd, named Kane, I hear it growling in the basement like a motherfucker. I say to my kid sister, 'Go downstairs and keep him quiet,' because Kane was a mean dog. So she goes downstairs, and when she does, the two guys immediately stand up. The big guy yells, 'Sally!' and he grabs the little guy by the shoulders and spins him around so that they're facing each other. Because just a second before, the little guy was standing right in front of my mother with his hand in his jacket."

According to information obtained later by actual federal agents, Harold, afraid that Sally Bugs was about to shoot Mrs. Castellito, had gotten in his way and decided to abort the mission for the time being. Harold gave Mrs. Castellito false names for the two of them and said that her husband could reach them at the F.B.I. office in Newark. "When my father got home that night, my mother told him there were a couple of F.B.I. men that came by," Anthony Castellito Jr. recalled. "He told her, 'They know where to find me.' She made him a sandwich and a cup of coffee. He put on his slippers and watched a Western on TV.

"I could tell something was funny about it. When the big guy asked if my father was home and I told him he was working, he said, 'What's his work?' I'm wondering, Now how could the F.B.I., if they're investigating him, not know where he works? Also, since when does any F.B.I. man wear argyle socks and pointed shoes? And the F.B.I. sure as hell don't put their hands in their pockets, which is what they'd done."

Soon Harold hit upon a new plan. They would ambush Castellito at his country house, in Kerhonkson, New York, about two hours upstate from Manhattan. He and Sally Bugs recruited a few more utility hitters, including another Salvatore: Big Sal Sinno, a trusted confidant of Tony Pro's who was also on good terms with Castellito. Big Sal was six feet three and broad in the beam, with a Roman nose, a pompadour, and a baritone that would have made him a good Othello. At the time, he was operating an illegal floating monte game in New York for Tony Pro. Harold gave Big Sal orders to lure Castellito to Kerhonkson, but he was not to lay a finger on him. That task remained solely with Harold and Sally Bugs, experienced hit men.

At around 9 A.M. on June 5, 1961, Castellito parked his union-issued Cadillac near the Local 560 building, ate breakfast at a diner, and was approached by Big Sal. According to court testimony and F.B.I. interviews with some of the principals, Big Sal told Castellito that Tony Pro had a friend who was on the lam from authorities. As a favor to Tony Pro, Big Sal asked, could he let the lamster hide out at his farmhouse for a few days?

Castellito agreed. It was politically wise to appear friendly toward his colleague Tony Pro, and he was sympathetic to life on the wrong side of the law. Over the years, he had raked in plenty of money by permitting illegal gambling and shylocking in his "barns," or member trucking companies. So he and Big Sal picked up the purported lamster—actually a longtime enforcer for Harold—at a house nearby.

Then, Castellito, Big Sal, and the lamster headed north on the New York State Thruway.

In photographs, Castellito's retreat in Kerhonkson suggests the wiseguy pastoral ideal—prefab, with knotty pine paneling, a summer kitchen with a poured concrete floor, and a long driveway separated from the road by a chain. "We had 185 acres, seven horses. He liked to cut the grass, bale hay, stack it up in a barn," said Anthony Jr. "My father loved that farm better than coming into Jersey City with his Cadillac."

Harold and Sally Bugs were hiding inside Castellito's house. As soon as Castellito came in through the kitchen, Sally Bugs struck him on the back of the head with a railroad-car hose that had been filled with lead. The blow threw Castellito to the floor but was not enough to knock him out, and, with his head propped against the kitchen sink, he fought back.

There wasn't much time for any of them to think about their original assignments. Big Sal joined in and tried to restrain Castellito. Harold strode to the porch and ripped a length of cord from the venetian blinds, and Sally Bugs and Big Sal drew the cord across Castellito's neck and pulled. In a minute, it was over.

The group set about disposing of the body. Castellito had wet his pants in the struggle, and there was blood all over the place. Harold found a bedsheet in the linen closet to wipe up the floor. To rid the corpse of evidence, he stripped it down, then hoisted it into the trunk of Castellito's car.

At this point, according to a confidential F.B.I. report, "the 'lamster' was very excited and started asking them why they did it and why they had not told him their plans. He was advised not to worry and that everything would be all right and he subsequently quieted down."

Harold drove the body into the woods, where another member of his crew was already digging a hole. He heard a horn honking and a voice calling out from a few hundred feet away.

"Hello?" It was one of Castellito's neighbors, a real estate agent who happened to be doing some work on an adjacent cottage. Harold zipped back to meet him. The man introduced himself and asked what Harold was doing there.

Harold replied that he was looking for gravel. Quickly, he added that he had a couple of friends with him and they were interested in buying property.

"Well, look, if you are looking for property, let me show you what I have," the neighbor said, according to subsequent testimony. "I build bungalows, and we're selling land." He spent his lunch hour showing them several houses, including his own.

As soon as they could extricate themselves, Harold and the others caravanned to Freehold Township, New Jersey, to find a makeshift burial site. The lamster's parents had recently moved into the area, and he located a dumping ground near their apartment. They dug a hole four feet deep and laid in Castellito's corpse, face up. On the way home, Harold cashed a $425 paycheck he'd found on Castellito. The next day, he and Sally Bugs cut up Castellito's car and sold the parts to a junkyard.

Harold went to Tony Pro's office a week later. By way of an alibi, Tony Pro had flown to West Palm Beach with his girlfriend on the day of the hit and married her. Now Harold flung an arm around him and kissed his cheek.

"Very good," Tony Pro said. He handed Harold an envelope.

The same week, state authorities questioned Harold and Tony Pro. They were obvious suspects because of rumors that Tony Pro saw Castellito as a threat to his leadership. Moreover, Castellito's realtor neighbor in Kerhonkson had called the state police to report his bizarre run-in with strangers on Castellito's property. After he heard a noise that sounded like someone shoveling in the wooded area, he'd taken down the license-plate number. It checked back to a trucking company in Hackensack that was known by police to be a front for Harold's rackets. The neighbor identified a police photo of Harold as one of the men and said that the other two—Sally Bugs and Big Sal—had been in shirt-sleeves, "sweating profusely." Also, police noted, "he remarked that both appeared to be Italians and looked like gangsters."

The officers who interviewed Harold minuted that he was unhelpful, the state police searched Castellito's property but found no significant clues, and the case remained unsolved.

Tony Pro was comfortably reelected president of Local 560. He promptly named Sally Bugs a business agent, then appointed his own brother, Salvatore (Sammy Pro) Provenzano, to fill Castellito's trustee position in the union, and later made another brother, Nunzio (Nunzie Pro of course) a business agent. But, instead of delivering on the payoff he'd promised Big Sal, Tony Pro cut him off from his share of their monte game. Big Sal complained. Soon he went missing and was presumed dead.

Tony Pro was embarking on a cleanup operation. He withheld Harold's piece of the union profits, too, and in December 1962, set a trap for him at the Cabana Club in North Bergen, New Jersey (one of many hotels and recreation facilities that Harold had taken over in lieu of loan payments). According to an F.B.I. report based on what several of the participants later said, Harold walked into the bar of the club and saw Sally Bugs peering out from behind a curtain and one of Tony Pro's brothers behind the bar. (Two other men whom he didn't see were lurking as well.) Instead of retreating, Harold tore through the kitchen, pulled a stove out of the wall, and barricaded the door. Tony Pro's boys tried to coax him out, begging him to talk things over, but for five hours

Harold wouldn't budge. Through a barred window, he eventually saw a salesman he knew, and persuaded him to pry the bars open with a tire iron. As Harold fled, Tony Pro's crew started firing. He was hit, but flagged down a passing motorist and paid him twenty dollars for a ride home.

One of my grandaunts told me that Harold's mother-in-law was visiting when he stamped in. "Come upstairs," he said to his wife, and when he took off his sports jacket, she saw that his shirt was soaked with blood. She brought him to a safe house, where, according to one of Harold's associates, a Mob doctor extracted four bullets and thirteen buckshot pellets from his body.

Harold vowed revenge, but bosses told him that Tony Pro could not be killed so long as Local 560 remained a cash cow. A few weeks later, though, after leaving an office on the first floor at union headquarters, Tony Pro took one step into an empty elevator shaft and fell twelve feet to the basement. "Nobody said it wasn't okay to break Tony Pro's ribs," recalled Hoyt Peavy, an F.B.I. agent, who believes that Harold pushed him. "Kayo was respectful. He was good for his word."

The Mafia's higher-ups pronounced Harold off-limits to Tony Pro as well. Blessed as Harold was with plenty of other Mob contacts, he went on with his work. He was more upset that Tony Pro had ripped him off than he was about the attempt on his life. And for years he did not have to give much thought to the body near Freehold Township.

Castellito's family hesitated to call on the police for help the morning after he didn't come home. It was conventional Teamsters wisdom that law enforcement had it in for them. Meanwhile, Castellito's secretary told Anthony Jr. that his father had an appointment in his book for four the following afternoon, so he and his mother waited through the day, until the hour came and went without Castellito showing up. When Anthony Jr. called the Local 560 headquarters to ask Tony Pro if he knew what was going on, Sammy Pro told him that Tony Pro was in Florida with his girlfriend and was not to be disturbed. He said, "I'm sure your father's fine. Maybe he's with a girlfriend, too." The newspapers reported that Tony Pro was offering a $50,000 reward for any information leading to Castellito's whereabouts.

Anthony Jr. took two weeks' leave from work. He and his wife and daughter all slept at his mother's house, "to comfort her, but also because we all wanted to be there in case Dad came walking in," he said.

About a year after the disappearance, Castellito's sisters held a memorial service in Hoboken. The priest was the only person who spoke, because the Castellitos felt they had nothing to say. Anthony Jr. would just as soon have gone to a movie. He says that most of the people who would have wanted to come were "too scared to be seen there anyway." He left the church "expressionless" and then everybody went out for a big breakfast. It upset him that the service wasn't referred to as a funeral, but as a "remembrance."

About seven years after the disappearance, Anthony Jr. brought his mother to the Bergen County courthouse, in Hackensack, to have his father legally declared dead. He told her that by then they really had no choice. "She was shaking; she was a very frail woman," Anthony Jr. said. "It was one day after work. They had us sign a form. That was it."

THREE

Uncle Harold

I MADE MY FIRST VISIT to Auburn Correctional Facility in the summer of 1998. The village of Auburn, a former mill town that went bust more than half a century ago, is a small collection of dun-colored storefronts against an otherwise handsome mid-state landscape of gorges and Finger Lakes. Auburn is the oldest operating prison in New York State, a maximum-security home to 1,785 inmates. The place resembles a gray-walled medieval fortress, built entirely of limestone, with a wooden minuteman standing watch from a crenellated tower.

Harold has been in prison since October 22, 1963, when he was put away on an extortion charge. (The murder conviction that has him imprisoned for life came much later—and almost not at all—as the extortion sentence was winding down.) The other places where he has served include Dannemora, Green Haven, Attica, Stormville, Great Meadow, the Hudson County Jail, the Somerset County Jail, Nassau County Correctional Facility, Sullivan County Correctional Facility, Sullivan

State Prison, Trenton State Prison, the Metropolitan Correctional Center in lower Manhattan, Riker's Island, the U.S. Penitentiary in Danbury, Connecticut, the U.S. Penitentiary in Atlanta, and the U.S. Medical Center for Prisoners in Springfield, Missouri.

An officer had me empty my pockets, then traced my limbs with a metal detector. Another stamped my hands with invisible ink and waved me into a dark foyer as a set of bars slid shut electronically behind me. I raised my hands toward a guard in a booth in front of me, so that an ultraviolet light could bring the daily code into view. A second set of bars slowly hummed open. The visitors' center was a large, open room with rows of small tables. I waited at the edge of the room before a cardboard backdrop of a beach scene. To my right were the window partitions and handsets used for no-contact visits, a couple of imperfect lipstick kisses on the plate glass.

I told a guard that I was meeting Harold for the first time. He smiled slightly.

"Nice guy?"

The guard raised his eyebrows but didn't answer. The guard standing beside him said, "You'll see."

A heavy steel door opened and there was Uncle Heshy, in forest-green prison garb and work boots. He was big and fat around the midsection, with bandy legs, a bloodshot nose, and hooded eyes like a rooster's. Other than that, he bore some resemblance to my late grandpa Leo—the shyly optimistic carriage and thick white hair, "a head of hair that people would pay a lot of money for nowadays," as my grandmother would say.

I stood and extended my hand, which he ignored. "What the fuck kind of way is that to greet family?" he said, and gave me a kiss on the mouth. He stepped back to regard me, then handed over a laminated card from a funeral home announcing his wife's death from cancer two months earlier. He asked after most of our living relatives by name, people he'd never met. He was showing off.

"It's a funny thing," he said. "Family don't seem to mean anything anymore." He had not, he said, received a single condolence card when his wife passed away. "After my mother died—may she rest in peace, God rest her soul—Leo and my sisters sat shivah for me. Like I was dead." He didn't think his mother would have tolerated this. "I'm probably the only Jewish person alive whose brother and sisters have disowned me."

He had me buy him four Dr Peppers and two ice-cream sandwiches. One of the ice creams got stuck in the vending machine, and a guard helped me pull it out. "What are you, a cripple?" Harold said.

My granduncle was as strong as an ox and seemed in rude health, although he claimed to suffer from emphysema, diabetes, bursitis, arthritis of the spine, rheumatism, migraines, and high blood pressure. He told me that he could have got out long ago but has repeatedly turned down offers to testify against other mobsters.

"The windup is, you think your freedom is worth your self-respect?" he said. He burped, like someone who could burp the alphabet. "The government is dishonorable. Listen, I used to be somebody. I used to have the power of life and death. You know what that means? It means the government didn't decide, we did."

"Decided what?"

He rolled his eyes, annoyed. "Oh, you couldn't believe the kinds of things we decided. This thing won't die." (This thing: the Mafia.)

A guard walked by and said, "Show me the money, Harold."

He looked around. "Where is it?" He had apparently not seen *Jerry Maguire*.

Harold slugged down one Dr Pepper after another, arranging the empty bottles in a row between us. I asked how he could drink so much soda. "I'm doing it, ain't I?" he said. He stood up. "I'm going to the turlet."

He had a slight limp but moved quickly, with a herky-jerky rhythm. I watched him emerge from the bathroom with his hair slicked back and stoop to kiss a woman in lavender sweatpants who sat in the visitors' area. ("I knew her father," he explained later. "She's visiting her brother.")

"I saw that, Harold," a guard yelled from the corner of the room; inmates aren't allowed to talk to other inmates' visitors. "One more time, I'm gonna have to call my supervisor."

Harold waved his arms in the air without turning around to look at the screw who had reprimanded him.

When he returned to our table, he pushed his chair close to mine and held his right hand up to my face. "Do you see this?" he said. His knuckles were shiny and swollen. "Here, I tell you what kind of guy your uncle is. There was a Spanish kid three days ago giving me shit. You learn certain Spanish words when you're in prison, such as *maricon* means 'fag.' So when I heard that, I knocked him out cold and started trying to kick him in the balls. The other Spanish kids held me back, but by then he was already in another world."

I asked why Harold had solicited me. "I'm thinking about taking the story of my life and fictionalizing it some," he said, spreading his hands out wide. "Then we sell it to those Weinstein brothers at Miramar." The title he had in mind was *From the Ashes of Hell to the Power of Heaven*. "It would be about an adventurer who travels the world. The ashes part involves him running up against a greater power—Robert Kennedy persecuting me." As attorney general, Kennedy had waged a highly publicized war against organized crime, distancing himself from the shadowy associations his father had formed when he built the family dynasty. "Robert Kennedy started all this shit on me," Harold said. "I knew the reasons. He felt that I was a pretty dangerous guy." The power of

Heaven would come when our hero is released from prison and reunited with his family. "And the windup is—" he paused. "The windup is a lot of fucking things."

I explained the circumstances of the magazine assignment that had brought me to him. This seemed to appeal to Harold's sense of self-importance, though it hardly won him over. He proudly claimed that in 1968, Random House, Time-Life, and M-G-M Pictures got together and offered him a large sum of money to collaborate with a writer. His face reddened and he smacked the table. "Do you think if I didn't do it for Bennett Cerf I'm gonna do it now for a cocksucker like you for free?"

I flinched. "I ain't gonna hit you," he said, suddenly calm. "You know, you got your grandfather's nose?"

But Harold did talk to me—through ten visits over three years. I have learned things I have no idea what to do with, and I have wondered whether I have a right to keep such information to myself—and whether I have a right not to. I assure myself that the fact of our shared lineage is unimportant, and that I am free to write about Harold as a journalist. But I cannot doubt that he was talking to me only because I am a blood relative. And, because I am a blood relative, much of what I have learned I wish I didn't know.

Sometimes our visits lasted all day. Other times, they just seemed to. Harold's demeanor shifted wildly and without notice. He could be furious one minute over the tiniest perceived slight, such as if he saw me asking a corrections officer to make change. "You're killing me all over again, talking with these fucking guards," he said once. "These people are the enemy."

More than once, he asked me to bring in an eight-by-ten photograph which I had shown him the first day I visited, a picture of Leo and Frieda's entire brood gathered at her eightieth birthday party. All three generations of us are in baseball caps that my dad ordered for the event. "Now, that's a complete family," Harold said one time.

He was not at all as I'd pictured him. I wasn't exactly expecting Warren Beatty as Bugsy Siegel, but perhaps a luggy, fly-off-the-handle type—Joe Pesci in *Goodfellas*? Or maybe Fredo Corleone, the brother with something to prove? Harold was nasty, brutish, and short-tempered. And he was certainly unlike any relative I'd ever met. Older relatives were people who asked if I'd found a girl yet, or whether I mostly ate out in New York or cooked for myself. I knew that he was a hit man. I knew that a prison was the setting for our encounters. Still, on some level, I'd imagined a relative who would fuss over me, tell me what a bright boy my father had been, what a saint my grandfather was.

Harold's very presence was disorienting. He looked so soft at first glance—dimple-fleshed, with bulbous and heavy features—but his eyes were almost always fixed in an expression that could only be described as intensely blank. He stared straight at me for hours on end. There was also the matter of his voice. Each time he opened his mouth, I was startled by its dissonance—"a voice like a razor," his sister Ruthie said. Grandpa Leo, by contrast, had a lilting, musical voice.

On the occasions when I happened to forget I was talking to a murderer, something always happened to quickly remind me. One day, he was telling a grisly story about how Albert Anastasia had ordered a hit on a subordinate, how the murder had been a warning shot to all of Anastasia's soldiers. I asked Harold if he was the one who committed the act.

"That's not important."

"So who did?" I said. "Why was he killed?"

Harold stared at me but didn't answer.

I thought of what Robert Stewart, a former organized-crime prosecutor in New Jersey, had said when I told him I was writing about

Harold: "Do you want to get yourself killed? I wouldn't want him reading my name saying something he doesn't like."

Harold took a chicken wing off a small plastic vending-machine tray and sucked all the meat off without pulling apart the bones.

"You know," he said, "I didn't think I'd ever enjoy these." Then he asked about my career goals. He offered that if I really hoped to succeed as a writer I had to go cover a war. "You take a guy like Edward R. Murrow," he said. "He'd have been a nothing if he never saw some fire. He was always the one I liked on the radio. He had some voice, didn't he?"

I'm not sure which Harold threw me off my hinges more, hot or cool. I came across a trial transcript in which the judge, his patience worn thin by Harold's tirades as his own lawyer, had ordered him to settle down. "Yes, sir, Your Honor," Harold replied. "When I get calm I'm dangerous."

People talked about a bivalent quality to Harold that made him so ingratiating. He was as bumbling as he was shrewd. He had a sense of humor, or, at least, a sense of absurdity, where nobody else would have. He had no sense of humor where anybody else would have. For somebody who committed such clinically antisocial acts, he could be warm and even needy. For somebody who had to know that his actions were shameful, he could be shamelessly, amusingly self-righteous. He was scary and he was disarming.

Ivan Fail, a Springfield guard with whom Harold had run-ins, recalled him alone in his cell late at night, practicing scary faces in front of a mirror. "I had no use for his value system, but I did have a grudging respect for his moxie," Fail told me. He said that Harold threatened him several times, and that when he reported it to the prison, Harold retaliated with a $175,000 defamation suit. Harold didn't dispute the threats; he merely took issue with Fail for calling him a "thug" on the record.

When the F.B.I. managed to bring him in on charges of possessing stolen goods, he challenged the agent who arrested him to a battle of push-ups (and won). In 1964, he sued a prison warden for failing to repay a loan Harold had given him while an inmate.

Once, Harold sensed that the state police might be closing in on him while he was in the process of planning a homicide. He phoned the detective captain at home and offered to speak with him "to straighten out any trouble." When they met up at the police station, Harold volunteered that not only was he involved in nothing illegal but his shylocking operation employed thirty men whom he had taken off the street and saved from a life of robbing and stealing. For this, the captain's report noted, "KONIGSBERG said that he should be given a medal by law enforcement authorities."

I found Harold cartoonishly winning at times, with his fancy words and malapropisms, which, because he had to teach them to himself, threw into relief how alone he was. He complained about the "durances viles" of a life in prison. He told me that he would never be paroled. "You know why?" he said. "It's discretional." He remembered his father's "reciditing" hairline.

It wasn't as though there was a lot of sympathy going around for Harold anymore. One night when he telephoned me, I offered condolences because Edie, his oldest sister, had passed away the week before. It turned out that nobody in the family had bothered to let him know. After I clicked off, I went to make another call but I could still hear Harold on the phone. He was talking to the man in Queens—an old lackey of his—who'd helped him reach me via a three-party call. (Harold didn't have the prison's authorization to call me himself.) "Do you believe that?" Harold said. "Not a word, nothing."

"Things happen," his friend said, trying to console him. "What you gonna do?"

"Yeah," Harold said. I realized he was blubbering.

More recently, I was at Bayonne Hospital to visit Aunt Beattie as she recovered from a minor operation. Her phone was ringing nonstop—everybody was concerned about her. When a niece who was fielding the calls informed her that Harold was on the line, Beattie's face, though she was still mildly sedated, came alive. "Absolutely not," she said. "Hang up." His sisters haven't taken his calls for forty years. "He doesn't learn," Aunt Ruthie said. "What an asshole. His entire life's been spent locked up."

The screws at Auburn liked to taunt him. One morning, Harold and I noticed a guard named Lang silently hovering above our table. We tried to ignore him for a while, but he was theatrically taking some kind of food from a paper bag and enjoying it as loudly as he could. Finally, Harold asked what was going on. "I don't know what *you're* doing, Harold," Officer Lang said, "but I'm having homemade bread my wife made, and, damn, it's good."

Another guard, Officer Cuttey, told me he'd seen Harold's older daughter in the visiting room many times. "Sometimes she brings her son up here," he said. "The kid hates him. He says, 'You're not my grandfather—you're in prison!' " He said the boy screams "Don't touch me" when Harold tries to kiss him. "Harold's just a miserable guy, always in an argument with somebody," he went on. "He brings it on himself."

Harold certainly knew how to play for my attention. I'd come to Auburn, after all, out of an interest in being his link to his family, in doing what nobody else would do. He once asked why I was the only one among six cousins who wasn't pursuing an advanced degree. We had three in law school, one getting an M.B.A. at Wharton, and one—my brother—in medical school.

"I like to do my own thing," I said.

"Seems to me you're a bit like your Uncle Harold," he said triumphantly.

Somehow, I took from this a measure of satisfaction.

FOUR

Made in New Jersey

MY GREAT-GRANDFATHER, Mendel Konigsberg, left eastern Gali-cia in 1886. At the time, the region was under the harsh rule of the Austro-Hungarian Empire. Georges Clemenceau's essay "Impressions of Galicia" describes the Jewish citizens of Mendel's day as a people "on the alert for every chance that presents itself, the soul ever ready for combat." What presented itself for 236,000 Galician Jews between 1881 and 1910 was the opportunity to flee—some to Israel, and many more to the United States.

The story in my family goes that, when he ascended the gangplank of the boat that brought him here, Mendel had sewn into the soles of his shoes seventy dollars in U.S. currency, including a twenty-dollar gold piece. Fif-teen years later, he would put that money toward the first-class passage of one Fannie Breitbart, a young Galician lady whom his wealthy American uncle had arranged for him to marry. He saved enough to bring over his brother, and they landed jobs at a trouser factory on the

Lower East Side of Manhattan, toiling every day but the Sabbath. Payment was a dollar a day, plus room and board and all the pants they could wear. He moved to Bayonne at the turn of the century, when his uncle found him a job with a contracting and demolition business.

Bayonne is an arrowhead-shaped peninsula that hangs from the base of Jersey City. To the south, across the Kill Van Kull, is Staten Island; to the northwest, across Newark Bay, is Newark; and to the east, across Upper New York Bay, is Brooklyn. Although Hudson County is cut off from the mainland of New Jersey, it's hardly an island of tranquillity, and, in fact, it is the most densely populated county in the state. In 1866, Port Johnston Coal arrived in Bayonne, erecting docks along Bergen Point. Next came Standard Oil, which laid down the longest pipeline in the country, stretching some eighteen hundred miles to Indian territory.

Bayonne became an industrial capital of New Jersey, the home at one time to 235 manufacturing plants—a "fantastic maze of tanks, lights, pipes, towers, and smoke trailing flame," in the words of one local historian. Another history of Bayonne, published in 1904, noted that nearly 85 percent of the inhabitants of the Centerville and the Constable Hook neighborhoods—where Jews were settling—were "of foreign elements," and went on, "While some are of an objectionable class, taken as a whole they are an industrious, hard-working people, and have been the means of building up a thriving business section in these localities." Bayonne's Jewish population jumped from 1,200 in 1905 to 10,000 in 1912. The greatest number of them came from what used to be known as Russian Poland and the Dnieper Valley of the Ukraine. By and large, they settled, like my great-grandparents, in the area between Sixteenth and Twenty-fifth Streets, west of Broadway.

Mendel and Fannie Konigsberg spoke Yiddish and English with their children, and Polish with each other when they didn't want to be understood. Their house was built of brick and stucco and had the same floor plan as most of the two-family houses in Bayonne: a parlor at the front of each apartment, and two bedrooms, a kitchen, and a bathroom in the rear. They rented the ground floor to another family and lived on the second story. Edie and Beattie were in one bedroom; Fannie shared a bed with Ruthie, her youngest daughter; Mendel and Leo slept on sofas in the living room; and when Harold came along he got the den.

"That sleeping arrangement is what hastened Leo and your grandmother's marriage," Harold told me once, laughing.

Mendel was short—five feet six on a good day—but rugged, with enormous workman's hands. In 1930, he poured the concrete that anchored the New Jersey side of the Bayonne Bridge, which connects the peninsula city to Staten Island. When he was old, he liked to say that he had dug three-quarters of all the cellars built in Bayonne during the first half of the century. "He didn't do construction like *construction*," Grandma Frieda says of her father-in-law. "He dug holes. He never went to school and he learned how to figure a job by square feet, God bless him."

He was aloof, abrasive, and perpetually cranky, but venerable in his small way. When my father was a little boy, he chanced upon Mendel and his dump truck on Thirty-first Street one day. "He was down to one dump truck when I knew him, because none of his kids or their husbands had joined the business," he recalled. "I was so proud to see that Grandpa had men working for him. It was like seeing a celebrity—somebody I knew, running a business."

He was also a bootlegger, and later, after the repeal of the Volstead Act, a purveyor of homemade hooch. Several relatives told me of how he had operated a "tiny" still in his attic, which produced slivovitz, a hundred-and-eighty-proof plum brandy. At the public library in Jersey City, I looked up Mendel's name in the *Jersey Journal* index and found that he'd been mentioned a few times. The first was back in 1912:

BAYONNE MAN'S GOAT IS MISSING

Another headline, from 1946, told of a police raid on his still, which turned out to have been not so tiny:

SEIZE 3,400 POUNDS OF SUGAR

AND BOOTLEGGING EQUIPMENT

OWNER OF RENTED

GARAGE ARRESTED

When I showed this to my father, it came as news to him but not a shock. "I can't say that any of us ever really knew Grandpa Mendel very well," he said, then chuckled. "I guess it's clear by now that this family tends to block things out."

But Mendel looked after his own, and prospered. It was a point of pride that he'd been able to pay cash for their house on Avenue A at Twenty-second Street. The neighborhood was predominantly Polish and Italian, hardly Bayonne's gold coast, but it provided a source of income when he rented out the ground-floor apartment. His brother, by comparison, had a small candy store and lived in a flat behind it. Mendel believed in property, both as an investment and as a method of looking after his daughters.

"Papa kept everything close," Aunt Beattie says. He bought up the land leased by a gas station on his corner, then purchased four proximate garages, one of which would later serve as Leo's coolhouse. He built a home on a lot diagonally across the way—so that he occupied three of the four corners at the intersection of Twenty-second Street and Avenue A—and gave it to Ruthie when she got married. When Beattie wed and had children, he converted the attic for them.

In my father's earliest memory of his grandparents, Mendel is in wire-frame glasses, a felt hat with a stiff brim, corded suspenders, wool pants, and high-top work shoes laced all the way up; Fannie stands over the stove, in a floral cotton housedress and a full-length chef's apron.

"She spent all day in the kitchen; her cooking was legendary," a first cousin of Harold's, Marlene Altschuler, says. "Everybody ate her chicken." Fannie wore the same shoes that Mendel did, because she was heavy and that hurt her feet. She had a bulging, compressed figure, and long gray hair fastened in a bun with sturdy, V-shaped metal hairpins. "I never saw hairpins that big," my dad says. "She only took her hair down when she went to bed. It went all the way to her waist." Fannie served dinner in the dining room, on china, and used real drinking glasses instead of jelly jars, but she never sat at the table herself. Even if she and Mendel were the only two eating, she served him in the dining room but ate her own meal later, in the kitchen.

Leo worked on the Sabbath, and, since his mother wouldn't leave the house, he made a special delivery to her every Saturday: a dozen eggs, a pint of sour cream, a pound of butter, and a "cottage cup"—eight ounces of cottage cheese. My father usually accompanied him, and she served them leftover chicken from *Shabbos* dinner the night before. She rarely went out anyway, mostly just to walk to the synagogue and to the dentist's—she had dentures that never fit right. Her dying words, it is said, were "Take care on your teeth" (prepositions also gave her trouble). When my parents were married, Fannie called my mother to offer advice. "If you're cold, you ask for another blanket," she said.

Their synagogue was named Agudas Ahim. Mendel was a frum Jew, very observant, and had been a founding member, so the Konigsbergs had their own row near the front. "It was mostly old men; there were rarely bar mitzvahs," my father says. Agudas Ahim was a small Orthodox shul that couldn't afford its own rabbi, so the cantor led services. For the High Holidays, a rabbi was imported from New York and stayed all ten days. Eventually, the rabbi became an overnight guest at Mendel and Fannie's house. Because Harold was in prison by then, they gave the rabbi his bed.

•   •   •

"Even as a child, the patient was quarrelsome, temperamental and could not get along with other children," reads a psychiatric evaluation conducted during one of Harold's first prison stays. "He has never been able to make an adjustment in school, in the community, or his home."

His childhood contemporaries remember him as a boy who was held back in school three times, so that he truly towered above his classmates. "He was a rough kid, a dead-end kid," one of them recalled. "If you wanted to look at a deck of cards with fifty-two dirty pictures on them, he was the guy to go to." Another, Hy Rappoport, remembers school recess hours spent playing penknife, "a game where everybody takes turns throwing a penknife into the dirt, to see who can get it deepest. Harold threw it right at my hand. I was bleeding bad enough that they made me go to the nurse. He told me it was by accident."

Cornelius Gallagher, a contemporary of Harold's who went on to represent Hudson County as a U.S. congressman, says that to grow up in Bayonne was to hear a million tall tales about Kayo: "The first time anybody heard of him, I think, was the story about this kid who's coming out of school, eleven years old, and walks into the DeSoto dealership on Hudson County Boulevard, and says, 'Jesus, that's a nice car. I'd like to take a ride in it.' The salesman says, 'Yeah, kid, when you grow up, maybe you can buy one.' And Konigsberg says, 'No, I mean now,' and he sticks a knife under the guy's chin. He says, 'Gimme the keys.' And the guy, obviously, acquiesces. Then the kid drives it right through the plate-glass window onto the Boulevard."

Occasionally, when he could sit still, Harold listened to baseball games on the radio. He liked Dizzy Dean and, later, his famous line, "Let the teachers teach English and I will teach baseball. There's a lot of people in the United States who say 'isn't,' and they ain't eating." Although Leo played semipro basketball at gyms all over town, Harold never went along with his family to watch, because he was either out getting into trouble or being punished for it. Grandma Frieda told me that she once saw his report card, and he had failing grades in everything, except for an A in math.

At one point, Mendel tried to steer him toward a vocation. "Papa thought maybe Heshy could go into junk collecting," Ruthie says. "He started letting him ride in his truck when he was doing house wrecking. But all Heshy wanted was easy money. He wanted a paper route—Leo sold Eskimo Pies when he was a little kid—but Papa was afraid Heshy would steal the papers and try to sell them. Papa was well known in Bayonne; that made it worse for him. He used to say, 'If I ever fixed Heshy up with a girl, her father would come after me.' That's Jewish humor."

Young Heshy was prematurely tall but overweight until adolescence. He paid little attention to his appearance or to grooming, though he was embarrassed by his acne. Truancy was a given. "I had to go to school, but I didn't have to go to school," he told me once, and shook his head with satisfaction. "The tactic was you went in at the morning and you was in. Then you're let out for lunch. So I do what I want in the afternoon. Go and play cards, go steal a little bit here and there—the candy store, little A & P stores, places they only have one or two people working in there. You see, I had nothing in common with the kids in school.

"I was always a troublemaker," Harold went on. A story of legendary grotesqueness involves him and his aunt Rosie's cat, Hitler. (Why a Jewish family—or any family other than, perhaps, a Beer Hall Putsch-era branch of the Addams family—would have a pet named Hitler is beyond me, though Harold's explanation was, "This was before the war, and Tante Rosie had a strange sense of humor.") When Harold was ten years old, he threw a rope around the cat's neck and hung it from the perch of the steam shovel that sat in the family's yard. "My defense was, 'Well, he's Hitler, ain't he?'" Harold recalled. "I got a beating for it that didn't stop. My father was a little bit of a guy, but he had hands twice my size. He could give some beating."

Long before Harold arrived, Hudson County had established itself as a thoroughly corrupt municipality. From 1917 to 1947, Bayonne was ruled by Frank ("I am the Law") Hague. Hague's title was Mayor of Jersey City, but his influence stretched beyond city, and county, limits. He once had the New York crime boss Dutch Schultz arrested for not asking his permission to pass through Newark. Which is not to say that Hague minded seeing shady characters set foot in New Jersey. His entire political machine was built from illegal gambling rackets, ballot-box stuffing, and bogus patronage jobs ("Foreman of Vacuum Cleaners"). He made city employees fork over 3 percent of their salaries on an annual occasion known as Rice Pudding Day.

The next elected mayor of Jersey City, John V. Kenny, was no better. A Superior Court investigation found that he had funneled city funds to Abner (Longy) Zwillman, a gangster based in Newark. Zwillman, who'd also had ties to the Hague administration, had bankrolled Kenny's election, by putting up $350,000 to buy votes. In return, Kenny approved a steep fare increase for a commuter rail line in which Zwillman was a part owner.

Zwillman was one of the most powerful and influential bosses in the country. During Prohibition, he and a business associate had made millions shipping whiskey into Port Newark from the Bronfman family distillery in Montreal, but his great contribution to organized crime came when he convened in Atlantic City with a group of bootleggers from around the country and drew up plans to structure everybody's rackets around a single system of regional "federations." By minimizing turf wars and competition, Zwillman's scheme turned the alcohol and gambling businesses into Mob staples and in effect gave organization to organized crime. As for the governance of the New York area, Zwillman and five others—Meyer Lansky, Bugsy Siegel, Lucky Luciano, Frank Costello, and Joe Adonis—formed a half-Jewish, half-Italian governing body that J. Edgar Hoover referred to as the Big Six and which, when the Jewish leaders ceded control to Luciano and Costello, formed the basis of the five local Mafia families that still exist today.

Zwillman was tall—hence the nickname—coolheaded, and elegant (shirt by Sulka; inquest by Senator Kefauver). He dated Jean Harlow and kept a lock of what he said was her pubic hair in his wallet to show friends. The file the F.B.I. kept on him listed his build as "athletic," and under the category of special features were noted, "heavy eyebrows, large nose." At the peak of his career, he became Harold's mentor.

One day at Auburn, Harold explained to me how the relationship, and his entry into organized crime, came about. He said that he was thirteen years old and running a crap game on a vacant cement lot one block west of his family's house when an older boy demanded that he and his friends turn over a dollar a day, as protection. The boy's father was affiliated with the Black Hand, a precursor of the Mafia. "This kid and his brothers got their own game a block away," Harold said. "Now they want in on mine." There were several inconclusive fistfights, until, one day, the boy came around and Harold pulled a gun on him. (A thirteen-year-old with a gun? "It was the *Dee-pression*," Harold explained.)

"I didn't have no common sense," he said. "I put the gun right in his eyeball. I said, 'Go ahead, move my hand.' He was begging me not to hurt him." Harold and his friends surrounded the boy and forced him to empty his pockets; he had two hundred dollars on him. "That was a big mistake. I had no idea at that time what was organized crime. I began to understand." He smiled.

Word quickly got around the neighborhood that he had messed with someone from the wrong family. In Harold's version of the story, Mendel called on Longy Zwillman to ensure his protection, escorted him to Zwillman's office himself, and willingly participated in the draft deal that followed. I have verified that Harold indeed went to work for Zwillman around this time, but while Mendel, as might have been inevitable for someone in construction—not to mention bootlegging— could certainly have had a working acquaintanceship with organized crime, it's not clear that he knew Zwillman or would have wanted a favor of this sort for his son.

Harold said that the meeting took place at the offices of Zwillman's cigarette-vending business, the Public Service Tobacco Company. It was in Hillside, New Jersey, at the edge of Newark. "He says to me, 'You're a tough guy, huh?'" Harold said. "I'm frightened to death by this guy. My father was very upset and angry. But Abe"—people close to Zwillman rarely called him Longy—"says to tell him the story in my own words. So I tell him." Harold said Zwillman looked approvingly at him—he had already reached his adult height and had begun to fill out—and put him to work at fifty dollars a week. Harold and his friends corralled all the alcohol business between Twenty-fifth Street and the Kill Van Kull. Soon, Harold was making more money than the rest of his family put together.

"We learned how to run numbers, and pretty soon I was what they called a controller," Harold said. In Mayor Hague's day, nearly every citizen of Hudson County played a lucky number, hoping it would match the last three digits of the day's total mutual handle, or the take, at a given local racetrack, a figure reported the next morning in the New York *Daily News*. Every afternoon but Sunday, a team of runners brought to Harold the day's play—all the bets, which had been placed at candy stores and newsstands around town. He sealed the play in canvas bags, which he delivered to the basement of the Bayonne Democratic Club, on Twenty-seventh and Broadway. At 8 P.M., he went back to the Democratic Club and picked up slips listing who was to be paid and how much he was to distribute to each runner; by midnight, he returned to the club with the receipts. A winner's return was six-tenths on the odds, with the other four-tenths going to the racketeers—a portion of which went to paying off the local beat cop, his captain, and the chief of police. Harold's take was 5 percent of the gross receipts for the day, minus the hundred dollars that went to pay off two local detectives.

"You know what Abe used to have me do?" Harold said. "It was 1940, '41, and the Germans had these Bund organizations, meeting halls up on Eighty-sixth Street in New York. Abe used to send us in to disrupt these guys—and I mean *disrupt* them." He dipped his shoulder and tore down an imaginary door. "That's why I still idolize Abe. Once a week, he organized fifty, sometimes a hundred of us and gave everybody a hundred dollars apiece. There were boys from Jersey and some of Meyer's kids from the Lower East Side, and all of them doing it were Jews. We were instructed to break legs, arms, shoulders. We were instructed never to hit them in the head, but sometimes they got hit in the head."

I asked Harold if they told the Germans they were Jewish.

"The only thing we told them was with a baseball bat," he said.

Zwillman made Harold his driver and bodyguard, and Harold dropped out of school. "Every day at six o'clock, I'd pick Abe up," he told me. "I was fourteen the first time he had me for dinner. When you was in his house, you could ask for anything and it'd be there." For Zwillman, there had been no Great Depression. He lived in a three-story Tudor mansion in West Orange, with manservants in the kitchen and a study full of law books. "He married a real socialite," Harold said.

I asked if he had wanted to be rich like Zwillman and he brushed the question aside. "We always had money," he said. "My mother gave clothes away." I asked if Zwillman was "just a businessman" or if he killed people too. Harold threw a hand on the table.

"Aw, you got a lot of shit you don't know," he said. "Anybody high up in organized crime, if that was you, you had to do that probably half a dozen times. Fuck, how the fuck you gonna get people to respect you?"

Their relationship brought Harold into contact with "everybody that was everybody that was in that world." He told me about Frank Costello's froggy growl—"I can still hear his voice telling me as I'm driving to Philadelphia with my window down, 'Shut it.'" About coming up through the ranks with Vincent (the Chin) Gigante, who is believed to have been, until recently, the Mafia's boss of bosses. About the wedding, at the Pierre Hotel, of the daughter of Joseph (Joe Bayonne) Zicarelli, who was at one time the head of the Bonanno family. About being on the business end of an interrogation from Vito Genovese, with his "soft brown eyes." He said, "It wasn't vicious eyes, not like Lilo."

(Lilo was Carmine Galante, who once, as the two of them drove home from a Mob gathering in Canada, gave Harold orders for a hit on a fellow gangster who had just professed a serious aversion to prison life, declaring, "I did five years of that. I can't take it no more." In the car, Harold recalled, "Lilo says to me, 'You heard what he said, didn't you?' I says, 'Uh-huh.' He says, 'Take care of it,' and that was all it was. I knew I had to take care of the guy.")

Harold spoke about Zwillman with filial awe. "Abe had a daughter who didn't appreciate him. I was maybe like a son to him," he said, never acknowledging that Zwillman—as I had learned from his biography—was close to his stepson. "He loved me. Ever since that point in my life when I met him, I was a different person entirely."

By the time Harold was twenty-three, he had been arrested twenty times, mostly for robberies and assaults. In one case, he was charged with stealing a diamond-studded wristwatch, a sapphire ring, a car, and two hundred dollars in cash from a married couple in Paterson, New Jersey. According to the *Bergen County Record,* which dubbed the case the "striptease robbery," the woman of the house testified that young Harold had taken her upstairs, tied her arms behind her, and "pulled her robe down to her waist and told her he'd like to do something to her." Harold claimed he'd been hired by the woman's husband to carry out a phony robbery, and the man admitted in court that he had just recently taken out a two-thousand-dollar insurance policy on the jewelry. Harold was acquitted.

Harold's sisters have always characterized his criminal life as something independent of their family, as if a mutual abandonment occurred the first time he showed up with a black eye at *heder,* or Hebrew school. "My mother ignored what was happening," Ruthie told me. "She stayed in the kitchen and wouldn't look up from her chickens. When the police came to the house one night, she thought they were saying '*Please!*' She said, '*Please* what?'"

At first, Mendel, the sole family member to comprehend the gravity of what Harold was up to, tried to keep his son out of trouble. He persuaded the chief detective at the Hudson County prosecutor's office to come by the house and give Harold a talking-to, but Harold cursed at the detective and told him to get lost. But Mendel—whether or not he did indeed sell Harold down the river to Zwillman and the Mob—was inextricably mixed up in his son's wayward development, and at times he abetted it more than anybody else was comfortable with. "Papa made me testify as a character witness when Heshy was in that striptease trial," Ruthie recalled. "Can you imagine?"

Not even Harold was oblivious of the antinomies. He bragged to me about his father's prominence in Hudson County and credited him as "the one that got me into all this." But, in a more somber moment, he noted that although Jews and Italians had built the business of organized crime as equal partners, "the Jews were smart enough to leave it after they made some money. Listen, they wanted their children to be somebody. Once you get money, money is meaningless. So if you got a child, what are you going to do getting him into this godforsaken business?"

Several relatives concur that Mendel exposed both Leo and Harold to his illegal distillery operation. One day, he enlisted the boys to stow twenty single-gallon cans of his bootleg slivovitz under the floorboard of his Dodge and accompany him to the Lower East Side, where a rabbi had a standing order. Harold wasn't old enough to drive yet, so Mendel asked Leo to do it. Just outside the Holland Tunnel, a policeman pulled them over. As the cop approached, Leo began rubbing the steering column. He explained to his father, "I'm trying to get some grease on my hands"—to give the appearance that he was merely a driver, who was unaware of what was hidden onboard. He was so nervous that he wet his pants.

"My father saw that his other son didn't have the stomach for that kind of business," Harold told me. "You couldn't talk him into anything that was against the normal ways of doing things. He was so pure, Leo. But he had to work, with his hands. You think your grandfather had five million dollars in the bank like I had? You think he had a million shares of U.S. Glass?" He held up a paper towel. "He couldn't steal this."

Harold was both dismissive and sentimental toward his brother's inability to be anything but normal. "The time I had a hijacked truck of Polish hams that came to me—your grandfather wouldn't even take them," he said. "He could've sold them and made sixty thousand dollars. Instead, he told me to get lost and he didn't make nothing. Leo worked every single day since he was a baby. Listen, that was the pleasure of his life. I can't dream of anybody saying anything bad about my brother Leo." He grabbed the table between us and shook it forcefully. "This table ain't big enough for his heart."

He said that Leo had tried to straighten him out once. "I was eight-een, nineteen years old. He wanted me to find legitimate work—go work for my father, something like that. I told him to mind his own fucking business. I said, 'You do your thing, I do my fucking thing. Don't butt into me.' My brother, you know what he said? He didn't say any more. He seen he had a losing hand. He folded."

I wondered whose resolve admonishment from Leo could ever have dented. When I was in the tenth grade, he asked if anyone ever offered me drugs—"pills, dust, dope"—and warned, "If they do, you just tell them, 'Hey, I don't need that, man.'" Even my grandmother had laughed at how unconvincing he was.

FIVE

A Shande *to the Goyim*

AROLD'S LIFE TRAJECTORY was counter-historical. For a Jew to become involved in organized crime after around 1940 was unlikely, and to the community in which he'd been reared, Harold's descent into corruption represented not just failure but regression. In 1908, Jewish teenagers had constituted 58 percent of the population of New York's juvenile detention home, a statistic that was heavily publicized at the time. But the significant involvement of Jews in crime was "a one-generation phenomenon, a social and economic consequence of the immigrant experience," in the words of Deborah Dash Moore, in *At Home in America: Second Generation New York Jews.*

And to some, even that was one generation too many. "Jews maintained, almost as an article of faith, that 'THERE OUGHT TO BE NO JEWISH CRIMINALS AT ALL,'" the historian Jenna Weisman Joselit writes in *Our Gang,* a book about Jewish criminality in the first half of the twentieth century. "When it came to crime, exceptionality was not simply a part of the Jews' traditional belief in the Chosen People notion or merely a source of ethnic pride; it was also a weapon, a tool of survival."

A case in point can be found in some correspondence from 1934 between the director of the International Jewish Statistical Bureau and a member of its advisory committee, Dr. Cyrus Adler of Philadelphia. The bureau's director had just completed a study on Jewish criminality and was requesting assistance from board members in getting it published. Dr. Adler, in a squeamish reply, questioned "whether just this moment is the moment for such a publication." After all, he explained, "Among the numerous charges that are being bandied about now against the Jews is not that of excessive criminality. . . . I think every individual criminal is a blot upon the Jewish name."

And wisely so, perhaps, because when the Jews did err, America's ruling class offered a refrain of anti-Semitism and nativism. Around the turn of the century, Frank Moss, a civic-policy shaper, described the Lower East Side ghetto as a place where "the criminal instincts that are so often found naturally in Russian and Polish Jews come to the surface . . . in such ways as to warrant the opinion that these people are the worst element in the entire make-up of New York life."

The bulk of the Jews who rode the wave of New Immigration to America between 1880 and 1920 were, of course, Russians and Poles. They lived four to a bedroom in cold-water flats and supported their families with piecemeal work in light industry, manual labor, pawnbroking, and, in some cases, such sublegal pursuits as gambling, prostitution, and theft. By contrast, the German Jews of New York and Newark had been established in America for fifty years as bankers and merchants, members in good standing of the Harmonie and Progress Clubs. Hell-bent on assimilation, they'd quickly embraced American

Reform Judaism, and saw a serious P.R. risk in the sudden appearance of so many unwashed and penniless—and Orthodox—Jews up and down the Eastern seaboard. "They feared that, if the Russians were not rapidly Americanized, they themselves would be discredited because non-Jews would associate them with the Russians," the historian Edward S. Shapiro writes in an essay anthologized in *The New Jersey Ethnic Experience.*

In New Jersey, one result of the hand-wringing was the formation of a dozen or so agrarian colonies, for which the German Jews enticed the Russians, in exchange for housing and occupational training, to abandon their pushcarts. Although, as the wife of an administrator at one of the colonies wrote, the officially stated goal was to teach the wonders of a life lived close to the land—"The Russian Jew, who of necessity has become solely a trader, might yet, . . . as a farmer, rejuvenate his race"—the communities served the additional function of moving the Russian Jews out of view.

The way that Harold's family dealt with his disreputability was not so different. Of course, nobody could have wanted a violent criminal for a son or a brother, and for a family to try to ignore or minimize a black sheep's transgressions is perfectly common. But, like the German Jews', my relatives' discomfort had complex origins. I wondered whether Harold's unlawful livelihood signified to the Konigsbergs how far they had been forced to travel in order to leave the ghetto behind, or how close to it they still were.

The first big sentence came down in 1950: fourteen years, for robbing an appliance store of $450 and severely beating its owner. My father, who was eight years old at the time, was told his uncle Heshy was out of town and working for the government. Only when he discovered a letter with "Drawer N" in Trenton as the return address did he learn the truth. Frieda didn't discuss what Harold had done, just that he "got in trouble for taking something that wasn't his" and seemed to have gotten a raw deal out of it. "He's just a kid," she said. "He's twenty-two years old, and by the time he gets out he'll be middle-aged."

Because it sickened Mendel and Fannie to see him locked up, the responsibility of maintaining contact fell to my grandfather. On Sunday afternoons, Frieda, my dad, and his sisters would ride to the penitentiary with Leo and wait in the car as he visited his brother. "I suppose it was a strange way to spend our Sundays, but it was my father's only day off, and Mother insisted that he spend it with us," my father recalled. My grandmother, whose nature is to accentuate the positive, and, failing that, the benign, remarked that even Harold's foodways were out of step with his family's. "Oh, Heshy gave his parents such a list of things to have us bring—the cooked chickens, the Tropicana, the Genoa salamis and cheese," she told me. "Leo had three men at the warehouse working on it for a day or two. Nonkosher salamis—nobody else ate that."

While Harold was paying his first lengthy debt to society, my grandfather was quickly coming into his own. To some it might have seemed as if Leo's success was brought on by a kind of newfound freedom—his reputation and ambition finally unencumbered by Harold's ignominy. But the fact is that Leo had already set out to achieve as much distance from his family as the narrow peninsula of Bayonne would allow.

"Grandpa was like me in that he made his own life," my father told me. "Once he started that business and was truly on his own, he never looked back." According to Frieda, Leo had no interest in working for his father. "He didn't want to be under his thumb," she said. "Mendel was meddlesome."

I wonder if more than independence was at stake, whether Leo knew that there was something unscrupulous about Mendel's business practices and feared for his own reputation. Even back when they were newly married, one of Frieda's first moves as Leo's bookkeeper was to stop letting him dip into the cash reserve on Friday nights to loan his father money. Because Mendel paid for his business expenses in cash, he was never liquid, and had never had qualms about borrowing from Leo to cover his payroll. My grandmother tells the story proudly, giving half the credit to Leo: "That was how we made it clear we weren't going to be pushed around by my in-laws."

What does it say about Leo that although I was already out of college when he died, I can barely recall the sound of his voice? In that household, it was Frieda who did all the talking. My grandmother is a formidable woman. She used to smoke floral-print Virginia Slims in a long cigarette holder and once, when a man at a restaurant leaned toward her table and told her, "You know, I like you very much but I don't like your cigarette," she replied that she liked her cigarette very much but didn't like him. Just recently, she says, she was riding a bus into Manhattan when another passenger recognized her, introduced himself, and inquired after Harold: was her brother-in-law still alive and in prison? She told him, yes, he was, and then she called him a bastard for asking.

Frieda has always been above self-doubt. If any of her kids came home from school upset about a poor grade or a playground skirmish, she would issue the instructions "Erase it from your mind," and rub the child's forehead for effect.

As for Leo's financial success, my father says, "All of his ambition came from Mother. I think she simply told him to be successful."

Frieda's childhood had been poorer than Leo's. Her father, Moshe Fox, was handsome and kindly, but soft—the family mascot. When he'd arrived at Ellis Island from Russia, he didn't know his real birthday, so, like many immigrants, he chose the Fourth of July. He could piss away an entire week's salary in a Friday-night poker game. He was out of work for a twelve-year stretch that began during the Depression, and when he finally landed a job, as a matzoh inspector on the Manischewitz assembly line, he had to lie about his age in order to keep working past sixty-five. Frieda's brother, Sammy, supported the family during their father's unemployed period, having turned down an invitation to play shortstop in the Yankees' farm system for dependable work at Colgate-Palmolive.

After high school, Frieda got a job at the Maidenform brassiere factory, bringing home $13.65 a week. She married my grandfather, her brother's best friend, in 1937, when she was nineteen and he was twenty-two. "They were tall together," Harold remembered. Indeed, Leo stood a full six feet, and in heels Frieda was not much shorter. Leo was a good catch. He worked and he had a car. On dates, they simply went for drives; he had no money for meals. Years later, they had to bring their children home early from a vacation in Niagara Falls because they'd run out of money. "Grandma made it into fun anyway," my dad recalled. "For one meal, we pulled over and made cream-cheese sandwiches in the car. She turned it into a little picnic."

By this time, Leo was driving a route for his uncle's butter-and-egg business. The uncle, Morris Padwe—Leo called him "the old man"— eventually let his son-in-law Abie and Leo buy into the business as his equal partners. Leo was much more capable on the route than Abie, who "liked to stay in the office and saw himself as some kind of executive," my father remembered. "Leo thought Abie was lazy. I always picture Abie in a blue blazer. His sons were popular in school."

There were four food wholesalers in Bayonne in the forties and fifties, all of them Jewish and on friendly terms with each other, and they shared the understanding that poaching customers was forbidden. But Leo single-handedly brought in so many new clients that, by the time the old man decided to retire and leave his third of the business to Abie (thereby giving him twice Leo's stake), Frieda didn't see any point in remaining partners. So she talked Leo into forming his own company.

Within a few months, Leo L. Konigsberg Foods was not only thriving, it was running the M. Padwe Company out of business. Leo was a soft touch, and no request was too large or too small. Unlike Abie, he gave customers a line of credit when they couldn't pay their bills on time. "Everybody loved doing business with Leo," Harold recalled. "The people didn't like Abie. Abie was a miserable bastard."

Mendel's sister begged Leo to come back into the fold, accusing him of destroying the family. Leo felt terrible, and against my grandmother's wishes joined up with Abie again. Leo worked hard while he was there, but the company was still, mysteriously, hemorrhaging money. "How long can you put up with this?" Frieda asked him. This time, after much agonizing, Leo decided to leave for good.

His first real coup was getting the business of the Arlington Diner, in Bergen County. The place was huge, with famously rich cheesecake they moved in tremendous volume. He was proud to be one of the few wholesalers who was able to get thirty-pound cans of cream cheese (others sold it in three-pound loaves). Once, when the diner ran out of cream cheese at two in the morning—baking was done at night—Leo got in his car and made a special delivery. Soon, he was *really* buying in bulk—30,000 pounds of American cheese at a time, for example, hauled straight from the factory in a trailer that had been piggybacked on a flatbed railroad car, which saved him three cents per pound. "We had dealerships with Kraft and Hellman's, so we could carry stuff and sell it to the other butter-and-egg men in town," my father says. "This made him a very important wholesaler. I mean, little Leo Konigsberg from Bayonne!" Soon, he bought out Cousin Abie's business.

Leo was well aware of how indispensable Frieda was in all this, and when customers arrived to make good on a bill, he told them to come in and pay his queen. "Mrs. Konigsberg kept the most organized, thorough books," Tony Margetis, who owns the Colonette diner in Jersey City, said. "She was so fast on the adding machine. You'd see her sitting at the desk, and her hands were flying, clack-clack-clack."

She was very protective of Leo and how he was regarded. (Even after his death, she has continued to dramatically inflate his high school academic record.) "She made my father into something bigger than he was," my dad says. "She acted like he was the world's greatest husband or father or businessman. She'd say, 'Such a strong man,' and speak of him as somebody powerful and significant, even though he was a simple man."

But Grandma Frieda really did see my grandfather as a patriarch, because he did all the things she couldn't. He worked late while she went home to do the parenting. He drove places. (She only once took the car beyond Bayonne—with my father as navigator—to run an errand in Jersey City, never veering off Hudson County Boulevard.) He was a good *hondler*—somebody who knew how to negotiate. "But Grandma was the one who joined a Christmas club at the bank," my dad says. "He decided who to do business with, and she determined at what value this would be, and when and how to expand. She wanted the authority, but not at his expense. So, over and over, she went through the exercise of declaring him responsible for everything they got."

In return, Leo idolized his wife. They spent their time however she declared they would, went where she wanted, spent their money at her direction. A typical Sunday, if they had free time, involved a visit to Frieda's Hasidic jeweler on Canal Street. She would dash inside, pick out a present for her birthday (or Mother's Day, or their anniversary), and send Leo in to make the purchase. Using this method, she procured a three-carat emerald ring surrounded by sixty marquise diamonds; a diamond tennis bracelet, which she received for her fortieth wedding anniversary; and the ring she calls her "top banana"—a white-gold banana the size of a .44 shell, half denuded of its yellow-gold peel and covered with rows of tiny diamonds. Her taste is fanciful. She has a thing for rhinestone sunglasses, fruit-hued slingbacks, and handbags with large logos (Gucci, but long before the Tom Ford revolution).

To question her level of sophistication would be missing the point. "She didn't get these things to show off to anybody else," my father says. "She never cared what anybody thought, because other people didn't really figure into her world." Thus, what social life my grandparents had—friends they met on their honeymoon, or at the Link, a sort of Jewish Elks' Club—petered out when Leo went into business for himself. "Grandma and Grandpa didn't share their time with other people," Dad says. "I don't remember us going to other people's homes or having guests over, not even our cousins."

Frieda was willing to cut others loose if they proved themselves to be a drag on the momentum that she and Leo needed to get where they were going. Penny-ante disputes with two of Leo's sisters, over the handling of Mendel's estate, culminated with her decision that she and Leo would simply not speak to them again, and the fallings-out, while scarcely acknowledged in so many words, lasted for decades. After Leo died, Frieda decided to let her sisters-in-law back into her life, but they continued to tread lightly. Whenever I've visited Bayonne and called on Beattie or Ruthie, the first question I've been asked is always, "Does Frieda know you're seeing us?" My grandmother, Aunt Beattie once explained, "does not like to share."

It wasn't just Leo and Frieda who could be aloof. The Konigsbergs were a sort of walled city, and as everybody got older, walls within walls continued to go up. "All Mendel's kids were distant from the rest of us," I was told by one of Leo's cousins, also named Harold Konigsberg. "I would never have asked Leo or his sisters a personal question the way I would any of the other cousins. Listen, an open door to go in and out of the Konigsberg home on Avenue A—we haven't had that since I'm six or seven years old, when the Kayo stuff started happening. We took it for granted that they had their problems and you leave them alone."

This Harold Konigsberg is known within the family as Good Heshy. (There were, actually, three Harold Konigsbergs of that generation in Bayonne; the third changed his named to Mark.) Good Heshy, one of five children born to Mendel's less prosperous brother, Zelig, was a pharmacist in Hudson County. He was talking to me by phone from his retirement community in Florida. When I asked him if his name had ever made for problems in his business, he quickly said, "No. I did my work and I kept my head down and that was enough."

"But you felt you had to keep your head down."

"It was a can of worms for the whole family, this very decent family," he said. "Your father, your grandfather, I'll bet they never even liked to gamble—this is the Konigsbergs. But you don't see what I saw. You're out there earning a living, writing your writings. Your father's out in Omaha—nobody's going to give him a hard time. But the rest of us were local. Three-quarters of the cops in Bayonne had some dealings with Kayo over the course of their lives. When I had the drugstore, the cops all came in and met me eventually. And they saw there is another Harold Konigsberg."

In the years since I'd begun to learn about Harold, I'd taken to showing up at family events—mostly funerals and shivahs, unfortunately—as the sole representative of my immediate family. I was enjoying seeing more of my grandmother, and grew very fond of my grandaunts. I liked to walk around the sooty time warp of Bayonne on sunny days and look at my father's grammar school (No. 3 School), the hospital where he'd had his broken leg set, the playground that his maternal grandfather took him to.

Still, there were times, such as on the phone with Good Heshy, when I felt stealthy and unwelcome. Good Heshy is a relative I do not know well but who, I was sure, resented my sudden interest in him and our family. Where had I been all these years when they'd gotten together over the High Holidays? I couldn't win with him now. Whether I was avoiding my relatives or asking them to talk about the uncle nobody wanted to talk about, I was guilty of holding myself at a remove from them.

On the other hand—and this is something I was aware of every time I saw a Konigsberg relative—a good deal of slack is always given to me not just because I'm family but because of my place in it. I come from a long line of overachieving firstborn sons, and, among all the descendants of Mendel's father, I have yet to be made aware that somebody is more revered, admired, or beloved than my father. My father is kind, wise, unfailingly ethical, and handsome, but none of these attributes approaches the significance of the simple fact that he is a surgeon. I'd have thought that just being a doctor was probably enough, except that once, Aunt Beattie described her very bright and successful older daughter, a psychiatrist, to me as "not a doctor like your father, but still sort of a doctor."

While I was talking to Good Heshy, I couldn't shake the memory of the time I had met his kids, who grew up in Bayonne and are both around my age, at a cousin's engagement party several years earlier. Good Heshy's son had turned to his sister after they chatted with me and said—my mother overheard him—"Well, at least we didn't get the cold shoulder."

On the phone, Good Heshy said, "You know, the name Harold Konigsberg has never hurt me."

He paused to reconsider. "I met a guy in the card room down here. He says, 'What's your name?' I tell him, Harold Konigsberg. Turns out he was a judge in Newark. He says, 'I know all about the Konigsbergs.' Well, he didn't know all the Konigsbergs. He knew Kayo Konigsberg. But he sat there telling stories to everybody in the card room, about the so-called 'all the Konigsbergs,' right in front of me."

While my grandparents scaled ladders of socioeconomics in situ— Frieda had no interest in abandoning Bayonne to live someplace where everyone hadn't known her as the prettiest girl in her high school class—for much of American Jewry, moving up often coincided with moving out: first, out of the ghetto to nicer neighborhoods (uptown Bayonne, Crown Heights in Brooklyn, Crotona Park in the Bronx); then, quitting the cities altogether, to the suburbs. The Jews of Newark and Hudson County settled in Bergen, Passaic, and Morris Counties, in Bloomfield, Tenafly, and the Caldwells; or, if they really hit it big, in the Oranges, Maplewood, and Millburn. Philip Roth—who grew up in Weequahic, a Jewish enclave of Newark similar to the Bayonne of Harold's era—describes the exodus in *Goodbye, Columbus:* "The neighborhood had changed: the old Jews ... had struggled and died, and their offspring had struggled and prospered, and moved further west, towards the edge of Newark, then out of it, and up the slope of the Orange Mountains, until they had reached the crest and started down the other side, pouring into Gentile territory as the Scotch-Irish had poured through the Cumberland Gap."

The Irish and the Italians, by comparison, frowned on social mobility, says Joshua Michael Zeitz, a historian at Cambridge and the author of the forthcoming book *White Ethnic New York: Religion, Ethnicity, and Political Culture, 1945-1970*. "The Jewish immigrants' Catholic contemporaries put much more stock in the church and local institutions, in their established hierarchies—even, to some extent, local criminal mobs," he told me. And they were reluctant to leave the urban strongholds they'd established. "When new immigrant groups and blacks arrived, the Italians dug in their heels," Michael Aaron Rockland, a professor of history at Rutgers University and a coauthor of *The Jews of New Jersey*, says. "Where the Jews have a history of wandering, uprooting themselves when they had to, Italians have a real connection to the land, to the physical roots to their heritage." Nor did the Irish hold much of a brief for mobility and risk. They bought homes as quickly as they could and were more likely to reject the uncertainty that came with entrepreneurialism for the security of the service occupations: teaching, the police force, municipal politics.

In Gerald Gamm's recent book *Urban Exodus: Why the Jews Left Boston and the Catholics Stayed*, the author attributes the divergence to religious doctrine: "The Catholic church is a permanent structure, consecrated to God and built around a permanent altar," while "[in] Jewish law, the Torah is holier than any synagogue structure, and Torah scrolls are entirely portable." Citing an earlier study of Jewish flight (from the west side of Chicago), he notes that "the Jew was eagerly moving out to a higher-status district, and 'fleeing from his fellow Jews who remain in the ghetto.'"

The era, for Jews, of rapid ascent and prosperity that followed the end of World War II happened to coincide with the moment at which Harold and his criminal career were first coming to public attention. Despite—or perhaps because of—the Jews' success, it was a tricky time. "On one hand, there was a new commitment in the courts to legal reform: restrictive covenants and gentleman's agreements that kept Jews out of certain jobs were no longer allowed," Deborah Dash

Moore, the historian, told me (and, in fact, the movie *Gentleman's Agreement* was just out, in 1947). "On the other hand, anti-Semitism and resentment of the Jews was still quite reputable. Not much time had passed since the Holocaust." This was also the era of the Rosenberg trial. "American Jews were very aware of both how good they had it and what a vulnerable condition theirs was."

Of course, as Moore was quick to point out, questions of self-regard can't be completely answered by sociology. "Don't discount family dynamics," she said. "I had a great-uncle who went to jail for theft. My aunt still says he was about to return the money when he got caught."

For two years during the late fifties, a sociologist named Marshall Sklare studied more than four hundred Jews in "Lakewood," a pseudonymous affluent suburb on the outskirts of "Lake City" (which were later revealed to be Skokie, Illinois, and Chicago), to examine their habits and their views on Jewish identity. In response to the question of what qualities were most essential in "a good Jew," Sklare found that the fifth most popular answer was "Gain respect in the eyes of Christian neighbors." It ranked behind "Lead an ethical and moral life" and "Accept his being a Jew and not try to hide it," but ahead of "Know the fundamentals of Judaism," "Belong to a synagogue or temple," and "Attend services on High Holidays."

"The Jews have been under siege for a long time, and have had to move cautiously for the last thousand years at least," Nathan Glazer wrote in *Commentary* magazine in 1952, in an article entitled "Why the Jews Stay Sober." "Perhaps the siege has been raised here in America, but most Jews as yet are not, very deep down, sure that it has been." He pointed out that the majority of America's Jews had been here for only one or two generations. "We are all closer to the ghetto than we think," he wrote.

"Do you know the word *shande?*" Aunt Beattie said once, when I asked how it had felt to watch her brother become a household name in Bayonne. *Shande* is the Yiddish word for shame. "How do you think it felt? A *shande* to the *goyim*!"

My father, a good student all the way through high school, certainly had no intention of staying in Bayonne or even New Jersey when the time came to leave home. So he applied to Harvard, Yale, Dartmouth, and Cornell, but not Princeton. He was turned down by all of them and enrolled instead at his backup, Rutgers, the state university of New Jersey. Though he wasn't devastated, he chided himself for having thought college admissions would be so easy. He studied hard enough in college to get into a choosy medical school (Tufts), and hard enough in medical school to get into an even choosier residency (Cornell). Before he met my mother, he spent his summers loading Leo's trucks. Every year, people asked if he was back for good and joining his father's business. "This one?" Frieda would laugh. "Are you joking?" My father has always said that it's a good thing he actually wanted to be a doctor, because his mother never gave her only son a chance of becoming anything else.

The overall college matriculation rate for the Bayonne High School class of 1959—my father's class—was about 25 percent, but almost all of the Jewish students were in that group. One typically overachieving friend from the neighborhood, Steve Roberts (from the Russian Rogowsky), went to Harvard, became a reporter for the *New York Times*, and married up and out: his wife, Cokie Boggs (now Cokie Roberts, the television pundit), came from one of the most prominent political families in the South. In 1970, already the paper's Los Angeles bureau chief, Roberts returned home to chronicle his ten-year high-school reunion for the Sunday *Times Magazine*. He assessed the career goals of his former classmates ("They are neither movers nor shakers, and that is all right. They are content. They get along"); thanked his childhood neighbor Barney Frank—who later became a U.S. congressman from Massachusetts—for persuading him to join him at Harvard; and noted that "next to oil refining, Bayonne's biggest business is probably crime." He cited a Mob investigation that centered on Harold.

"You have to understand, the Jews of Bayonne were all very aware every time Kayo was in the news, that this was the Jewish criminal," Roberts told me. "I was very aware that he was related to my friend Harvey—your dad—and I'm sure it embarrassed my parents." It didn't surprise me to hear Roberts characterize Harold as a sort of village freak, but I resented the possibility that he'd pitied my father because of it. "This person totally defied the aspirations they had for their children," he added. "And, look, things were shaky for Jews in Bayonne. I mean, most of our parents still spoke Yiddish to each other."

On the other hand, Barney Frank insists, not all of them took Harold's infamy so hard. "My brother hat-checked once at the Jewish Community Center for a Konigsberg family event and Kayo was there; we were excited about that," he told me. "We loved the fact that he was one of us. I mean, here's a guy who had—you know, he wasn't just an accountant like Meyer Lansky. I remember teasing one of your father's cousins about him. She'd get upset, but most of the Jewish kids I knew were sort of worshipful of Kayo. We used to follow him in the papers."

Frank went on to liken Harold to Mark Bingham, the gay rugby player who died valiantly in the September 11 attacks, helping to fight off the hijackers of his plane and bring the vessel to a crash that undoubtedly saved many lives on the ground. "There was just this enormous pride in the gay community over Mark Bingham," Frank said. "He was one of us, and he was a true hero. He defied the stereotype that we're weak and effeminate. That's what Kayo sort of did for Jewish teenage boys in Bayonne at the time. We were very conscious of being known as cowardly, people who never do anything physical."

If Frank felt a kinship with Harold as a fellow Jew, I asked, did he also feel chagrin or awkwardness?

"Jews are pretty much over that," he said. "They ought to be."

Philip Roth writes in his memoir *The Facts* of a night he was pursued by rowdies from a rival—and Gentile—Newark school. Not only was there no embarrassment in running away from a fight, but "by and large it was considered both shameful and stupid for a bright Jewish child to get caught up in something so dangerous to his physical safety, and so repugnant to Jewish instincts. The collective memory of Polish and Russian pogroms had fostered in most of our families the idea that our worth as human beings, even perhaps our distinction as a people, was embodied in the incapacity to perpetrate the sort of bloodletting visited upon our ancestors."

Perhaps it is because so many Jews in America today have reached a high level of deracinated comfort that the onetime existence of a Jewish organized-crime empire is not an automatic cause for embarrassment for all. "What the son wishes to forget, the grandson wishes to remember," goes the line by the historian Marcus Lee Hansen. Paul Breines, a historian at Boston University and the author of a book from 1990 entitled *Tough Jews*, notes that the Jews' own notion of themselves as a passive people (which he traces to the second century A.D., when the Roman army, after overtaking Judea, quashed several revolts by the Jews) fell to pieces in 1967, with Israel's stunning victory in the Six-Day War. "That was when it hit home to American Jews that there were Jews who were fighters, Jews who were warlike and aggressive," Breines told me.

That era of Jewish resistance spawned not only several dozen novels of Israeli heroism—Leon Uris's books, including *Exodus*, were wildly popular—but also, Breines theorizes, a slew of books and movies about

American Jewry's involvement in organized crime, such as *The Rise and Fall of the Jewish Gangster in America,* by Albert Fried (1980), Jenna Weisman Joselit's *Our Gang* (1983), and Sergio Leone's epic film *Once Upon a Time in America* (1984). Indeed, the last thirty years have made clear that there are Jews who are willing not only to acknowledge the history of Jewish gangsters but, in certain instances, to celebrate them. Sometimes they are evoked as a quaint oddity: one such volume is entitled *But—He Was Good to His Mother.* Sometimes shrewd: the great social critic Irving Howe, of all people, writes of Arnold Rothstein, the godfather of Murder, Inc.: "In his own way, he was still another Jewish boy who had made good." And, most troublingly, they have been celebrated as folk heroes, a mythopoetic antidote to the onetime stereotype of Jews as weak and easily bullied.

That Meyer Lansky's son graduated from West Point is something Harold trotted out to me as proof that people like them were able to deliver a legitimate life to their children. America has a short and pliant memory. But Longy Zwillman's closest relatives in New Jersey chose to remain anonymous and changed their name to Willman. Recently, on an assignment to cover a movie screening, I met Blair Zwillman, a lawyer whose father had been Longy Zwillman's first cousin. "When Longy was just getting started in bootlegging, he asked my grandfather on the other side of my family if he could borrow a truck for illicit purposes," Blair said. "Longy was only nineteen or twenty. My grandfather would not let him use the truck. Longy said, 'I don't want to see you or your family in the Third Ward again.' For me, being related to the guy was a source of shame as a kid. The whole of Essex County knew his name. Wherever I was, I'd hear, 'Oh, he's related to a gangster.' It was even from the Jewish kids."

Blair told me that he was hesitant to say more. "I'm up for a judgeship, and I wouldn't necessarily want attention being paid to this," he said. Earlier in the evening, I'd overheard him introducing himself to Norman Mailer and laughing when Mailer asked about his surname. "That's right, I'm a *legitimate* Zwillman," he said. To which Mailer replied, "And how am I to interpret *legitimate?*"

One woman whose father, an associate of Harold's and Zwillman's, was once one of the premier bookmakers in the country, told me that she hadn't told her adult children about their grandfather. "Come on, I never even told my first husband," she said. "It's not that I'm ashamed. If you or your parents were immigrants, normal opportunities just weren't available. My father and Meyer and Abe Zwillman—what they did in their little meetings was not something they brought home. My father was a money man."

Their little meetings?

"Don't take this the wrong way," she said. "But, I mean, I don't think my father ever killed anybody."

Harold was released from the state prison in Trenton in 1958, after serving the better part of eight years. Time had hardly stood still for him, he wanted it known. One of the first weekends after his homecoming, he sat at Fannie and Mendel's kitchen table blustering to Leo and his family about the connections he'd made in the Big House. (It was during this stint that his name, in association with older, well-known gangsters, began to appear in the F.B.I.'s Mafia files.)

Shortly thereafter, when his sister Edie was embarking on a spinster's holiday in the Caribbean, Harold gave her a lift to Idlewild Airport and—because it was too awkward for Leo and Frieda to say no—my dad was allowed to ride with them. Harold had a new Cadillac and a Patek Phillipe watch, and he flashed a giant wad of cash at the tollbooth. He talked about resorts he knew in the Caribbean. He offered to throw everybody a party at the Copacabana; he said he could get a good table. "We almost never saw him after that," my father remembered. "My parents started protecting us from him."

Leo and Frieda had a rule between them not to accept any gifts from Harold. They broke it only once, in the case of a legendarily tempting silver tea set. "It was big and ostentatious and he brought it over to your grandparents' anniversary party," my father said. "Everybody assumed it was stolen. He certainly hadn't gone to Grand Street and picked it out himself." It was elaborate—with service for tea and coffee, and a small bowl for the tea leaves after they'd been leached. "Oh, what a party!" Grandma Frieda said. "I wore the most beautiful turquoise gown. It was one of the first long gowns that year—they had just come back." Leo was mortified by the gift. He said they should get rid of it right away, but he and Frieda couldn't decide how to do that, and she put it in a closet.

Harold had shown up at the party "with his arms draped in mink coats," his cousin Marlene told me. "He wanted to sell them to us at deep discount." My dad's younger sister got drunk and drove Leo and Frieda crazy when she tried one on for size.

At first, Harold's sisters thought his illegal dealings were funny. "Ruthie would say, 'Oh, he's got such moxie,' or you'd get 'Look at our baby brother, he's some kind of little *shtarker*,'" Marlene recalled. I could see why it was easier to write Harold off as a two-bit blowhard than to take him seriously. Even today, they explain away his criminal reputation as the product of empty boasts. "He was nothing, a big nothing," Aunt Beattie said. "Who are these prosecuting attorneys telling you he ever did anything big?"

When Harold announced that he'd incorporated a business in his father's honor, E. M. Konigsberg Trucking, nobody believed him, but it was true. And so—some honor—Mendel's name appears on countless F.B.I. reports.

•   •   •

One of the first things Harold asked me when I arrived at Auburn was how my family spoke of him. When I told him that I'd grown up not knowing about him, he kicked the legs of an empty chair near us.

"That's not right," he said. "Listen, in our family I was the one who was always there for anybody." He claimed that he had once physically threatened the man whom Ruthie's husband, Artie, worked for when he heard that the guy was giving Artie a hard time over pay or hours or some such thing. His cousin Ruthie Greenfield, who owned a leather-goods business with her husband, admitted to me without much compunction that they once got Harold to settle a dispute. "We had a handbag situation," she said. "We couldn't charge more than five dollars for bags at the flea market because there was only one merchant there who was allowed to. Heshy made one call to the landlord and then we could sell bags for over five dollars again."

Harold's sister Ruthie was not so sanguine about the time he'd persuaded her to put up ten thousand dollars for an investment scheme that promptly tanked. "He said I should give him the business," she explained. A few weeks later, Harold offered to make her whole, showing up at her front door with a shopping bag full of cash. "He thought I'd be grateful," she said. "You know King Midas? Well, everything Heshy touched turned to misery."

Harold claimed that he'd once taken it upon himself to settle some "union problems" he'd heard Leo was having. When I asked him if my grandfather was aware of this, he raised his eyebrows. "Whoo! You kidding? He would've died. Leo was antiviolence in every way possible."

He went on, "I don't ask nothing of my own, none of my blood relatives, because my own are weak. I don't mean weak like you're thinking. I mean weak like if somebody calls you in and asks you something, you'd break down. Did I ever bring anybody to my house? My brother, my parents, did I ever expose them to anything? I don't do these things. Listen, I ran away from the house. Family—you give to them, you don't take from them."

Harold was finally cut off from his family for good after an incident that happened one Saturday night in November 1958. He was making his way home from New York via the Holland Tunnel when police apprehended him. The ticket that he'd used to pay his toll was from a stolen toll-commutation book; Port Authority workers were under instructions to watch for serial numbers from that book.

Three days earlier, the body of a longshoreman named Joseph Barbito had been found in a stolen car parked behind a diner in Kearny, New Jersey. Barbito was dressed in dark clothes and clean nylon gloves—"white net woman's type gloves," according to the police report—a burglar's getup. He had been shot three times in the head at close range. When the police returned the car to its owner, he noticed that his toll tickets were missing from the glove compartment. While detectives doubted the perpetrator of such a carefully orchestrated murder was foolish enough to try to beat a fifty-cent fare, it was a lead nonetheless. They also had a possible motive. Cops in nearby Parsippany had recently picked up Barbito for robbing a safe at a supermarket and questioned him about a plague of unsolved safecrackings that had hit Hudson County over the past few months. He made bail after he named several partners with whom he'd worked. Police surmised that Barbito's murder was revenge for squealing.

The toll tickets led to Harold's arrest as a material witness in the case, and when an alleged accomplice fingered him, Harold was eventually charged with the homicide. At his booking, police permitted him two phone calls, and he used one to call his mother. He told detectives that he'd bought the ticket book from a Bowery bum the night before. Asked if he knew the victim, he leaned back in his chair, spat on the floor, and said he considered Barbito "a punk," according to the police report. Anyway, Harold said, "I wouldn't use a gun to kill anyone. I'd use my hands."

He stood trial in January 1961. One of his codefendants, Louis Ferrini, was persuaded to testify against him. Ferrini was an interior decorator and small-time crook who had met Harold in prison and subsequently joined up with his criminal enterprise. By the time of the Barbito killing, however, Ferrini claimed in a signed statement for detectives that he was trying to "sever our relationship, which was nearly impossible." He just didn't know how to break the news to Harold. The day of the murder, Ferrini was at an intersection in Jersey City when Harold ran up to his car and asked why he was following him. When Ferrini said he worked in the area, he wrote, Harold "appeared to calm down some-what, but not before stating that it was only because he was so busy was the reason he didn't have time to kill me, as he did to others who interfered in his business. He then announced that he was my boss and that I would follow his orders."

That night, Ferrini said, Harold intimidated him into driving him, and two associates, to a meeting with Barbito. Five minutes after Harold got out of the car, Ferrini heard gunfire. Harold rushed back to the car, out of breath and smelling of burned gunpowder. When Ferrini asked if anything went wrong, Harold told him, "One of these days you're going to get the same thing."

Harold, however, had an alibi. A lawyer from Brooklyn testified that he was having dinner with him the night of the murder, and a man who owed Harold a number of favors said that he had seen him buy the stolen commutation book. The jury was gone for three hours and came back with a verdict of not guilty. (A subsequent F.B.I. investigation of the trial found "various accusations of irregularities and jury fixing resulting from Konigsberg's 'alleged influence.' ")

Harold wasn't satisfied with a mere acquittal. He sued Hudson County over lost income for the time he spent in jail awaiting trial. He won, and was issued a check for $1,095.

I have never ascertained precisely when Harold first killed somebody, nor what sort of psychological threshold it may have required him to cross. This case, at any rate, marked the first time that he was publicly accused of murder, and he became a tabloid staple. "YEGG SLAYING SUSPECT CALLED THE DEAN OF A CRIME COLLEGE," read a banner in the New York *Daily News.*

The significance of the case to his family, however, was that it inadvertently implicated Aunt Beattie's husband, Louie. When the police had nabbed Harold at the tollbooth, he gave his parents' address as his own, although he no longer lived there. Mendel and Fannie's house was searched, and in the garage and attic detectives found a metal strongbox with $14,000 in cash, neatly bundled in waxed paper, and an armory of "burglar's tools": acetylene tanks and torches; two automatic guns fitted to eject knife blades for picking locks; a key-making machine; a thousand keys; several pairs of nylon gloves; a book entitled *The Impression System of Key Fitting;* and diagrams of several commonly made safes, all of which, the police easily deduced, belonged to Harold. It so happened that near the cash pile there were also some bankbooks belonging to Louie. Wondering if Louie's financial records were possibly connected to the Barbito murder, the police decided to book him and hold him overnight for questioning. As Beattie, in her housecoat, looked on and sobbed, an officer guided Louie into a squad car.

Louie's arrest made the papers, several of which noted that he worked as a field agent for the Internal Revenue Service. While the police quickly established his innocence and no charges were pressed, the scandal of his night in jail didn't sit well with his superiors at work. They put the squeeze on him to resign and, when he held his ground, transferred him to a dead-end job. "They put him in a corner at a fucking card table," says Ray Brown, who, in his dual roles as Harold's lawyer and Hudson County's king of municipal gossip, tended to know these things. "He was Hershey's brother-in-law and he was clean as a hound's tooth. So they just embarrassed him and limited him."

Beattie and Louie were demoralized beyond repair. I'd been told many times by my father never to mention the incident to Aunt Beattie, but recently when we were talking, she brought it up herself. "Next time you talk to my brother Heshy, ask him if he knows what it was like for me to go pick my kids up at the J.C.C. after that, slinking down so low in my seat and just hoping that nobody would see me," she said. "That was almost fifty years ago. You know that just a couple of months before, Louie and I had looked at property in Short Hills? We came this close to buying something, but I didn't want to leave Mama and Papa. Just think if we'd moved then how none of this would have happened." She sighed a grim, inward sigh and composed herself. "What is there to say? It's my fault."

When any of our relatives mentions "the thing with Uncle Louie in the garage," it is always as proof that no matter how clear of Harold one tried to steer, there was no such thing as clear enough.

Even so, nobody admits to remembering that the crime Harold was charged with was murder.

That same year, Harold met Catie, a little Italian lady with blazing red hair. Her parents owned a bakery on Wright Avenue in Jersey City, in the middle of his turf. She was widowed, with three children; it was said that her first husband had been killed in a Mafia intramural.

"I seen how she was in the neighborhood: not crying out loud, not with this guy and that, like all the other cunts," Harold recalled. "I could tell right away that there was compatibility. She had good ways."

On their first date, for lunch in Chinatown, Catie brought her kids. He wooed her for six months. "I always would buy her boxes of cookies from Sutter's, on Greenwich Street," he said. He noticed the place did a brisk business, and so he had it robbed and found $140,000 in the vault.

Harold's family learned about Catie through the newspapers, following one of his arrests in Hudson County. He'd refused to answer questions until the police delivered Catie to headquarters. "You know, there are only two things that mean anything to me, my family and my girl," the New York *Journal-American* quoted Harold as telling an officer. "I'm absolutely in love with her and I've seen her every day since we first met."

Leo and Frieda were at the butter-and-egg warehouse one day shortly thereafter when Ray Brown paid them a visit. "You know, your brother plans to marry this young woman," Brown told them. "She's a Roman Catholic, and he wants to make sure you're comfortable with that." My grandparents could only laugh. "Every week we're reading in the papers about this arrest, that arrest, and we should have a problem with him marrying outside of the faith?" Frieda said.

Harold proposed with a four-carat diamond solitaire. They made their home in Lodi, six towns into New Jersey from the George Washington Bridge. It was a big house—five thousand square feet, with five bedrooms and a finished basement. It had cost more than $100,000, the F.B.I. noted in a memo, "but is designed to look less expensive," and had new furniture, which they kept under plastic sheeting. Their two daughters were born in quick succession, and he gave both the girls names with his father's initials. "He thought the babies were like toys," Aunt Ruthie told me. "When he'd come home late at night from doing his thing, he'd want to play with them, so he'd make Catie wake them up."

He was out of the house most of the time, though he was not the sort of gangster who kept criminal and family life entirely separate. One of the more fearsome thugs under his employ went steady with Catie's sister; there were even double dates. The wife of another accomplice recalled having dinner at their house and described Harold's wife as "a lively woman. She made a wonderful meal, pasta and meatballs followed by a meat course."

Later, when Harold was sent back to prison, she truly learned what it was like to be his workhorse. "He had her running here and there for him, places she'd never had to go in her life," Ruthie recalled with sympathy. He was constantly imploring his wife to visit him or attend his courtroom appearances, and then would send her home to convey messages to men who worked for him. She was so much under his thumb that, during a long period of incarceration at a prison in Springfield, Missouri, he required her to take an apartment near the prison—relocating with the children—in order to handle his legal correspondence.

For a time, Harold's new family remained separate from the family into which he'd been born; his parents and siblings had by then cut both their ties and their losses. But when he was put away, Catie's sisters-in-law befriended her. I wondered why the Konigsbergs let her into the family. They certainly were under no familial or social obligation, and they had little in common with her.

But the way my grandaunts and my grandmother discussed Catie, it was as if they identified with her for being stuck with Harold. "She was a nice person," Beattie said. "And she did a good job raising those girls on her own." Grandma Frieda said, "I felt so bad for her. Who would ask such a thing as to be married to him?" They understood that nobody who was with Harold had ever meant to be in that position. And perhaps they felt that by keeping the family open to her, they were redeeming themselves for whatever their brother put her through.

Although Harold's daughters were infants the last time he was out of prison, they are quick to say that he raised them. One is a lawyer and the other is a corporate executive. One has described him as "my best friend, a wonderful father." Harold, for his part, spoke to me much less about his adoring daughters than he did about the family that had exiled him, but he was proud that both women earned bigger salaries than their husbands. Years ago, Harold provided his wife and daughters with a house and money. After his well ran dry, he said that as a favor to him, Moe Dalitz, a gambler and hotel tycoon in Cleveland, furnished them with five thousand dollars a month. When Dalitz died, in 1989, Catie went to Boca Raton to see Gerry Catena, another aging gangster. He gave her ten thousand dollars but asked that she not come to him again.

As always, Harold's stewardship had its price. According to Ruthie, after he was locked up for good, he warned his wife that if she ever left him for somebody else, he would have her and their children killed.

Not long after I first met Harold, I was introduced to his older daughter at a cousin's wedding in Texas. She was rubicund, with full lips just like his. She wore sturdy gold jewelry and a tone-on-tone silk dress. She had traveled halfway across the country for the night, even though she barely knew the cousin because, she said, "that's what family does." When I told her that I was writing about her father, she became upset. "Who on earth wants to read about that?" she said. "Nobody who knows me knows about this. You have no right to play God and resurrect it. Do you think anybody will hire you after they find out who your uncle is?"

Just as Harold did, she feared that his being written about would hurt his chances for parole. "Don't you read the papers?" she said. "They're setting convicts free after six years because the prisons are full. And these are men who killed innocent people."

We pleaded with each other for a while. I told her it didn't seem like I was going to change her mind. "That's right," she said. "I'm a Konigs-berg."

Not that anybody else had become more open to the idea of my telling Harold's story. The argument I heard most frequently was that it would upset Frieda. "Who needs that kind of trouble?" Aunt Ruthie said. My aunt Barrie, who had known Harold only when she was a little girl, hung up on me when I called to ask a question. I stayed at my grandmother's house while I was doing research in Bayonne and Jersey City, but after a couple of days she told me to find a hotel. "I just feel so complicit hearing you interviewing people on the phone at Grandpa's desk," she said. Then she made me breakfast.

After we ate, I went into the den and packed up my things, stowed the fold-out bed, and turned off the air conditioner. The room, with its crimson carpeting and dark-paneled walls, has been the setting of magical memories for my brother and me. It was where we were allowed to stay up late on Saturday nights to watch Archie Bunker on the solid-state TV—which is still there—with a remote control that actually rotated the knobs on the set. It was where we slept when we flew out to visit alone the summer I was eleven (whenever we visited with our parents, we stayed at a Marriott at the Newark Airport; Dad explained that Jews don't crash on couches). That summer, we played marathon games of Ping-Pong in the basement and got to eat Chicken McNuggets for lunch every day. We watched Bjorn Borg beat John McEnroe in the 1980 Wimbledon final, during which Grandpa Leo explained that, even if we liked Borg better, Americans were supposed to root for the American.

My grandmother was kicking me out, but she was obviously having a difficult time of it. She gave me an antique silver mirror to take back to my apartment. She told me about how embarrassing it had been for her parents when the police busted Mendel's still. "My parents had feelings about my being married to a young man from that kind of a family," she said. "I wanted them to be proud of my husband."

And that was it from her. If I had thought I was doing my relatives a favor by pushing them kicking and screaming into the therapeutic age, talking their way through the dysfunction and unhappiness of the past, I was mistaken.

Once, when I was at Auburn, Harold sent me back to my hotel with a copy of a parole appeal he'd recently submitted on his own behalf. "I want you to see what I been through," he said, nodding solemnly. "And read what I wrote in there about your grandfather."

I got a booth at a Greek diner nearby and paged through all manner of accusations of frame-ups, rants against anti-Semitism and mistreatment in the correctional system (kosher meals not delivered on Passover), and a promise to work with youth at risk should he ever be sprung. "My beloved wife," he wrote, underwent "a woman's change of life with woman problems"—menopause, which had happened many years before and was exacerbated by his inability to be home with her and offer comfort. It was 120 pages long, single spaced and all in uppercase. And he'd devoted considerable attention—ten pages—to our family's history, dating back to Eastern Europe and focusing on Mendel's early stages as an immigrant. On its own, it was impressive: my father knows almost nothing of his ancestry beyond his parents, and Frieda and my grandaunts even less.

Harold told the government about his brother a few pages in, citing him as somebody who could vouch that he'd been at home—and not at the scene of the crime—on the night half a century ago when he was nabbed on his first major robbery arrest. He lovingly described Leo as "solid" and "honest," with an august reputation throughout Hudson County. He added that Leo had never been arrested for anything, "including vehicle violations." It wasn't much of a paean in my eyes, and Harold neglected to warn the esteemed members of the parole board of the difficulties they would have in locating his brother, who'd now been dead for nearly a decade. But regardless of the appellant's motives or reliability, I was grateful for the opportunity to be alone with Grandpa Leo in my thoughts.

It has been a great relief to learn nothing that would cause me to doubt his probity. That life is inherently more complex than my relatives' united-front recollections would have me believe only deepens my admiration for him. Leo, after all, was a cynic. How could he have been otherwise? "Whenever there was some kind of political scandal in the papers, his reaction was that everybody's a crook: the big businessmen are big crooks and the small guys are small crooks," my father told me. He said that Leo's by-the-book business ethics were neither a function of moral purity (that an honest living was the only living that he could truly conceive of a person making), nor of superiority (that the normal way was crooked, and he had to be better than normal).

"If I had to attribute it to something, I'd guess that when Grandpa pissed his pants on that bootlegging trip into New York, it really affected him," my father said. "He probably realized that whatever the consequences were of living that way, they scared him. And he made a very conscious effort never to find himself in a position like that again."

He went on: "And maybe it even helped that when Grandpa Leo first joined his uncle's butter-and-egg business, it was an honest business—I mean, as far as I ever heard, it was—and that was how Grandpa learned to operate. Or maybe it was just a matter of his following Grandma Frieda's lead. She was extremely principled, stubbornly so. But he wasn't stubborn enough to declare himself philosophically different from the people around him." Perhaps, Dad said, if Leo hadn't been fortunate enough to marry her, things might have been different. "If he'd first learned the business from some *goniff,* maybe he would have said, 'this is how it works,' and been the same as them. Maybe he was more lucky than unlucky."

Part II

Shooting Angles

SIX

"This I Do Not Like to Use"

HAROLD BUILT HIS C.V. in a remarkably short time, and was most active from 1958 to 1963, between incarcerations. His portfolio—everything from bookmaking to nightclubs to resort hotels to hijacking to trucking, to even, according to a man who claims to have been his partner in the venture, a clandestine abortion clinic—owed its breadth to his equal-opportunity relations with the Mafia's various families. The Genoveses and Bonannos were especially equal; both, although based in New York, were heavily involved in Hudson County's trucking and gambling rackets.

A meat-hauling company in which Harold had controlling interest operated out of a truck stop in Hackensack. It had a few hundred tractor-trailer drivers on its payroll, according to the testimony of an office manager, in addition to at least eight bookkeepers and salesmen (and also, for a spell, Harold's wife). Don Hockstein, who sold insurance in Bayonne, recalled the time Harold stopped by his office to inquire about having some of his trucks and real estate underwritten. "I submitted applications, but the insurers I tried said no because of his reputation," he said. "I remember when Harold came to see me, we talked about our families—how his father worked with my grandfather and whatnot. Meanwhile, I was calculating the potential costs for him on the adding machine. They were all odd, irregular numbers, and just before I pressed for the total, he shouted it out." Harold had been looking over Hockstein's shoulder, adding the numbers in his head while they chatted. "He was right, down to the penny."

Harold's businesses had names almost comically vague—New Jersey Branch Farmers Co-operative Marketing Associates was a trucking company; Howell Distributor Systems, Inc., was his loan-sharking operation in Bayonne. ("Collectors and buyers of accounts receivable and delinquent accounts," read his business card, which listed him as "executive vice president.") He owned a beachfront hotel in Jamaica. One of his front-page appearances in the *Times* came after a wiretap caught him offering to procure Frank Sinatra as an investor in a casino on the island. Through a Bonanno family boss, the F.B.I. believed, Harold got involved in running guns and ordnance to the Dominican Republic. He told me one day at Auburn that he'd purchased the weapons from Samuel Cummings, a famous arms merchant based in Monaco, and had also sold them to civil-war-riven countries—Venezuela, Liberia, and the Congo. "Both sides at the same time in the Congo," he said.

"Really?" I said.

"*Really,*" Harold said, as if I'd asked the dumbest question in history. "Listen, I been all over. I did a lot of things, with a lot of countries. A lot of very important transactions and acts."

I asked who hired him for the transactions and acts. "I don't get hired. Fucking punks get hired. I been my own boss since I'm thirteen years old, fella!"

On a wiretap the F.B.I. set in 1962, the boss of a crime family in New Jersey was overheard puzzling over Harold's incorrigibility; he had broken a golden rule and beaten up two members of La Cosa Nostra without the appropriate permission. "He ain't a bad kid, after all. Only he was brought up wrong," the boss said, adding that other Mob bigwigs, having lacked the fortitude to ever stand in Harold's way, "taught him that he can do anything he pleases." (Another gangster responded that Harold was trouble long before that: "He had a habit of beating up Italian kids.") Gerald Shargel, a defense attorney who got to know him in the course of representing a number of his contemporaries, told me, "I always thought of Kayo as a guy like Mongo in *Blazing Saddles*. Even the other gangsters were afraid of him."

I'm not sure whether Harold ever had the kind of money he says he did. I know that, even after he got sent up for the last time, it was twenty years before his wife had to find herself a secretarial job. When the F.B.I. placed a bug in his office, he could be heard discussing his stock-market investments of $150,000 here, $180,000 there, and so on. He had enough, according to an F.B.I. informant, to play in a regular crap game in Jersey City and not pay any mind to losing $4,000 in one night, and $7,000 and $12,000 on other single nights. Later, however, he began filing *in forma pauperis* claims in court, requesting exemption from fees as he made his legal defense from prison. (Most of the businesses he took over were never in his name, and when his ties to the Mafia deteriorated, it became much harder for him to get his hands on any money.)

Harold had few friends other than perhaps the people who worked for him—an ever-shifting arsenal of blunt instruments. A Justice Department memo described one of his associates thusly: "Edward Skowron, AKA Eddie the Polack, DOB May 1925, is not a Mafia member. He is known as a hoodlum hanger-on and as a shylock strong-arm man.... His criminal record dates to 1939," and included convictions for rape and for the bribery and assault and battery of police officers. "It is known that Skowron is Konigsberg's 'slave'—he does Konigsberg's bidding, and he always has," another memo states. "He is dependent on Konigsberg for everything he owns—at the present time, Konigsberg is paying Skowron between $50 and $100 a week. The agents who know Skowron best confirm that he is a 'punk'—a minor, insignificant hoodlum who is subject to Konigsberg's beck and call."

Another member of his circle was Bob Whisnant, a professional gambler who evidently should have kept his day job. After he accumulated massive debt to Harold, he was permitted to pay back his loans first by giving tips at the horse races, and then, eventually, by conspiring to fix the races. He also helped Harold as he learned to read. On the telephone from Florida, Whisnant vouched for Harold's good humor. "We had a great time playing the horses," he told me. "I couldn't believe a guy that sharp couldn't read, and I watched him teach himself. We used to ride along the Jersey Turnpike and read the signs out loud. Some words, he'd say, 'What the hell is that?' and he'd laugh at himself for not knowing.

"We went down to the races in Florida, and I took him to the Boca Club. I think he might have felt out of place being introduced to the fancy sorts of people they had there. He could dress like a slob and of course he didn't talk so distinguished. People were looking at him funny. He was very shy, believe it or not. Then he tried to impress them and started talking in a voice that was too loud about how he owned hotels and resorts down in the Caribbean. Well, nobody was interested. They just turned and went on talking among themselves. He never said anything about it, but I could tell he was embarrassed."

Whisnant described Harold as all business. "He liked to work, there was no question about that," he said.

F.B.I. surveillance of the office Harold shared with three accountants at 19 West Forty-fourth Street in New York City, near the Algonquin Hotel (and in the same building where I now go to the dentist), recorded Harold and various associates discussing real-estate deals in the Philippines and Argentina; an opportunity to invest in a new "foam birth preventive" that has not been approved by the F.D.A.; petty shakedowns in Hudson County; the bootlegging of phonograph records; the commercial possibilities of controlling a dog track in Paris and indoor tennis clubs at an undetermined location; the distribution of stolen watches, clocks, and a single fur piece; and the purchase of B-25 and B-26 bombers, which, the F.B.I. noted, "could be used against Cuba," as well as a deal, already in place, to sell arms to Cuban revolutionaries. They talk about a recent election in South America, fretting that the new president will "cancel all oral contracts." Harold expresses his interest in an offer to shake down an emerging television star in California who has secretly fathered an illegitimate child. The baby's mother wants $2,000 to $3,000 to keep quiet, but Harold thinks he can get $50,000.

Harold works late some nights. He naps on his couch. He returns from the Copa. He dashes off to the bank to convert $3,500 in singles into larger denominations. His secretary tells a visitor to beware of his temper. Harold advises the secretary against going on holiday the next week and leaving him in the lurch. He adds that she wouldn't enjoy her vacation anyway, as she does not shoot craps, play cards, or play tennis. Harold becomes "very upset" when informed that a thirty-five-dollar check drawn from his account has bounced, and he gives an associate thirty-five dollars in cash to deposit immediately. With Harold out of earshot, another man in the office notes that "Harold is a child," and the subject is changed.

•   •   •

Harold ascended the organized-crime ladder swiftly, and largely by dint of his violent reputation. Even as he cooled his heels awaiting trial on a minor charge, a detective in the Hudson County prosecutor's office told the *New York Post* that the squad was under shoot-to-kill orders if any of them should catch Harold in the act of a mere burglary or hijacking. In a confidential memo dated October 3, 1961, an assistant U.S. attorney general submitted the following to J. Edgar Hoover:

> *The Department has received the following information. . . . Konigs-berg is described as being in his early thirties. . . . He seldom wears a coat or tie. He has a car with a souped-up engine capable of going over 100 miles per hour. . . . Konigsberg is said to carry a small length of rope with him, which he utilizes to strangle people. . . . Konigsberg brags about the fact that he has 40 "soldiers" working for him who are paid $250 a week for their strong-arm activities. . . .*

And from the profile the F.B.I. began to amass on Harold while he was still at large:

> *Information set forth concerning Howell Distributing Company, Howell Distributing Systems, Inc., Frigid Express Company, Frigid Freezer Company, Inc., and P & H Trucking Company, all of which allegedly are part of KONIGSBERG's operation. KONIGSBERG allegedly taking over Tippy Tu's Charcoal Haven, Bergenline Avenue, North Bergen, for non-payment of shylock loan. Louis LE PORE, AKA Louie the Breeze, backed by KONIGSBERG's money, is now operating Modern Motors, Columbia Park, North Bergen, N.J. . . .*
>
> *KONIGSBERG allegedly took over the Peter's Cocktail Lounge,*

*Union City, and which place was insured for $40,000 on 11/21/61
and burned on 12/21/61, fire being of suspicious origin. . . .*

*KONIGSBERG called . . . unstable and without emotions by
law enforcement authorities. . . . He is connected in high places, both
politically and in La Cosa Nostra. . . .*

*KONIGSBERG CONSIDERED A RUTHLESS KILLER BY
LAW ENFORCEMENT AUTHORITIES. HE HAS BEEN
KNOWN TO USE A GUN IN THE PAST. HE SHOULD BE
CONSIDERED ARMED AND EXTREMELY DANGEROUS.*

Money lending remained his bread and butter. F.B.I. agents who
raided his office in Bayonne in 1963 found a stack of immaculately kept
ledgers and, in a kitchen drawer, thirty pairs of handcuffs. The U.S. Attorney General's office estimated that Harold was taking in $50,000 per
week as a shylock. In 1961, a wiretap caught him comparing rackets
with Angelo DeCarlo, a boss in New Jersey, over dinner at Dowd's
Steakhouse. "Use a little common sense, go and book horses," DeCarlo
suggested. He thought loan-sharking was too slow a business, with all
that sitting around waiting to be paid.

"We don't never sit," Harold said. "We call three, four, five, six
times a day."

Harold told DeCarlo that for a $5,000 loan, his standard interest—
the vigorish—was $250 a week; if he lent out $20,000 for a year, his
profit was $52,000.

DeCarlo was impressed. "Two-fifty a week? We get a hundred dollars a week for five thousand dollars."

"You're scabs," Harold said. "You'll have to organize you guys."

Harold delighted in the extortion process and regularly told clients that
he hoped they wouldn't pay. His friend Bob Whisnant, who often hung
around Harold's office in Bayonne, recalled, "One time he said, 'Come

on with me, I got to see somebody,' and we drove to this bar in New York. The guy was behind the bar—he owned it. And Harold just took the part of the bar that lifted up and broke the damn thing off. He made him open the cash register, took everything out of it. He tore the guy's pants pockets off to get his wallet. Harold really knocked the guy around and he bled really good. He pounded his head against the rubber rack on the floor that you walk on behind the counter, to keep from slipping, and on the side of the damn wall. The guy was screaming in pain, asking him to stop. The whole action was probably a minute or so. There must have been thirty people in the place and nobody did a damn thing. I've never seen somebody so violent.

"When we were back in the car, I said, 'Harold, what the hell?' and he said, 'The guy owed me money.' Now, you know as well as I do that Harold could get as worked up over fifty dollars as he could over five thousand, and he never even said how much this guy owed him. He was just chuckling to himself, slapping his hand on the steering wheel."

Harold liked to cast himself as the lone upright party in a money-lending deal. Violence just meant he was keeping his word: it was his client, after all, who had broken the compact. This is an old Mob saw, and even lawmen have been known to buy into it: "Most of the people who they killed are the people who deserved it," says Robert Stewart, the former Mafia prosecutor.

"The curse of my business," Harold told me philosophically, "is you got to do business with a lot of scumbag cocksuckers."

But Harold's prey were often perfectly ordinary people conducting legal transactions—if somewhere along the margins of commerce. In 1963, he was charged in two separate extortion cases, one in Philadelphia, the other in New York. The two arrests were, in the end, what slowed him down enough for the government to begin an effective pursuit. When I read the testimony and wire-tapping transcripts that arose from the two cases, the despair of Harold's victims was palpable. They had no idea what they were getting into.

One such client was Joseph Zavod, a real-estate speculator in Philadelphia. At a public auction on June 24, 1963, Zavod and three partners had purchased the West Philadelphia Jewish Community Center for $90,000. They planned to resell it immediately, through a prearranged deal, to the Cobbs Creek Civic Association for $150,000. Unfortunately, they had miscalculated the amount needed for a down payment. They discovered themselves $13,500 short and their check was about to bounce.

Joseph Zavod had never been much of a businessman. In a good year, he'd made maybe $8,000 before taxes. He was a happy-go-lucky type, an enthusiast for magic tricks and hypnotism. "He was crazy about animals," his son, Alan Zavod, told me. "We had chimpanzees, monkeys, parrots in the house." He started a pet-and-aviary-supply store and, when that failed, worked as a buyer for a drugstore chain. In 1963, he was diagnosed with polycythemia, a condition that caused his body to overproduce red blood cells. Treatment was simple: he got his blood drained every few months (the Zavods disposed of it in their garden, producing the best roses in the neighborhood). The main symptom was constant fatigue, which forced him to look for a desk job. "Real estate seemed easy enough," his son recalled.

One of the first opportunities that came Zavod's way was the J.C.C. deal, and he really needed it to work out. He was thirty-nine, with three children, no disability insurance, and no savings to speak of. He stood to make at least $15,000 from the resale. Zavod later testified that, through a tenuous connection of one of his partners, he contacted Harold, and late at night, Zavod and the partner drove to Bayonne.

The windows of Harold's storefront office on Hudson Boulevard were clouded by grime and the front room was full of broken furniture. He sat in the back, at a large desk, flanked by leather chairs and two of his "bookkeepers," who were there to serve as extra muscle. Zavod detailed their plan to flip the J.C.C. and requested a $13,500 loan. Harold reached into a drawer and pulled out a fistful of large-denomination bills.

"He stacked them in front of him and they made quite a nice pile," Zavod testified. "He counted off $13,500, put a rubber band around it and pushed it out on the desk, and put the rest of it away." Nervously, the borrowers agreed to Harold's outrageous terms: $25,500 for the $13,500 for thirty days, to be paid on an installment plan over the course of the month.

Zavod asked if they had to fill out any promissory notes or loan papers.

"No, just a handshake is enough," Harold said. He took a long bone-handled revolver from his desk, pointed it at Zavod, and broke open the cylinder to show that it was loaded. "This I do not like to use in order to collect my money." Then he picked up a fourteen-inch-long piece of rubber hose that was filled with lead, and whacked Zavod's partner on the knee with it. "That hurt, didn't it?" Harold said. "I would much rather use this."

Zavod and his partners missed the first deadline; their resale settlement was stalled. Harold granted a couple of extensions, but, according to the testimony, the arrangement quickly dissolved into an exchange of pleas and threats. The culmination was Harold's unannounced appearance, on August 27, on Zavod's doorstep in Broomall, a suburb west of Philadelphia. "My sister let him in," Alan Zavod told me. "I could tell it wasn't exactly a social visit. She was twelve. I was seventeen that summer. She told him where the bedroom was and he marched straight upstairs and closed the door behind him."

"I went a little crazy with this guy," Harold told me.

Zavod was laid up with a complication from the blood disorder. "Where is your goddam money?" Harold demanded. He rifled through Zavod's closet and drawers. "You can't even afford to buy your wife any decent jewelry. There is nothing in here but junk." He said that if Zavod could not deliver $13,500 within another month—and if he wanted to save his own life—his home was his only collateral. Harold would pay Zavod $25,000 for the three-bedroom house.

Since Zavod still owed more than $9,000 on his mortgage, Harold explained, that left him with about $1,500 to buy a new one.

Zavod looked up. "I would rather not. Do I have any choice?"

Harold drew up a bill of sale. Zavod summoned his wife upstairs to co-sign it.

It was a busy year for Harold. During the summer of 1963 he was charged in four separate cases, and was facing a ten-year sentence for possessing a truck full of stolen menswear. He'd been caught with the goods—three thousand suits—in an abandoned garage adjacent to a bar he owned called the Hoo-Ha Club. "This is the first legitimate arrest the F.B.I. ever had me for," he declared when agents shined their flashlights on him.

On September 12, while he was out on bail, Harold flew with his wife to Denver, where a businessman named Albert Hayutin was requesting his services. Hayutin had grown up in Colorado, survived nine days surrounded by Axis forces in the Battle of the Bulge, and worked in the oil business and in residential real estate. In 1963, he met Joseph Cannistraci, a twenty-nine-year-old stockbroker—well dressed and smart (an intercollegiate chess champion while at Fordham, he never hesitated to point out)—who offered to cut him in on a deal to take control of a land-development and mining company. Hayutin had put up

$100,000 in cash and securities, obtained mostly through personal loans from several banks and prominent friends in town. But when he learned that Cannistraci was not paying the company's bills and that construction had ceased on some of its building projects, Hayutin tried to bail out. Several times, he left messages with Cannistraci demanding his money back, but his calls weren't returned. Meanwhile, Hayutin's lenders were getting so impatient, he testified in the eventual case against Harold, "that it was almost unbearable, and I was hesitant to answer my own telephone."

In desperation, Hayutin decided to hire a collector. He had learned about Harold through an accountant in New York. Over the phone, he consented to Harold's 30 percent commission, plus $5,000 in expenses.

The first day Harold was in town, according to testimony, Hayutin returned to his office from lunch and found Cannistraci, who weighed some three hundred pounds and was known to colleagues as Fat Joe, stripped to the waist. Harold was sitting beside him holding a revolver.

"What's going on here?" Hayutin said.

Harold said that he and Cannistraci had reached "a complete understanding."

"Like an evil genie unwittingly released, the sadistic defendant rapidly assumed the entire direction and control of the conspiracy," reads an appellate brief from the case. Back in New York, Harold stormed into a Wall Street brokerage company where Cannistraci was a principal and pored over the firm's ledgers. He threatened to throw a trader out the window unless the man turned over stocks as partial payment. Later, Cannistraci had the gumption to point out that he didn't owe Harold, he owed Hayutin, whom he would therefore repay with a check to his bank in Denver. Harold countered that if Cannistraci really insisted on maintaining this naive view of the deal, he was taking his chances.

"You can do what you want and I'll do what I want," Harold said.

"You won, kid. You won a fight that you never won. You became the champion of all losses."

When Hayutin asked Harold if threatening Cannistraci was really necessary, Harold told him to stop asking questions unless he wanted a beating himself.

Cannistraci traveled to New York to look for other assets that he could liquidate. Hayutin followed him there, then asked his wife to fly out. "Al was very scared of Mr. Konigsberg and what he might do," she told me. "He called and said he needed me there with him for the moral support."

Cannistraci was unable to come up with the money, of course, but what really got him in trouble was showing up two days late for an appointment at Harold's office. As his only defense, he brought his friend Earl Humphreys, an ex-marine from Dallas who was trying to get a career as a lounge singer off the ground. He had an album out on Verve Records and was in New York to perform on Johnny Carson's *Tonight Show*.

Harold was furious. He told Cannistraci that it was no longer about money but a matter of "respect." Off came Harold's wedding band, his watch, and his jacket. He rolled up his sleeves.

"He then told me either I'm going to die as a man or die as a coward," Cannistraci told a grand jury. Putting up resistance, Harold explained, was dying like a coward. "But if I did not die like a man, then he would proceed to kill each member of my family, including my son when he reached the age of thirteen, and there was no business discussion at all." From the adjoining room, according to testimony, an unseen person handed Harold a plastic sheath filled with copper wires. Over the course of four hours, he struck Cannistraci fifty or so times on the arms and head, then landed a blow above his ear, opening a cut.

Humphreys, who was permitted to mop the blood from Cannistraci's neck with a handkerchief, spoke up. "If he has any more of this coming," he said, "I would rather take them than watch them."

This so impressed Harold that he gave Cannistraci a two-day reprieve.

Cannistraci repaired to Humphreys's sublet to soak his swollen body. The next morning, they went to the Manhattan District Attorney's office. Detectives installed a bug near Harold's desk and tapped Humphreys's phone. "Kayo called me up five days later, after Fat Joe missed his next appointment," Humphreys told me. "He'd taken a shine to me. I got the feeling he wanted to be friends."

"Looks like the people you had faith in ain't so honorable, are they?" Harold said to Humphreys. "You know what bothers me more than anything in the world? That you were man enough to . . . suffer for him, and this man didn't even have the audacity, or the integrity, rather, to protect you and . . . at least keep his word, you know, by showing up." He offered to help Humphreys get singing gigs at a nightclub.

Investigators dispatched Humphreys and Cannistraci to Harold's office and set up watch from a building across the street. Even though he knew they were right there, Cannistraci was nervous as he stuttered through his lines, still promising to borrow money in order to pay Harold: "I'll go to my father's and say, 'Dad, I need this money for my business. I'm going to lose everything.' On a financial basis, my father will give me the money. He did it before when my sister got married."

"You got yourself a deal," Harold said. He conceded to one last payment schedule, and promised Cannistraci that there would be "no more calls," and "nobody looking up at your mother's house or your brother's house anymore." He asked Cannistraci why he'd moved his wife out of Denver.

"She was nervous and very high tension," Cannistraci said. "She's expecting a kid in less than a month."

Harold, who measured quite a few cubic inches less than Fat Joe, looked him up and down. "How do guys like you make babies, anyway?"

Harold was arrested for extortion several days later, on October 23, 1963. Two detectives in the Manhattan D.A.'s office called him down to headquarters for questioning, and my granduncle, with the brazen self-assurance of a man of clear conscience, rolled straight on in. The same week, extortion charges were made against him in Philadelphia; Joseph Zavod, too, had gone to the F.B.I.

Even after he turned Harold in, Cannistraci continued to scramble. According to financial documents later seized by detectives, he got himself into one mess on top of another over the next couple of years. Cannistraci was being investigated by the Queens district attorney on suspicions of ripping off seven people in a real-estate scheme in Colorado, and he was allegedly running a scam wedding-planning business. In 1965, the state of New York barred him from trading or selling securities because, it was alleged, he'd put up customers' stock as collateral for personal loans. A neighbor on Long Island, where he had a home, later told *Newsday* that Cannistraci "came over like confidence-plus" to persuade him to invest several thousand dollars in a fraudulent stock deal.

Cannistraci and his wife and children went to live with his parents in the Bronx, then separated when he took a hotel room in Manhattan. He owed a lot of people money, and while the government wanted to protect him as its star witness against Harold, who was in jail awaiting trial, it took a long time—until September 20, 1966—for a judge to even slate the extortion case for trial.

That night, Cannistraci called his wife. "Joe told me that he may or may not have money for me the next day, as I was in need of food money," she later told investigators, according to a transcript of her interview. She asked her husband if she should go on welfare.

"No, everything will be okay," he told her.

The next day, Cannistraci was found murdered on the Long Island Expressway.

The killing was never solved. Recently, Cannistraci's sister told me politely that she had no idea why it hadn't been, "not that I had any idea what he was doing back when he was alive." It turned out that, while the Nassau County Police Department had let the case slide decades ago, it was officially still open—though very cold. And although Harold was in jail at the time of the killing, everybody had suspected his involvement.

One morning in August 2002, I took the Long Island Rail Road to the town of Mineola, where the Nassau County homicide squad had agreed to let me view the old investigation files from the case. Police headquarters was a large stone structure set off against the boulevard by a well-tended lawn. Upstairs, a lieutenant showed me to a small interrogation room with a two-way mirror and pointed to five footlocker-sized files on a desk. I left the door open—New York was in the middle of a heat wave, and the hotbox was poorly ventilated—and carefully set the contents of the first folder on a desk. It contained phone records, an autopsy report, a chemist's analysis of the scene of the crime, and photographs—eight-by-ten glossies of Cannistraci's corpse, first on the side of the highway near Lake Success, and then naked at a morgue, his head propped up by a cardboard takeout container.

He had been shot three times at close range with a .38, twice in the chest and once in his left shoulder. A trail of blood that pooled at his corpse began, according to a police report, twenty-four feet up the road; apparently, he'd tried to crawl away after he was shot. His topcoat and dress shirt were unbuttoned and spread out beside him like airfoils. He'd lost one of his shoes. The shirt came from Sid Klein Fat Man's Shop Inc., on Third Avenue and Tenth Street. Among the contents of his car were a deflated toy football, a "gross amount of cigarette ashes" on the floor well, and four empty cases of Hi-C.

Fingerprints on the armrest in Cannistraci's car were compared with those of more than a dozen suspects in the murder, including Harold, and matched to one Philip (Philly Lucky) Giaccone. Philly Lucky, I learned, was a Mafia figure of some stature. (He was later rubbed out, and in 2004 his remains were discovered in a Gotti-crew burial ground near the Brooklyn-Queens border.) Documents in the second and third sets of files revealed that Cannistraci had called on Philly Lucky to settle a dispute he was having with his co-owners in another floundering venture, a restaurant in the East Fifties called La Polonaise. When he got in his car for the last time, he was on his way to a meeting with Philly Lucky to talk about "a new business deal." It was easy to imagine that, in order to get out from under his debt, Cannistraci had let the Mob take over whatever holdings he had left. While Philly Lucky seemed to have been the prime suspect in the murder, he was never charged. The lone surviving detective I could find from the case told me that he couldn't remember why not.

The last two files in Mineola were full of personal effects: a cheap watch with a Twistoflex band, house keys, a desk diary, the Mother of Carmel ribbon he wore around his neck, and lots of photographs of him with a woman and toddlers whom I took to be his family—on a picnic, laying out a buffet in their apartment, wearing pink party hats and clapping their hands as they sing to each other. They had all been found on his person or in his hotel room, and I wondered if his wife hadn't ever tried to reclaim them.

What I found so rattling was not just that Cannistraci's murder hadn't been solved, but that the clues didn't point to Harold. Up to this point, I had been safe in the knowledge that his effect on people was to disrupt their lives—and I mean *disrupt* them. The inventory of monstrous detail was upsetting, but there was a sort of moral order to it: Harold was a catastrophic force that visited suffering upon other people. But what if those people were fully capable of screwing up their lives on their own?

The question was not resolved any better when Joseph Zavod's son drove me to his family's former home in Broomall, outside Philadelphia. Alan Zavod, who is married without children and works for a car dealership, is solidly built and had a salt-and-pepper goatee. He wore a leather bomber jacket with exposed rawhide lacing up the front. It was a Saturday, a snowless morning in December. The house, which has turned over twice since the day that Harold had tried to throw the Zavods out on the street with $1,500 to their name, sits on a cul-de-sac at the bottom of a hill. It has new siding and windows. The subdivision, Marple Heights, went up in 1955, one hundred and fifty identical split levels. Alan said that all but two of the original owners were Jewish. "We watched them build the house," he said. "My parents bought extra land in back for five hundred dollars, so the kids would have somewhere to play."

Joseph Zavod had not escaped Harold altogether unharmed. According to federal prosecutors, before Zavod went to the F.B.I., Angelo Bruno, the reigning Mafia don of Philadelphia, learned of the loan and, disapproving of a North Jersey gangster shylocking on his territory, temporarily forbade Harold from returning to collect. Only after Bruno's protection from Harold wore out did Zavod call the authorities. Zavod still struggled to find work after that, and Alan dropped out of Temple University in his freshman year to support the family with a succession of jobs in sales. Whether it was a favor for not assisting the government's crackdown on the Bruno family or because, as Alan put it, "nobody else wanted to hire my dad when he was in the papers for doing business with a loan shark," Joseph Zavod's next employer was a mortgage-placement company owned by one of Bruno's captains. I.R.S. audits, two indictments, and one conviction ensued.

"A lot of people don't realize the Angelo Bruno family were great guys," Alan said. "They paid back my father's loan to Konigsberg and then forgave it. One of Bruno's guys would say, 'Hey, Al, can you use a new suit?' and send me to pick out whatever I wanted at the men's store on Ninth and Passyunk. It was all an interesting experience. Anytime these gangster movies are on, I've got a little bit of insight."

Joseph Zavod died of heart failure, in 1985. During the last decade of his life, he opened a pizzeria with his wife and three children. "It wasn't so bad, all of us working together," Alan said. "We didn't need anyone else."

We took the West Chester Pike—a midcentury drag of automotive shops, package stores, funeral parlors, and rehab-equipment dealers—to the former West Philadelphia J.C.C. Now it is the Philadelphia Baptist Church, but the original carvings in the arched doorways remain: a Magen David, a menorah, Torah scrolls.

"For a long time after everything happened, my father and I would drive past this place, just to look at it," Alan said.

An elevated train roared by.

"Just like we're doing now. And then we'd discreetly flip it the bird, both of us."

SEVEN

Little Lambs

THE AFTERNOON OF Harold's arrest in the Cannistraci case, October 23, 1963, turned out to hold great significance. It was the last afternoon, to this day, that he spent outside of captivity. Here began the second career of Kayo Konigsberg, eluding the law from behind bars. The amount of time and energy he spent gumming up the government's wheels once he was locked up was extraordinary. The story of this mutual antagonism is a window on not just his criminal mind but also the Feds' tenderfooted efforts to fight the Mafia in the sixties.

Immediately, Harold gave up on appealing the smaller convictions in New Jersey and began serving three consecutive sentences at the Hudson County Jail in Jersey City. As a prisoner there, Harold was immune from a New York State writ of prosecution; no trial against him in New York could start until the D.A.'s office could get him moved.

He had good reason to stay, having bought off the warden during an

110

earlier hitch. "I ran that place," Harold told me. "I had money and I knew everybody in Hudson County. The warden was a sucker."

Harold's setup made the prison scene in *Goodfellas* look like prison. He had a private apartment done over for him in the third-floor jail library, with his own TV, telephone, radio, refrigerator, hot plate, desk, sofa, and what one inmate described to the *Daily News* as "parlor chairs." "He had candelabras and a wine-colored rug," a fellow prisoner, Michael Hardy, recalled. "On Rosh Hashanah he made sure all the Jewish cons got invited to services. He sent the guards out for pizzas." According to testimony in an eventual case against the warden, any inmate who paid Harold twenty-five dollars a week or came to him with the right recommendation was looked after. Harold took his meals alone with the warden. A grand jury in 1965 was told that one of Harold's frequent guests was twenty-five-year-old Marilyn Jane Fraser, identified by the U.S. Attorney's office as a heroin addict and a fifty-dollar-a-night call girl. She claimed to have been a Rose Bowl Queen (University of Southern California). At the time, stories circulated that Harold kept a prisoner as a cook and threw dinner parties when *Peyton Place* was on. Some evenings, it was said, he left the jail to collect debts, and some afternoons he and the warden went to the racetrack together.

In Gay Talese's *Honor Thy Father,* just after the Mafia heir Bill Bonanno arrives at jail, a guard presents him with some magazines, newspapers, and candy bars and says they are a welcoming gift from Kayo Konigsberg. "Your uncle always impressed me," Bonanno told me recently. "No matter where he was, he found a way to manipulate the situation."

He had a knack for getting under people's skin, doing favors that left them indebted or ensnared. David M. Satz, a former U. S. Attorney who prosecuted Harold in New Jersey, recalled, "Anybody that Harold drew into his vortex, they became his property. He overwhelmed people so they were like little lambs." There was, for instance, a lawyer who made a lot of money off Harold's investment tips, and another who had the poor judgment to frequent his parties at the Jersey City jail.

Teddy Stein, who'd grown up with him and joined the Bayonne Police Department, once testified to Harold's alibi in a robbery case. "They said to me point blank I could never go anywhere in the department if I did it," he told me. "All Kayo wanted me to do was say I saw him in Bayonne on the night of a robbery in Jersey City, and I had. It cost me a promotion." As a token of gratitude, Stein said, Harold stole a 1947 Dodge straight from a dealer's lot and left it in front of Stein's house. Though Stein didn't keep the car, he considered it a "touching" gesture. "Let me tell you something about him, if he liked you, he was an all-around individual."

Harold put a restaurateur cousin, Shimon Konigsberg, in business on the Lower East Side. Seymour Kaye's steakhouse (he Americanized his name) was legend for its backroom bazaar of hot furs and jewelry. Besides Harold's daughters, Shimon is the only relative who still takes Harold's calls. Not long ago, he made a surprise appearance at a family funeral. "Heshy sent me," he explained. "The last thing I need is to be on his bad side."

"He made me crazy," Frank Lopez, one of Harold's lawyers, told me. "When he was on trial in Manhattan once, he asked me go to Joe Louis's hotel and hand him a thousand dollars to sit with his supporters. He thought it would endear him to the three black jurors." Louis showed up, but Harold lost anyway.

Ivan Fisher represented Harold in one case and successful appeal, but abandoned it before the retrial. "He takes too much," he said. "And he's terrifying physically." He wanted to know if Harold was still angry with him for quitting.

"By the way," Fisher asked, "how old is he now?"

"Seventy-three."

"That helps," he said.

Exasperating demands and intimidation were woven through my own encounters with Harold. Each visit and letter carried requests: for a certain edition of a pocket dictionary or a brand of red felt-tips; for me to take up his parole with people of influence in New York State, or investigate the jurors who had found him guilty in a trial more than twenty years ago. He wanted to know if I had a problem with posing as a state official or if I was willing to hire a private eye—someone he'd read about in the *Times*—to do so. He never got tired of asking, and when I said no, he took it as an insult and called me "dishonorable" for effectively siding against him.

To sit there listening to Harold was an exercise in patience. I could go months without seeing him, and then the moment I'd show up again, he'd ferociously resume whatever plaint he'd left off talking about the last time. He could return from the bathroom after a long afternoon of gangland epics and evocations of Leo's preternatural ability as an egg candler—holding one egg at a time to a light box to look for blood spots on the yolk, my grandfather could go through 120 dozen eggs per hour—and stare at me as though he'd never laid eyes on me before.

Without my knowledge, he put me on his list of paralegal assistants (I wasn't the only person, or even the only relative, on whom he'd conferred this status). The arrangement made me uncomfortable, but I met with Harold on his terms because, he'd cautioned, it was our only assurance of privacy.

Harold was filling his days by suing everybody. He had complaints in play against Auburn, other prisons, his lawyers. He showed me entries from Westlaw, the legal-research database, that quoted from his successful appeals. "You get interested in something, you start reading about it," he said. He passed me a copy of a suit he'd filed against St. Paul Fire and Marine Insurance, which had paid him a claim of $916.87. The money had been awarded in 1971, but the check didn't get to him until 1992. By his calculus—factoring in inflation and the successful run of the securities he would have purchased with the money, not to mention damages—he was now owed $1.35 million. Then he had me take a look at the form letter he'd gotten in response, from an administrative agent of the insurance company.

"Look at that guy's signature," he said. "It's small, like some chickenshit. Do you know what that means? It means he's weak and lets people tell him what to do all the time." Harold smiled vauntingly. "Now, I've got a name, somebody to go to. I'm going to keep working on this cocksucker until I get due diligence."

He set a tote bag he'd constructed from plastic wrap and layers of packaging tape in front of us and pulled out a rabid and confusing letter he'd written to the judge who was arbitrating in his suit. "I want you to see how I work," he said. "You don't like my style of writing probably, but that's how I bring them to the table. See, I just shoot angles at the guy."

I tried to earn Harold's favor by listening patiently through his perorations—he liked to pick stocks and handicap elections, and was particularly keen on Hillary Clinton's long-term future. "She's like a palm tree," he said, holding an open hand in the air and slowly flexing his arm at the elbow. "She bends." To illustrate a point he was making about politics in New York State, he brought up the name of the onetime head of the Republican Party in Sullivan County, a man who had held court at Grossinger's, the Borscht Belt lodge. Recalling my grandmother's stories about trips to the Catskills, I asked Harold if he'd ever stayed at Grossinger's.

"Now, these are some fucking questions," he said. "Who didn't go there? Everybody was there that was Jewish." His gravid lap heaved up and down as his breathing became excited.

When he was really angry, Harold got rather businesslike, folding his hands in his lap and lecturing me. One day when this happened—he was upset by my apparent misunderstanding of his methods in brokering a meeting between Joseph P. Kennedy and Vito Genovese, and of how long another gangster had served in prison—I gathered my notebooks and stood up to leave.

"What are you doing?" he said softly. "We still got a few minutes."

"*Geh gesunt,*" I said, from a farewell that he'd taught me, meaning go healthy, go in good health, peace be with you.

"*Geh in gesunter hayt.*" Harold was walking away, finishing the saying under his breath. "*Shalom alechem.*"

He turned to face me again, and what he said gave me goose bumps. "Remember, by the mouth the fish dies."

Although he knew that I was writing about him and had taken to asking me what information from our interviews I'd already passed on to my editors, he continued to throw out Don Vito–like remarks from time to time. He was used to dominating everyone around him, or at least he'd convinced himself that he still could.

But I was starting to find Harold truly frightening. Once, when we got onto the subject of a policeman who'd recently been shot, I'd inquired about the Mafia lore that held that lawyers, cops, and reporters were off-limits. "You're wrong about that," he said. "Didn't you ever hear of Victor Riesel?"

I had. He was a syndicated columnist who was leaving Lindy's coffee shop on Broadway late one night in 1956 when a young man ran by and threw sulfuric acid at his face, blinding him for life. A member of the Lucchese crime family was later charged with arranging the attack. His motive was revenge for Riesel's crusading coverage of Mob corruption in the labor unions.

•   •   •

Although I girded myself against giving it a lot of thought, the probability was growing that Harold was not going to like what I wrote about him. I doubt he could fathom that I would dare publish a word about him without his approbation. Deep down, even I wasn't sure I could go through with it. I had mixed feelings about sharing what I knew with the world. When I'd begun, I hadn't envisioned singing his praises, but I certainly hadn't expected him to be so hostile, nor that what I'd learn would be so unmitigatedly awful.

I had been staying at the Auburn Holiday Inn, within walking distance of the prison, but suddenly it gave me the creeps. Before I went to find myself some supper, I lay down on the bed and struggled to picture Harold in his cot, motionless and asleep. He struck me as somebody whose addled brain never completely quieted. The very thought, I could tell, was going to keep *me* up all night.

I found a hotel in Syracuse, forty minutes away. I had got in the habit of packing only one day's worth of clothes, telling myself that Harold would probably not see me and I'd get to go home. But not once did he turn me away. Who else was going to listen to him? His own ambivalence toward my writing about him was hardly the first thing I'd observed him feeling torn over; I'd seen many times the self-pity that alternated with remorse, and the sporadic groveling for his family's attention that broke up long stretches of his being quite happy to leave them alone. I attributed Harold's resistance to the notion that protesting allowed him to maintain plausible deniability. If he objected every once in a while to what I was doing, neither his daughters nor anybody in the prison system could accuse him of talking out of school or courting attention—which, by the way, he probably liked. In *Contract Killer,* a memoir written by a former Gambino hit man, the author recalls Harold proudly decorating the walls of his cell with his own press clippings.

At around 9 P.M., I called my parents. They were sitting on their patio in Omaha. My father, usually very interested in the details of my work, was always tired if I phoned from Auburn, or busy sealing a leaky showerhead. That night I made an extra effort to engage him with some of Harold's stories.

"He's a fat old man in prison," my father said, cutting me off. "Why are you doing this to yourself? Isn't it depressing?"

Harold was slow to emerge from his cell the next morning, so I talked with two guards. One of them told me how Harold's cot is so penned in by stacks of legal files that he can barely stand up. "He's always working on something, reading papers and writing letters," he said. "When he dies, they're going to have to name the prison library after him."

We watched as a voluptuous black woman in a red T-shirt dress sat down to visit with a white prisoner. He was balding, with a ponytail, glasses, and tattoos. "She's another inmate's wife," one guard said.

"She's here to pass on her husband's dope," the other said. "She'll go in the bathroom, put the packet in her mouth, then come back and kiss this guy and he'll swallow it." I asked him why they didn't try to stop it. "There's only so much we can do," he said.

I'd brought Harold kosher salami, rye bread, and jars of mustard. When we took our place at a table, he said he didn't want any of it, intending, I'm sure, to let me know that I needed him more than he needed me. He sent me to the vending machines for two packs of Lunchables. Like my grandfather, he was a big eater who ate daintily. He set the little stacks of crackers, cheese, and watery ham on paper towels and meticulously lined up sixteen three-tiered sandwiches.

I still found the challenge of trying to win Harold over invigorating. The way to get on his good side was to convince him that I'd beaten him at something—by waiting out a tirade without getting flustered, or acing one of his impromptu interrogations, in which he would wrest the interviewer's role from me and test my knowledge of, say, his defense strategy in old cases. In the middle of this, he might ask how much I was being paid to write about him, or if I ever wore glasses, or why, instead of dressing up and carrying a briefcase "like a professional," I came to see him every day in shirtsleeves, carrying a stack of loose notebooks. "How come you don't wear a suit of clothes?" he said. "I guess you prefer to look like a bum."

Harold waved to a corrections officer walking past us. "That cop's a good guy," he said. "He's Spanish, I think." I said that he was probably Puerto Rican, because he was wearing a collar pin that bore a tiny Puerto Rican flag crossed with the Stars and Stripes. "That's pretty good of you, being aware of things," he said.

Harold had opened up one afternoon, regaling me with childhood reminiscences for a while, when he suddenly narrowed his eyes and went quiet.

"Stop using that psychology on me," he said.

I told him I wasn't doing anything except asking questions.

"Well, it's working now." I wasn't sure if I was supposed to feel flattered or chastened.

Harold was especially proud of his command of the news. In addition to the *Times* and the New York tabloids, he takes the *Wall Street Journal*, *Time*, and *Newsweek*, and for years subscribed to the *Criminal Law Reporter* and the *New York Law Journal*. "If I didn't have that reading, I'd probably be sick," he said. He cocked his head toward the center of the visiting room. "Most of these guys, they've been here five to ten years and they've lost it. I still have my equilibrium."

He asked if I'd seen an item in the *Times* just after John F. Kennedy Jr.'s fatal plane crash, in which a retired gangster, taking a break from promoting a miniseries on Showtime, saw fit to rule out foul play. "From what we know, John Jr. had no political aspirations at this time," the man had been quoted as saying. "So no one I know had any vendetta against him." We agreed that it was kind of a strange question for the paper of record to even acknowledge.

Harold nodded and let out a conspiratorial laugh, as if we were two chums conversing over 19th hole cocktails. "You and me, we could tell some stories," he said.

He blew his nose into a paper towel and, before he waddled off to the bathroom, he instructed me to read a copy of his letter to the New York Department of Corrections: further allegations of mistreatment at Auburn, violations of his civil rights.

"I tell you, I got a lot of gems in there," he said. "Maybe you'll read it and see—'Maybe this bum can write a column in the *Daily News*.'"

He explained that he had a lot to say about current events, Jewish affairs, business, and, of course, the American penal system. And whereas most newspapermen rely on their own research, he said, "I don't have to. I know what's coming out of my mind and head and heart." He planned to go straight to the paper's multimillionaire publisher. "I'll sit down with Mort Zuckerman, convince him." I started to ask how, but before I even got off the question Harold said, "That's between me and him and God."

That day, I'd arrived late, and he'd grumbled that I was wasting his time, making him wait. The following morning, he greeted me with a big smile. "I figured it out," he said. "You got a girlfriend up here."

"No, I don't." He asked if I had anybody in my life. Back then, I didn't.

"I hope you marry a Jewish girl," he said. "But let me tell you, there's only one thing that matters—respect. If you have that, you can get through the rest of things."

•   •   •

On May 28, 1964, with trials for both the Philadelphia and New York extortion cases looming, a Hudson County prison guard discovered Harold in a "heavy sleep." His friend the warden reported that he had fallen off a chair while changing a lightbulb and hit his head on a bed frame. When he came to, a government physician diagnosed a brain contusion with a possible hemorrhage: "In answer to questions, he mumbles incoherently. He tries to speak, whispers in a repetitious fashion, but is inaudible.... He is not capable of standing trial at present time." Both trials were delayed.

In Manhattan, two sanity hearings were held, occupying between them nine weeks and generating some 2,400 pages of transcripts. Psychiatrists who testified to his incompetence gave conflicting assessments, attributing it by turns to: a brain trauma; organic paresis, a brain disorder not caused by physical injury; paranoid schizophrenia characterized by autistic thinking; and "chronic brain syndrome." At pretrial motions, Harold was brought into the courtroom on a stretcher, then positioned in a wheelchair. In a bathrobe, wrapped in blankets and with a towel around his head, he would sag for hours as though catatonic, drooling and humming to himself.

Away from court, according to government records, Harold was observed conferring with his lawyer, reading the *New York Times,* and playing pinochle with other inmates. A subsequent prison evaluation said, "The patient was able to get several other patients to wait on him and to satisfy many of his needs.... He was able to convince the hydrotherapist that he was unable to use his right leg whatsoever even when actually standing and walking on both legs."

After doctors at Bellevue Hospital finally concluded that he was malingering, he concocted another strategy for evading trial. Although Harold denied rumors that he had cooperated with the government ("I never caved in," he told me. "Nobody could find anybody like me in a hundred years. I never was a stool pigeon"), federal documents and subsequent interviews make clear that he did, in fact, cooperate, and persuaded the Feds, in return, to secretly try to shield him from justice.

The federal files pertaining to Harold's criminal career are not part of the public record and have been sealed by the government for four decades and counting. When I first tried to obtain them under the Freedom of Information Act, I received a form letter telling me that, without a signed waiver from Harold or proof of his death (these seemed equally beyond my abilities), the F.B.I. was under no obligation to even acknowledge having logged a single word about Harold. Eventually, however, in the storage rooms of state and federal prosecutors, and in the homes of retired government investigators, I found thousands of foxed pages, documents that were classified confidential and never admitted in court—surveillance, F.B.I. interviews, and correspondence among Justice Department officials. In time, I began to piece together what transpired during his phase as an F.B.I. informant, from 1965 to 1968. He confessed to carrying out a string of Mafia killings. At the time, some had already been fruitlessly investigated, with Harold as a leading suspect. Some had been, as yet, total mysteries to the law.

It was Harold who initiated contact. On January 11, 1965, John Malone, the F.B.I.'s top man in New York, got word from a prison official that Harold was interested in a visit "alone as soon as possible." His curiosity aroused, Malone rushed to meet with Harold the next day, and barely recognized him. As Harold later explained, he hadn't cut his hair or shaved in weeks in the interest of keeping up his non compos mentis appearance. He'd also stopped eating and had dropped a significant amount of weight.

According to a coded "airtel" memo from Malone to J. Edgar Hoover, Harold immediately declared that he might be willing to furnish information about La Cosa Nostra that included twenty murders. "He indicated that he is directly involved in many of the murders he will give us and when finished he would probably go to the electric chair and this he did not want to do," the memo went on. "His last condition was that the F.B.I. supply him with a sufficient quantity of sleeping pills with which to commit suicide. He was told that this was an utterly ridiculous condition which could not and would not be met. He withdrew it."

To test Harold, Malone asked what he knew about a $500,000 truck robbery that had just occurred in Paterson, New Jersey. All Harold would say was that two of the men involved were also in on a recent Wells Fargo robbery. Malone asked if Harold could deliver the leader of the Genovese family to the F.B.I. "I can give you him three times," Harold said. Asked for proof, Harold said, "I'll tell you where the bodies are and that should be proof enough."

The F.B.I. knew enough about Harold to be both skeptical and tantalized. He "seemed normal" in conversation, a federal official noted in another report. The only time he got emotional was when he talked about his wife and children and his eyes teared up, although, the report went on, "this too could have been an act."

And it wasn't as though Harold didn't have apparent motives. "When asked why he was doing this," Malone wrote in his memo, "he stated that now he is down and out, the hoods that he did so much for are abandoning him and giving him a hard time, and he wants to have the last say." Several of his rackets had been taken over by associates while he was in jail, and he was still furious with Tony Pro and his gang for depriving him of his share of the Local 560 action and for dropping his wife from the union payroll. Over the coming years, Harold made several attempts to squeeze hush money out of his old colleagues. In a letter to Sally Bugs Briguglio, he wrote, "What moneys you withhold from me you will spend ten times over in court litigation and in addition I will write to the United States Government in New York and New

Jersey and bring in the Federal government. Now you can call me a stool pigeon you got it in writing." He even sent his lawyer at the time, Frank Lopez, to convey threats. "I went to all the bosses—the Colombos, the Gambinos, Tony Pro's people," Lopez told me. "I told them Harold said, 'Look, you fucking guys, help my family out,' etc., or else Harold was going to testify." But nobody was persuaded.

As Harold began negotiating with the F.B.I., he asked that they provide his wife and children with protection and money. Hoover fielded suggestions on how to do this from within the Bureau. One supervisor liked the idea of a sliding pay scale, based on what Harold could produce: "For example, Konigsberg might be offered a flat sum for information and testimony leading to the conviction for a felony of any 'button' man"—a hit man—"or equivalent. A higher sum could be offered for similar information and testimony of a 'caporegima' [sic] and a still higher sum for an 'underboss' or 'boss.'" Harold requested $250 a week for his family for as long as he remained incarcerated; another agent proposed giving him $5,000 for the corpse of a missing person.

Though it remains arguably fertile ground for an ever-dwindling cadre of film and television producers, the Mafia has been all but dead for a while now. In 1999, for example, the *New York Times* reported that perhaps only twenty-five made men were operating in the state of New Jersey, while twenty years earlier, the number had been more like two hundred. During Harold's day, the Mafia's ranks were not only vast and largely unpenetrated by law enforcement but they posed a serious public-relations problem for the F.B.I. Even when a 1967 Presidential commission estimated that the Mob's annual income was $6 to $7 billion—more than what America's ten largest industrial corporations took in combined, pundits noted—J. Edgar Hoover still maintained that there was "no such thing as organized crime." As the director of the Bureau since 1924, Hoover felt that to acknowledge the Mafia and its increased pervasiveness was tantamount to an admission of failure. As the *Wall Street Journal*'s rackets-beat reporter, Jonathan Kwitny, pointed out in his book *Vicious Circles: The Mafia in the Marketplace,* Hoover's New York bureau had more than four hundred agents in New York "looking under beds for reds" but only four assigned to organized crime.

But in 1961, Robert Kennedy became U.S. Attorney General and made dismantling the Mafia his highest priority. He coordinated the twenty-six federal investigative agencies—from the F.B.I. to the I.R.S. to the Bureau of Narcotics—to pool their information on hoodlums. He hired a cadre of ambitious young meritocrats as prosecutors, one of whom, Earl Johnson, had recently completed an inspired academic assessment of the Mob, which, to this day, coworkers of his refer to as a sacred text. "At the hands of organized crime, America has endured the extraction of billions every year, the stifling of free competition in hundreds of markets, the maiming and murder of countless human beings, the systematic cultivation of human weaknesses in our population," Johnson wrote. "This is a horrible price for American society to pay. And yet organized crime continues unquashed and largely unscathed."

Between 1960 and 1962, the number of annual federal racketeering indictments rose from 17 to 262. Kennedy also pushed new antiracketeering legislation through Congress—laws that made it easier for prosecutors to provide immunity to witnesses, expanded wiretapping regulations to permit eavesdropping and phone taps, and made it a federal crime to travel across state lines for illegal business. In 1964, boasting to reporters of the various measures he'd been championing, Kennedy said, "It's because of this that we've been able to arrest Harold Konigsberg for extortion in Philadelphia," a reference to the loan-sharking case for which Harold was still awaiting trial.

Hoover, meanwhile, was in the position of playing catch-up, and

Harold presented a valuable opportunity. "The Mafia was still so tightly organized and powerful, it was an unusual breakthrough for an inside guy like Konigsberg to be talking," Edwin Stier, who prosecuted federal organized-crime cases in New Jersey from 1965 to 1969, told me. An agent in the F.B.I.'s New York office wrote in a memo to Hoover, "The NYO is of the opinion that if Konigsberg is ever made fully coopera- tive, he would seriously damage personnel in LCN's"—La Cosa Nostra's—"New York and New Jersey 'families.' "

Hoover gave the go-ahead for making a deal with Harold, but with- out promising money. "You should take into consideration that Mrs. Konigsberg is of Italian background and herself comes from a hoodlum- type family," he wrote to the New York office, and "they may not desire to be relocated by and receive financial assistance from the Govern- ment." Hoover instructed his G-men to be "most circumspect" in handling the informant, "bearing in mind the possibility of a devious trap being set by him for personal reasons."

A team of agents was assigned to visit Harold at the federal penitentiary in Danbury, Connecticut, where Hoover had moved him, "so as not to alert the District Attorney's office [in New York] to the possibility that Konigsberg is cooperating with the F.B.I." The first two who showed up, on May 12, 1965, signed their own names and titles to the visitors' register, but under the line for "Person Visited" wrote "Warden," in order to maintain Harold's privacy with the correctional officers. Then the warden himself brought Harold by wheelchair into his office, shut the door, and, at 10:45 A.M., left the agents and the prisoner to get ac- quainted.

Harold had no intention of making the process easy for the F.B.I. He began by playing dumb. "He rambled in speech, using the word 'Mary' numerous times . . . and on occasion pointed to a photograph of the late

President Kennedy on the wall of the room, stating 'Eisenhower,'" the agents recorded. When one of the agents asked him if he wanted a television in his cell, they continued, "This statement seemingly brought KONIGSBERG out of his act," and "he appeared in complete control of himself from this point." Harold complained to the agents about prison conditions. He cautioned them that he didn't want it to get out to anybody—not even his lawyers or his wife—that he was informing. And, speaking of his wife, he said, he was not happy that stories had reached her of prostitutes having visited him at the Hudson County Jail. He asked if the F.B.I. couldn't pressure the officers involved in the jail investigation to lay off on that.

The warden came by to tell Harold that his wife was in the waiting room. Harold returned to what the F.B.I. came to call his "Johnny the Dunce" persona ("Me no care. Me gonna die anyway"), and the interview was over.

The agents continued to show up at Danbury. Much as when I visited him some thirty-five years later, Harold's mood and his willingness to cooperate were unpredictable. He promised the F.B.I. that whatever information he gave was as good as gold, that they "would never find anybody as honorable" as he was, and that once he gave his word he would go "100 percent with the Bureau." He sometimes gave assurances, unsolicited, that he wouldn't offer information to any other branch of the government—not to the Federal Bureau of Narcotics, which "has no ethics or principles," nor to either of the local prosecutors, in New York and in Philadelphia, who were waiting to try him in the extortion cases. On another occasion, however, he told the F.B.I. that if his interview conditions—certain agents together, certain dates and times of day—were not met, he would furnish all of his information to the New York D.A. just to spite them.

Sometimes, he said he didn't care about immunity from what he admitted and would testify anyway. One day, he said that if he ever thought the Bureau had done him a bad turn, he would accuse the agents of promising immunity—although they hadn't—and going back on their word.

"He would give you part of a story because he said you already knew the rest of it," said John Connors, an agent who had tracked Harold since the early sixties. "He goaded you into asking questions he wasn't going to answer. But he got carried away. He liked listening to himself talk." In the first weeks, Harold outlined the power structures of Mafia families, who owned which rackets, which gangsters ate their daily marinara where. But when agents came to see him on May 24, he was bored with providing mere intelligence.

"This is nothing," he said to them. "Why be interested in nickels and dimes?" Soon he was cataloging his own Mob hits.

EIGHT

Confessions of a Hit Man

THE TABLE OF CONTENTS to Harold's F.B.I. confessions lists twenty murders, deaths, and disappearances.

On the afternoon that I obtained the confessions, I returned home and started in on them immediately, but soon lost my appetite. I had an intense headache. I began skimming the pages and fell asleep.

Harold's confessions, even though they were partially redacted, were at once sickening, grim, intriguing, and clinical. The statements detailed one violent and merciless homicide after another. The killings were recounted with bravado—for the murders themselves and for having gotten away with them and for being able to rub the agents' civil-servant faces in them while they hung on every word.

For some time now, I'd anticipated the moment when I would come upon some massive documentation of Harold's depravity and rush to share it with my father, Grandma Frieda, my grandaunts. Then they would no longer be able to shrug him off as easily. Instead, I wanted to shield their eyes. Who wouldn't?

My parents were in New York that weekend. Against my better judgment, perhaps, I told them over dinner about the new information I'd found. I asked what Grandpa Leo would have made of Harold's confessions if he'd somehow been impelled to read them. My father said that Leo would've just echoed whatever Grandma Frieda said, and that she would have claimed incredulity and glossed over everything. Even if I'd managed to access his private thoughts, he said, I would have had no evidence that he was emotionally stirred. "Grandpa wasn't much for deep feelings," he said.

My father asked if it was such a wise idea to be interested in a bunch of unprosecuted murders and whether there was any danger to what I was doing. I said I didn't think so, and reminded him that Harold was a fat old man in prison. My mother asked why I couldn't have become a sports-writer.

One of the first hits Harold admitted to was the 1958 shooting of Joseph Barbito. He was the longshoreman whose murder Harold had already been acquitted of—the case that had brought about "the thing with Uncle Louie in the garage" and Aunt Beattie's lifelong embarrassment over her husband's night in jail. Harold said that the murder had gone down almost exactly as the prosecution charged.

Buoyed by this new information, the F.B.I. launched an extensive reinvestigation, tracking down and interviewing the original witnesses all over again. But, whatever the agents turned up, it was insufficient to bring the case back to trial. Because Harold had already been tried and gotten off, an attorney at the Justice Department wrote in a memo to an F.B.I. supervisor, "issues of motive or co-conspirators are academic."

Patrick (Paddy the Priest) Martinetti and Marino Romito were two more victims. They were Mafia associates and had been shot on

Thanksgiving morning, 1957, and left on the floor of a parked car in Jersey City. Thirteen one-dollar bills were fanned out on the backseat above them. The tableau, and the fact that one of the men had taken a bullet in his mouth and one in each eye, led a supervisor to surmise in the *Jersey Journal* that they'd been killed as payback for a "gangland double cross." Harold's version of events confirmed this. He said that he and a team of mobsters had carried out the killings. The victims had been indiscreet in their handling of a truck full of stolen cobalt, he said, and the Cosa Nostra boss who assigned the hits "wanted to teach everyone a lesson."

There was Samuel Wolkoff, whose body had been found on June 6, 1958, in a parking lot near the West Side Highway. He was forty-two years old and a partner in a meatpacking company. Harold and two men whom the F.B.I. identified as Genovese soldiers killed him because he supposedly knew the whereabouts of a hoard of stolen cash and jewels to which the Genoveses felt entitled.

Harold had walked into Wolkoff's office on West Fourteenth Street, according to the statements he gave, and claimed to be an N.Y.P.D. detective sent to arrest him. He told Wolkoff that a surveillance operation had implicated him in a case, then let him call his wife from a pay phone to tell her he wouldn't be getting home on time. Wolkoff begged not to be put in handcuffs, so Harold held off until they got to his car. Harold's two accomplices were waiting for them in a cream-and-orange Mercury. They drove Wolkoff to a house in the town of River Edge, New Jersey, where they alternately tightened and loosened a rope around his neck and questioned him about where the money and jewels were. Harold told the others, "This guy isn't going to tell you anything because he doesn't know anything. Let's kill him now." Then, as he recounted to the agents, he and one of his henchmen took hold of the rope and strangled Wolkoff to death. "Subsequent events," an F.B.I. report notes, "proved that the 14th Street butcher never did have control of any alleged fund."

On and on it went, over the course of two years, with Harold doling out information in bits and pieces, depending on his mood. When he was unhappy with his prison treatment, the Feds would move him to a new facility. Sometimes, once he had established his own participation in a given murder, Harold would narrate in the third person, referring to himself as "you know who" or "the other guy." In some of the 302s, as the F.B.I. reports are known, Harold says that he was the person who fired the gun, or tightened the garroting rope, and so on. In others, he gives the credit to a collaborator or leaves his own role vague. In the descriptions of the latter type of confession, the agents' play-by-play leads to the moment that Harold and a couple of his thugs are about to commit a murder, then states elliptically that the victim "was killed" or "was shot," without naming the triggerman. There are also murders he discusses that he claims to have had no part in, explaining that he has merely heard about them.

"The assumption was, he had a primary involvement in these murders he was talking about," one of the F.B.I. agents who visited him told me, and two of Harold's lawyers confirmed this. "He wouldn't have survived in the Mafia, because they couldn't have controlled him. But they put him to work."

Given the sheer magnitude and dimension of the confessions, some people in the government who did not hear them firsthand were initially skeptical. David M. Satz, Robert Kennedy's newly appointed U.S. Attorney for New Jersey at the time, says that when the F.B.I. first mailed him the interview reports, "I thought this guy was just popping off." John Wilgus, an agent charged with running down Harold's claims, told me, "That's the coin of the realm with organized crime, how much these guys can say they've been involved with. They embellish prodigiously."

Indeed, despite the preponderance of cold-type classification, numberings, and warnings, the 302s could be indiscriminate in tone, with page after page simply quoting or paraphrasing whatever came out of Harold's mouth—unsubstantiated, unquestioned, largely unfiltered, with all utterances receiving equal billing. For example, a report on the ambush that Harold withstood from Tony Pro's crew at the Bergen County swim club read: "He stated the fourth person who was in the Cabana Club when he, KONIGSBERG, was shot was FRANK ROMEO. He stated he felt a little bad about furnishing his name inasmuch as ROMEO was his best man at his wedding."

Nevertheless, Paul Durkin, the primary agent assigned to interview Harold, told me, "In general, we felt he was someone to be trusted. There were follow-ups to things he told us. We just didn't get something and run with it. We had to verify those things."

To bolster his credibility, Harold sent F.B.I. agents to a Mob graveyard near the Jersey shore, where they exhumed the remains of at least two men whom they believed to be his victims, and hair and bone fragments that were thought to belong to a third. They had been buried on farmland owned by one of Harold's pet thugs. "You could write the script just by seeing what was in the garage," Kenneth Hackmann, the agent who supervised the effort, told me. "He had the front loader and a bunch of barrels."

Hackmann and I were sitting at the dining table of his airy retirement condo in Virginia Beach. He had prepared for my visit by locating an envelope full of photos from the investigations; he had mug shots of Harold and his old colleagues and pictures from the dig, which he kept referring to as the "Mafia Memorial Park." He flipped through the pile until he found a picture of himself at the site, in a crew cut and a woolen mac, shoveling in the woods adjacent to a house. The photographs were in color. The house was yellow.

"It had snowed the night before. We started with shovels and picks," Hackmann said. The government brought to bear more than seventy-five agents and detectives, a bulldozer, a backhoe, air compressors, pneumatic drills, and floodlights borrowed from the nearby naval air station so they could dig through the night. The digging began at 2 P.M., and by 4:05, when the excavation reached a depth of three feet, the first long bone appeared. It belonged to a suspected government informant named Angelo Sonnessa. He had been hog-tied and buried beneath the foundation of an old mash pit, exactly where Harold said he would be.

Hackmann pulled out a picture of a femur or a tibia—the bone was too caked with dirt to tell which. "Yep, there's Sonnessa," he said.

He flipped until he got to a photo of a rusted metal drum, which had been found beneath the cement floor of a demolished chicken coop. The drum looked empty but for a layer of sandy soil. These were the remains of the next victim, whose body had disintegrated so severely that the F.B.I. lab had to rely on his gold pivot tooth, a stainless-steel lingual bar, and his double-hernia truss in order to make an identification.

The excavation, which went on for two days, became an extended publicity op for the F.B.I., and cameramen from nearly every news outlet on the eastern seaboard were provided an unobstructed view of the diggers hard at work. "Mr. Hoover said that the finding of these bodies is a very graphic demonstration of the degree to which organized crime has established its own code of justice inside a legal society and makes it necessary that there be a continuing, all-out drive against this element," a federal press release read.

The Mafia heard of the secret informant's identity within a few days, and so did the *New York Times,* which noted on the front page that "the underworld was reported to be in a state of great anxiety." A criminal lawyer was quoted as saying, "They who are about to die, salute him. If it suits Kayo's fancy, he can turn in all the top boys. I think it will suit his fancy and I think they're all dead."

The first person brought low by Harold's graveyard maneuvers wasn't an organized-crime figure but a member of the U.S. House of Representatives. It began with the discovery of a pair of orthopedic shoes, which the F.B.I. traced to one Barney O'Brien, a down-and-outer from Bayonne. Harold told the F.B.I. that O'Brien had died of a heart attack while visiting the home of Rep. Cornelius Gallagher, of Bayonne, and that he had been called upon by the Mob to remove the corpse. Gallagher was a J.V.-level congressman on the rise, a close friend of the Kennedys, and, as it happened, a vocal critic of J. Edgar Hoover. He had gone so far as to denounce Hoover's spook tactics—keeping intelligence files on most of official Washington, for instance—on the House floor. In 1968, *Life* published the F.B.I.'s account of this episode in a story alleging Gallagher's Mafia connections. Gallagher denied the accusation, but admitted that he knew Harold. "I tell you, everybody knew Kayo," he told *Life*. "Kayo is an original."

"Hoover and his goddam fanatics were using Konigsberg to help them compile information, true or otherwise, on whoever they thought they might want to blackmail—celebrities, other politicians, union people," Gallagher said when I visited him and his wife at their home at the western edge of New Jersey, near the Delaware Water Gap. "Konigsberg was telling stories like Scheherazade because he wanted to stay out of a real jail. Eventually, when they said, 'Harold, what about that guy Gallagher?' they plugged in that story of a body in the basement."

Gallagher and his wife were gracious hosts, who served lunch on Royal Crown Derby china, and I enjoyed their company. But, like Harold, he may not be the most reliable narrator. He had recently, in his late seventies, finished serving a prison sentence for tax evasion, his second stint in the big house. (He attributed both to government conspiracies.) And while the federal investigation that followed was never able to establish a link between the corpse and Gallagher, his wife, or his home, Harold's story had legs, as they say in the news business. A storm of coverage followed, and Gallagher's political career eventually petered out. In 1964, just a year before Harold's confessions, he'd been considered a strong contender for the vice-presidential slot on Lyndon Johnson's ticket.

What the government wanted most was to pin the disappearance of the Local 560 secretary-treasurer Anthony Castellito on Tony Pro, who was a bigger catch than Harold. In 1965, labor corruption was reaching new levels. During the previous two years, another union challenger of Tony Pro's had been fatally shot outside his house. According to the F.B.I., he was heard uttering the names "Tony Pro" and "Sammy Provenzano" on his deathbed. In addition, Jimmy Hoffa and seven fellow Teamsters had been indicted for defrauding the Central States Pension Fund of twenty million dollars. In *The Enemy Within,* Robert Kennedy's book about investigating unions for the Senate's McClellan Committee, Kennedy described the Teamsters as "a conspiracy of evil," and "the most powerful institution in the country—aside from the United States Government itself."

Harold told the F.B.I. about murdering Castellito at the farmhouse upstate, but, before he would agree to testify before a grand jury, he demanded that the government drop the extortion charges against him in Philadelphia and New York. William Hundley, who ran the organized-crime unit of the Justice Department, was amenable, even recommending that Harold, as long as he helped them locate Castellito's body, be granted immunity from prosecution for any crimes he admitted to. As he assured his superiors in a memo dated October 7, 1965, "Since he is doing 10 years on his present 'rap' "—for the stolen suits at the Hoo-Ha Club—"I don't think we have much to lose." As to the New York indictment, Hundley added, mentioning the Manhattan D.A. by name, "I know I can handle that one informally." Meanwhile, the Feds quietly abandoned the case against him in Philadelphia.

The last order made no sense to J. Shane Creamer, the U.S. Attorney who'd been assigned to prosecute Harold in Philadelphia. In fact, until I called him recently to discuss the matter, he'd never been told that the dropped charges were Harold's reward for talking to the F.B.I. "The story I got from Washington was that he fell off a chair or something and we had to let it go," Creamer said. "It was very mysterious."

The government installed Harold at the Medical Center for Prisoners in Springfield, Missouri, protracting his hoax with another year of competency exams. Harold was in the acute psychiatric unit, on the 2-1-East wing, and put on a round-robin of various medications: high-dosage injections of a tranquilizing agent, Cogentin (an anti-Parkinson's drug), and a thousand milligrams daily of Thorazine, dispensed from large plunger bottles into Dixie cups like mustard at a stadium.

A staff psychiatrist reported that Harold viewed himself as a "grand manipulator of people and events in the legal area despite the fact that he never went to college, and [was intent on] showing people how smart he is. . . . His memory for immediate, recent, and remote events appeared to be excellent . . . particularly when relating to previous court testimony and past injustices." Another wrote, "Konigsberg views all social and interpersonal relationships as a struggle or an adversary-type of contest in which he has to get the upper hand or get defeated." One evaluation described him as "passive, depressed and mute," and one noted that when Harold was asked about loneliness or his family he often cried.

He told the doctors who examined him that he was in constant visual and auditory contact with one imaginary companion whom he called "the Judge," and another who had "magical powers." He accused the hospital staff of trying to brainwash him, rip his body limb from limb, and steal or poison his food. "When the patient finally allowed himself to eat he ate in a fashion that was as pathologic as his food exclusion," a doctor wrote. "He would ravenously eat such items as lettuce leaves or soup. He would literally scoop up large quantities of foodstuff and gorge himself, consuming three or four times the average portion in a matter of seconds."

Leonard Melnick, a Springfield parole officer who was assigned to monitor Harold through a window as he placed telephone calls to his lawyers, described Harold's manner as "relaxed" and "extraordinarily confident." Melnick told me, "I wouldn't say I was scared of him, but I would say he was very large." When Harold first learned Melnick's name, he smiled, shook his hand, and said, "Oh, a *landsman*."

According to a memo that the director of the U.S. Bureau of Prisons wrote apprising the U.S. Attorney General of Harold's time at Springfield, it was evident to Springfield's chief psychiatrist that Harold was putting on an act. However, the memo allowed, the chief psychiatrist agreed to certify Harold as "insane," under pressure from his supervisor.

Later, when three high-ranking officials at the Justice Department— their names were Henry Peterson, Fred Vinson, and William Lynch— moved Harold to a prison on the East Coast to coordinate having him testify against the Mafia, it dawned on them that a paper trail of mental illness might erode his credibility as a witness. Discussion ensued. Then, on an index card that was stapled to a routing slip and circulated, Vinson wrote a short note: "How about Lynch's suggestion that K. go back to Springfield and convince drs. that he fooled them?" And so the doctors at Springfield officially declared Harold "restored to sanity."

• • •

At Springfield Harold began to study law—in particular, the area of postconviction relief. He filed at least ten suits alleging mistreatment in prison, and to help with the paperwork, he retained Frank Lopez, a regular on the Mob's roster of defense attorneys. Lopez had fastidiously pomaded hair and a smooth complexion, and as a lawyer was blessed, a colleague said, "with more talent in his pinkie than most of us have in our entire bodies. He was kissed on the lips." Lopez came from Brooklyn and was married to the daughter of a Spanish diplomat. His gangland clients adored him and hewed respectfully to his advice. He was, however, courtly to a fault, that fault being an inability to say no to anybody. Harold made him suffer.

One day, Harold phoned Lopez to say he'd just filed a writ against the Bureau of Prisons. The guards at Springfield, he said, had stolen his watch, were anti-Semitic, and "a million other things," Lopez recalled. "He says, 'Frank, the hearing is set for Monday. When you get here, I'm going to give you a motion so you'll have something to talk about.' So for this I had to get out of everything else I was doing. I was running around New York trying to get judges to adjourn cases I was in the middle of. When I got there, I saw that over the weekend he had inflicted upon himself a terrible beating. He had a broken rib. He had scars. He was bloody. He said, 'We'll tell them the guards did it.'"

Lopez was soon flying out to Springfield every other weekend. "I'd sit with Harold and we'd scheme from nine to five, Friday through Sunday," he said. "If he was on one of his so-called prison fasts, it was my responsibility to sneak food in for him. So, 'Okay, Frank, go get the chicken.'"

When the time was right, the government secretly put Harold on a train to Newark, then transported him to the Somerset County Jail, where not even the warden knew his identity. On June 30, 1966, he led marshals to the scene of Castellito's burial, on farmland near Route 33, east of Freehold Township. "We looked for two days," Arnold Stone, the Justice Department's point man on the search effort, said. "We didn't find Castellito. Harold kept saying, 'It's gonna take a while.'" He had received a letter from his wife saying that she'd heard the body had been moved. It was hoped that laboratory tests could find traces of the corpse or its disinterment, but while Harold recognized the land, the roads, and the farms in the area, he couldn't pinpoint the exact location.

Without Castellito's body, the Feds' case, along with their attempt to keep Harold out of court, fell apart. On December 7, 1966, Harold's trial for the extortion and beating of Fat Joe Cannistraci finally began, in lower Manhattan. Here he attempted to bring about a mistrial by goading the judge into losing his cool. He announced that one of his lawyers, Frances Kahn, was a "spy" for the D.A. and fired her in order to represent himself. Then he convinced her along with Frank Lopez to serve as his paralegal assistants. (He loved making use of people in this capacity.) Both of them fed him notes from their seats at the defense table. "I was still learning to read and write in those days," Harold told me. "I had to have my wife sit alongside of me and look up words in a dictionary."

"People lined up outside 60 Centre Street to see the show he put on," Leonard Newman, one of the prosecutors, recalled. Harold wore the same mismatched suit every day, and what the *New York Times* called a "King of Clubs beard." There were the inevitable requests for Kentucky Fried Chicken and Tropicana orange juice (in unopened cartons, because he claimed that the Mafia, and perhaps the government, wanted to poison him). He bullied witnesses, and, when overruled, accused the judge, Abraham Gellinoff, of trying to hide exculpatory information. Whenever the judge wouldn't allow his line of questioning, Harold gleefully threatened to prolong the trial. One time, when Gellinoff remained seated while the rest of the courtroom stood for a recess, Harold said, "What's the matter, Judge, are your pants wet?"

The People were represented by Frank Rogers, an assistant D.A. Rogers was Black Irish, a pipe smoker who wore three-piece suits, a member of the law review at St. John's, a skinny fellow beginning to take on middle-age weight. "Frank was a street guy, not a traditional lawyer. He loved investigations, nuts and bolts; he was at his best around cops," said Michael Kavanagh, who worked as a prosecutor under his wing some years later. "He wasn't much of a people person. I went to see him once with a simple procedural question and he just dismissed me. He said, 'We made a mistake hiring you.' "

Although Rogers was arguing his first trial, he was already known to have designs on a future in politics. Harold homed in on him, denouncing him as a "bigot, sadist, a lowlife, reptilest, fork-tongue talker." He brought Rogers to the witness stand no fewer than four times. "Every time he runs out of witnesses, he calls me," Rogers complained.

Cross-examining a psychiatrist who had been brought in to establish his sanity, Harold took an hour setting up a hypothetical situation. "Now, Doctor, assuming everything I've said to be true," he said, finally getting to his question, "do you have an opinion as to whether District Attorney Rogers is crazy?"

Deep into the trial, when Harold's ramblings strayed further than usual, Gellinoff cut him off. "Mr. Konigsberg, listen, my friend, I'm—"

" 'My friend'? You got ten dollars, I'll sell you back your friendship," Harold said. "You're a miasma of perplexity. I just learned that one. How do you like that word, Judge?"

Gellinoff finally broke the following day. "Shut up when I'm talking," he said, after excusing the jurors. "You are the greatest faker in the history of the court that I know of.... You are one of the most brilliant people that I have ever seen as a defendant in this court. You have a keen, logical mind. I have said these things on the record so that you will know, Mr. Konigsberg—"

"That you're prejudiced?"

"You will not get away with this."

Those who wanted to like Harold were at a loss. The *Post*'s Murray Kempton, fond though he was of anybody who bucked the criminal-justice system, still had the decorum of a Roman senator, and Harold's scattershot approach led him to file a sorrowful dispatch: "One went ... preparing to salute one of the giants of the American struggle for Constitutional liberty.... One fled after the second hour with an idol crumbling in the dust behind."

"To be up there pretending to go along with what he was doing—oh, I was sitting in the loneliest seat in the house," Frank Lopez told me. "But the jurors liked Harold, they really did. The first time they came in, they were deadlocked on everything." After more deliberations, the jury found him guilty on four counts of extortion and one of conspiracy, but they remained undecided on four other counts and acquitted him of one.

On the day of sentencing, Harold refused to admit that he was the same Harold Konigsberg who had been convicted of two prior felonies. Gellinoff had no choice but to impanel a new jury and try a case simply to establish Harold's identity. Another five weeks in court, and Gellinoff gave him a stiff sentence of thirty to forty-four years but remarked, "You're turning into quite a constitutional lawyer."

Even with this conviction, Harold was still in the clear on his entire string of homicides. Peter Richards, a Justice Department lawyer who had spent the better part of two days interviewing Harold, pleaded to his supervisors in a memo dated October 31, 1967:

Realizing that if Konigsberg's New York State sentence of 30–44 years should be reversed (which it probably will be) and that his Federal sentence will expire in slightly more than two years, I feel that ultimately, all else failing, consideration should be given to prosecuting Konigsberg alone for one or more of the murders on which he has given statements to the F.B.I. It seems to me impossible to allow this man, who has confessed to more than twenty murders and who has told us that he will "go gunning" for his enemies when he is released from prison, ever to be released from custody.

Afraid that Harold's conviction was going to be reversed on the grounds that his courtroom antics had made a fair trial impossible, the Feds jettisoned the idea of using him primarily to get Tony Pro. Instead, they decided to turn the tables and use the admission of the Castellito murder as evidence against Harold himself. On February 20, 1968, the U.S. Attorney's office prepared an indictment, of Harold alone, and drafted a press release—only to drop the indictment soon afterward.

The problem was that with neither a body nor an eyewitness, there still wasn't enough evidence to prosecute Harold for the murder. And when government lawyers began to work through the possibility of trying him for Castellito's kidnapping, they found that a recent Supreme Court ruling would put in place a five-year statute of limitations; the case, by now, was seven years old.

All of which meant that the F.B.I.'s interviews with Harold had yielded nothing but humiliation.

When I spoke with the agents who'd spent all that time trying to cultivate Harold, they hardly sounded betrayed. In fact, they were interested in continuing to protect him. "I don't want to get into discussing our relationship," Special Agent Paul Durkin said. Why not? "It's because I liked him. We had a certain relationship and I honor that relationship." He said he was afraid of putting Harold in jeopardy. "Up where he is, he could get hurt from both ends." Special Agent Frank Donnelley, who was paired with Durkin for most of the interviews, asked me if there was anything he could do to assist Harold in legal matters or parole efforts. "I'd try to help him if I could," he said.

NINE

The Confidence Man

I NEVER *enjoyed* anything," Harold told me once, drawing out the word as if its very use signified a constitutional weakness. "Clothes, broads, money—that didn't mean garbage to me. Women are women. You go to bed, it's all over after ten minutes." He disdained "that guy Gotti, standing on the corner all dressed up and hollering pussy for sale." He sat up tall and exaggeratedly straightened his collar. "That's a figure of speech."

Harold certainly didn't possess the sensualist tendencies associated with gangsters of his day—the finely tailored dons and their ritualized high living. "He was much more interested in power than money," his lawyer Ivan Fisher said. "He needed money—to bribe people, say—but it held no allure beyond that." Fisher struggled to name something that Harold took pleasure in. "He liked to eat," he said eventually.

It occurred to me that Harold has never had any use for other people except as just that—something he could use. What motivated him above all else was the exhilaration of getting over. Although when he spoke to the F.B.I. he had hopes of self-preservation and Tony Pro's comeuppance, he did it mostly for sport. He liked nothing more than dissembling and putting people—especially those who had some kind of nominal control over him—through contortions. "Now, there's a lot of things I'm guilty of," he told me once. "I'm just saying, catch me on something."

Not long after he wrapped up the extortion trial against Harold in Manhattan, Frank Rogers, the D.A., and one of his detectives, Joseph Coffey, brought their great white whale in for questioning. "We wanted information on other people," Coffey told me. Because they didn't know the extent of what Harold had already told the F.B.I., Coffey said, "Rogers made the mortal fuckup of giving him immunity."

"They had no idea Harold was going to implicate himself," Frank Lopez, who was also in the room, said.

At the time, Coffey was investigating the homicide of Johnny Earle, a waterfront racketeer who'd been shot nine years earlier, in front of a lunchtime crowd at the Fifty-seventh Street Cafeteria, near Eighth Avenue. A possible motive, according to the *Times,* was that Earle had made off with the entire haul of $312,000 from a bank robbery in Queens, instead of sharing it with his colleagues. "It was the first thing every cop asked," Coffey told me. "I said, 'Who killed Johnny Earle?' "

"Yeah, I did that," Harold replied.

He proceeded with details. On assignment for the Genovese family, he had disguised himself with an Afro wig and dark brown makeup, followed Earle into a phone booth in the back of the restaurant, and pulled out a gun. The gun jammed, but inside his jacket Harold had another, and he got off three shots to Earle's face. Then he ran out the Broadway entrance of the restaurant toward his car, on Fifty-sixth Street. There was a ticket on his windshield. If the lawmen doubted him, he said, they could look up the parking summons.

Harold admitted to five more homicides. Rogers grew visibly nervous. "He's pacing as much as you can in a ten-by-ten office," Coffey told me. "Konigsberg's slumped over, being the slob that he is. Me, I'm elated. In those days, Mob hits were unsolvable. So when I found the summons, bingo."

Coffey went back into Rogers's office and said, "We got it." Rogers told him that they had nothing and explained that he'd foolishly given Harold immunity in exchange for information. "Rogers was devastated," Coffey recalled. According to the records of another detective in the room, the tape made of Harold's confession has since been lost. Coffey said the Earle case was closed as solved without arrest.

Coffey and I were meeting in the lounge of a midtown hotel. He is tall and imposing, and as he spoke, he pressed into my hand the actual parking-citation booklet, worn and clothlike. He'd saved it for all these years, the only shred of corroboration. On the second-to-last page, a police officer had recorded ticketing a white Mercury sedan with New York plates for a meter violation. He had done this at 12:35 P.M. on the day of the shooting, in front of the building at 1755 Broadway, which was right around the corner from the restaurant.

"He was an unusual guy, your uncle," Coffey said. "He didn't care about doing the forty-four years as long as he got over on the D.A.'s office. In his own mind, he showed he was smarter than everybody else. Because he made a wreck out of a top judge like Gellinoff. He sucked Rogers in, like, unbelievable."

I brought up Johnny Earle's name with Harold one day. "What do you know about that?" he said.

I told him I was aware of the homicide case, how he had killed the guy and got away with it, how the D.A. had a confession but was unable to bring charges.

Harold was silent. I tried to draw him out, feigning ignorance and fudging the circumstances. I asked if there hadn't been some sort of fight for the gun. If Harold hadn't killed Earle, I said, maybe Earle would have killed him.

"Now you're shooting angles," he murmured.

When I arrived at Auburn the next morning, Harold said, "Go and get me something, will you? Pretzels—I want anything that's rough, something I can crunch down on."

He tore open the bag with his teeth and split it down the seam, as if he were gutting a fish.

He sent me back for two bagels and two Mountain Dews. He told me to microwave the bagels and make sure they came with cream cheese.

The Johnny Earle case was still on his mind. "About this story," he said. "You had it wrong. They never caught me on any of that." A pause. "And I took out the whole gang."

There was of course no record of a "whole gang" getting killed that day at the Fifty-seventh Street Cafeteria, but Harold had no use for my nit-picking. He said if I knew so much about the case, then what was I asking him for.

"Tell me something," he said. "What did I look like, was there a disguise?"

"I've heard about the Afro and the blackface, Harold," I said. By now, calling him "Uncle Harold" sounded insincere and more familial than how I wanted to come across. And "Uncle Heshy" had gone out a long time ago.

"And what else?" he said. "Did you know I had thin gloves that made my hands look like a black's? No, I didn't think you knew that."

That set him off on another grand tale, this one about how he wore down an "incorruptible" New York City cop who was in the process of investigating him for the Earle murder. He said that the cop's supervisor, who was on the Mob's payroll, warned him that the cop had evidence and was on to him. "He says, 'He's got a .32, he's got witnesses, he's gonna link it to you.' I say, 'He can link his asshole to me. He has no fucking chance.' The windup is, I got this guy tickets to *Annie Get Your Gun*, I took my wife, and we sat behind him and his wife. Afterward, I took him to the Pierre, we had drinks and a snack, and we was a regular foursome for a year or two."

Eventually, the detective handed him the case evidence "in a valise" and closed out the investigation. "But he still wouldn't give me the witness lists," Harold said admiringly. He pointed out that he first began to win the cop's heart by telling him, "I like the way you show respect. I like that you're honest."

It shouldn't have come as a surprise to me that my attempt to find proof of the story of Harold and Officer Honorable was unsuccessful. The same went for his claim that he was once assigned by the Chicago Mafia to kill Bobby Kennedy, though at the last second none other than Frank Sinatra talked him out of it.

For that matter, it should not have surprised me that somebody who spent a lifetime in his metier lied about all kinds of things. His claims of having been framed by the government on various charges, while full of holes, were intricately crafted. I saw that he had worked the same details into his routine over and over, in legal motions and when questioned by law-enforcement officials. They were so consistently arranged over the decades that I wondered how long ago his mind had stopped separating them from the truth.

He told me of how, as a teenager, he was accosted by two Jersey City policemen at the Bayonne Diner and was threatened with arrest unless he relinquished his numbers racket to Mayor Frank Hague and the

Jersey City machine. Harold said that he leapt from his booth, pulled out a .45, and forced the counterman to relieve the cops of their guns. "Then I make them strip bare-ass," he recalled with a wistful laugh. "Then I take the guns, I take the bullets out of them. Then I throw it all, and their clothes, under their car." Then he left them there.

"Who ever defied Frank Hague in the manner I did?" he said. "Undressing those men was like undressing Frank Hague. I came home and my father told me what I did"—Mendel had already heard from authorities. "I said, 'So what.' He said, 'I'll tell zo vat, they're gonna kill you.'" He said that Mendel, through "some very high-placed political affiliations," arranged for him to lay low in Connecticut for a couple of months.

I think that Harold was looking for any chance to implicate his father in what became of him. I rejected the story on the philosophical basis that Mendel didn't deserve to go down in infamy with his youngest, and I had company in this position. The Mendel that Harold's sisters wanted to carry around with them was good—a petty criminal perhaps, but essentially good—and therefore not the one to blame.

It's also possible that Harold was simply trying to inflate Mendel's importance, both in the world at large and in the world that he came to occupy—Harold said that he saw them as the same, the spheres of organized crime and politics overlapping so significantly. This view allowed Harold to minimize the wrongness of his own life. Organized crime was a socioeconomic inheritance, and if you were born with it, that was how you lived.

But Harold's strongest motivation in aligning his father to himself may have been simply the desire to convey a close relationship with someone in the family.

And, of course, to remind me that it's the same family that I come from. In any case, the windup was that while he was hiding out in Connecticut, Harold was enlisted to aid the Israeli struggle for statehood. He said that Meyer Lansky and Longy Zwillman (two among the many Jewish crime bosses who claimed to have run weapons to Israel during this time) called on him, giving him seaman's papers and instructions to supervise a thirty-five-man crew on a ship bound for Marseilles. Their mission: to secretly deliver some 16,000 guns—rifles, machine guns, side arms—to Israeli militant forces. Harold said that their aid effort was met in port by David Ben-Gurion, Moshe Dayan, and Menachem Begin.

Then there was the spectacular yarn that I had to drag out of him, as he halted and stammered with convincing disgrace. In 1949, he said, he had led a group of soldiers from the Irgun—the Israeli underground commando army—on a Nazi-hunting mission into Chile. He recalled the maneuvers vividly: the battering ram he constructed by welding twenty tires to the front end of a truck, the daybreak raid on the "compound" of relocated Nazi families.

My skepticism was tested when Harold began to cry—actual tears—as he talked about how he and his fellow avengers made the regrettable decision that "nobody was walking out of there" and proceeded to kill even the women and children. "I don't feel so good about how that thing in Chile was handled," he said. "I don't want you to ever think about that again. I had a life. I take whatever punishment I get."

My granduncle's marbled hands were still. When an elderly prisoner limped past us, Harold winked to signal his hello.

"Guy was convicted of murdering a friend of mine," he said, perking up and adding that this didn't prevent them from getting on fine. "Business is business. He does what I tell him."

He pawed around in his bag of files and pulled out a heavily creased letter, dated 1983, from an adviser in the Israeli Prime Minister's Bureau. It was in response to a letter Harold had written to Yechiel

Kadishai—Menachem Begin's longtime political director—requesting help in an appeal. Although "it would be inconceivable that we would attempt to interfere or intervene in any way in judicial proceedings in your case," the adviser wrote Harold, "[w]e can only hope that your wife, children, and grandchildren find solace in the work you have done in the past on behalf of the Jewish people and the State of Israel." The letter could've meant anything. When I was back home, I tracked down a phone number for Kadishai in Jerusalem, where he is passing his years as a cranky old national hero. He told me that neither Harold's name nor the episodes he'd described rang any bells. "While I'm not aware of all that the Irgun ever did, I've certainly never heard of such a thing," he said.

I'd have bet my eyeteeth that the stories were complete fabrications, but still I wanted badly to believe them. They were mitigating folktales: He'd killed a lot of people, but here at least he'd killed somebody in the name of a cause other than himself. Every few months, I made an attempt to run down the stories, and while I knew that even if true, this sort of information would be difficult to verify, I was disappointed to come up with nothing—nothing to support Harold's gunrunning chronicle; no record among any Nazi-hunting group of such an arrangement or mission, no human-rights expert in South America aware of a vaguely similar massacre.

There was, however, the backstory of Morris (Cagney) Cohn, Harold's fictitious doppelganger. As a character in Sidney Zion's story tells it:

Morris Cohn in 1947 stole a warehouse full of guns and ammunition, right under the noses of the F.B.I. and the Treasury Department and he rode it out of here one night, from the Hoboken docks, straight to the Jewish terrorists. Three hundred thousand dollars worth of weapons, my boy, three hundred, when they were down to Matzo balls over there. And when I asked him, years later, whether the Israelis had taken care of him for that, he belted me in the mouth. "You Irish cocksucker," he said. "You think I'd take money from *us*?"

And, in a more comic vein, Peter Maas's King Kong Karpstein is rushed to Cuba by the Mafia after getting into hot water for breaking a police captain's jaw. He obtains a job working security in a casino, then one night roughs up a disorderly blackjack player and hands him over to the Havana police. The gambler is discovered to have been a German S.S. officer, with a warrant out for his arrest on war-crimes charges. He is extradited back to Europe to stand trial, and Karpstein receives a letter of gratitude from Simon Wiesenthal, the Nazi hunter, which he proudly carries with him.

I found the fictionalized accounts oddly satisfying. There was no reason to believe Harold's stories of self-aggrandizement, but as artifacts they had made their way into his mythology. Apparently, Harold had been telling this tale for many years.

"Listen, you ever go to California to the Simon Wiesenthal Center and see what they did to our women and children?" he'd said to me in the Auburn visitors' room, sucking out what remained from a foil packet of cream cheese. "That just makes me feel less sick about living with myself."

Then he'd raised his voice. "I did a lot of fucking bad things that I'm ashamed of and I been regretting it ever since." He was on the verge of yelling. "But I never went outside my circle. I never did anything to innocent people that wasn't trying to hurt me. I didn't go around burglarizing or raping or mugging!"

•   •   •

Harold's behavior never did yield itself to a cogent explanation. Nothing in his upbringing or early experience, as far as I can tell, seems on its own likely to have turned another child into such a demon. His life has amounted to the expression of a sick soul. The closest I came to a believable, though highly speculative, interpretation was in the field of forensic mental health.

In 2001, *The New Yorker* published my article about Harold. From my grandmother and grandaunts, there was virtually no reaction beyond Frieda's observation that a mug shot used to illustrate the piece was "a cute picture of Heshy." Not long afterward, I heard from my father's old medical-school roommate, Michael Weissberg, the vice-chairman of the psychiatry department at the University of Colorado medical school. Weissberg suggested that my understanding of Harold could be improved by looking at a few books about antisocial personality disorder (ASPD) and about psychopaths, the latter defined as people who exhibit a cluster of personality traits and deviant behaviors manifested, generally speaking, in an incapacity for empathy and a pattern of deceit. As a clinical diagnosis, the conditions associated with ASPD in the *Diagnostic and Statistical Manual of Mental Disorders* (*DSM-IV*) overlap with many of the conditions of psychopathy. (The term *sociopath* was once used interchangeably with *psychopath* but has since fallen from the diagnostic vocabulary.)

"You'll see the core of your dad's uncle in these descriptions," Weissberg said. "He's narcissistic. He has no remorse."

"Do you really think reading about a personality disorder will tell me how he got that way?" I asked.

He chuckled. "It'll tell you that you should stay away from him."

Another prominent psychiatrist had a similar take on Harold after the story appeared. Glen Gabbard, a psychiatrist at Baylor College of Medicine, published *The Psychology of "The Sopranos,"* a clever book for laymen dissecting the psychological themes played out on the TV series. Citing my article in a discussion of psychopathic killers, Gabbard named Harold as a textbook case—evidenced, for example, by his willingness to work simultaneously for more than one Mafia family.

The first in-depth examination of psychopathy was *The Mask of Sanity*, by the psychiatrist Hervey Cleckley, written in 1941. Cleckley's genius lay in realizing that there existed a certain type of cruel manipulator whose harmful actions were accompanied by an absence of delusion. The psychopath, he wrote, "does not hear voices.... In theory, the patient can foresee the consequences of injudicious or antisocial acts." In other words, a psychopath is a person who knows full well the difference between right and wrong and yet, without compunction, chooses to do wrong. Cleckley cited the protagonist of *The Incredible Charlie Carewe*, a novel by Mary Astor, as a quintessential psychopath. The jacket copy hit some familiar notes for me: "Charlie is a genius in reverse with dangerous charm. Sisters lie for him, parents defend him, friends obey him.... While calmly and casually, Charlie Carewe literally gets away with murder."

Cleckley's successor at the forefront of this field of study was Dr. Robert Hare, whose interest began while he was moonlighting at a prison near Vancouver during the sixties. In his 1993 book *Without Conscience*, Hare described an encounter with a dangerous inmate who again made me think of Harold: "The air around him seemed to buzz, and the eye contact he made with me was so direct and intense that I wondered if I had ever really looked anybody in the eye before." The inmate, whom Hare referred to by the pseudonym "Ray," had a winning personality, and used it to test the limits of what Hare would do on his behalf. "Ray had an incredible ability to con not just me but everybody," Hare wrote. "He lied endlessly, lazily, about everything, and it disturbed him not a whit whenever I pointed out something in his file that contradicted one of his lies." After Hare eventually managed to sever their relationship, he suspected Ray, whose most recent job had been in the prison auto shop, of sabotaging the brake line of his car. Frightened and intimidated by the experience, Hare felt that it wasn't enough for the clinical profession to simply attempt to understand psychopaths. His goal, as he stated it, was to come up with a diagnostic method by which to identify psychopaths "in order to minimize the risk they pose to others."

Over the next couple of decades, Hare and a team of colleagues devised a system of identification based on lengthy interviews with inmates and a detailed scrutiny of their case files. The standard forensic tests of the 1960s, such as the Minnesota Multiphasic Personality Inventory, relied heavily on "self-reporting" and were therefore extremely vulnerable to the subjects' manipulation. It was common for inmates to fake symptoms and rig their diagnoses. (At Springfield, for example, the M.M.P.I. found "simply no evidence" that Harold was malingering.) Such questions as "I lie (1) easily; (2) with some difficulty; (3) never" were not likely to yield useful data from psychopaths. As Hare put it, "Impression management was definitely one of their strong suits."

The result, Hare's Psychopathy Checklist (PCL), was first made available to the trade in 1980, and in its revised form (PCL-R) has become the standard measuring stick that clinicians use to diagnose psychopathy. The PCL-R, a quantitatively scored test, consists of twenty items, which are traits and behaviors. About half are personality traits that Hare says reflect the emotional and interpersonal makeup of a psychopath; the rest are behavioral traits, evidence of a particular social deviance. Scoring is simple: the psychologist or psychiatrist administering the test (Hare stresses that the checklist, which he sometimes refers to as "an instrument" and "a complex clinical tool" is for professional use only) works his way down the list of symptoms and scores the subject two points for each consistently displayed trait, one point if the trait is evident but with real exceptions or some doubt on the scorer's part, and no points if the trait doesn't apply.

Reid Meloy, a forensic psychologist at the University of California, San Diego, and a colleague to whom Hare, now in semiretirement, often refers cases, estimates that about 1 percent of the population would rate as psychopaths, and that about 20 percent of the inmates in America's maximum-security prisons qualify. (Of course, not all psychopaths acquire a criminal record. Many are nonviolent, and some, Meloy suggested, are thriving in business and politics.) "Typically, the way a person like this maintains an inflated view of the self is by devaluing other people, taking advantage of them," Meloy told me. "If you look at the trail of a psychopath, you will see it littered with wounded, angry people."

Meloy has served as the chief of forensic mental health for San Diego County and wrote the *DSM-IV*'s treatment-volume chapter on antisocial personality disorder. Since publishing his first book, *The Psychopathic Mind*, more than fifteen years ago, he has been one of the most visible forensic psychologists in the country, retained by the defense in the trial of Polly Klaas's murderer, and by the government to assess Timothy McVeigh and his coconspirator Terry Nichols. On a lark, I asked him how he would feel about administering the test to Harold, in absentia and over the phone with me, based on what I'd learned and observed.

To my surprise, Meloy was happy to oblige. "The PCL-R evaluation has proved remarkably accurate even in the absence of the examinee, so long as there is sufficient data to work with," he said. To be sure, my lack of a background in mental health, to say nothing of the biases and misinterpretations I undoubtedly brought to the process, can only have corrupted our triangular assessment. It also bears mention that plenty of Meloy's peers consider the PCL-R itself fundamentally flawed, in that it uses a numerical value, based on such imprecise characteristics as empathy and impulsiveness, to predict the risk that a person will behave destructively in the future. The numerically obtained likelihood of that risk, detractors argue, is not a fair basis on which to impose a more severe legal punishment, though it has been employed in such a way.

But still.

The first item on the PCL-R, as Meloy began to read from it, was "glibness and superficial charm." He elaborated: "The person can even be quite likable, but too quick and facile to be believable. They often use and misuse technical terms and appear to know a lot about politics, say, or science or the stock market."

I said that sounded like Harold. Meloy gave him the full two points.

Item two was "a grandiose sense of self-worth" (which, Hare writes, "often emerges in dramatic fashion in the courtroom. . . . it is not unusual for them to criticize or fire their lawyers and to take over their own defense").

"Two points," I said.

And so on. For item four, I was asked if the person in question has a pathological tendency to lie. Two points. Item six was expressing remorse for one's misdeeds while still arguing that one's victims or the criminal system are really to blame. Two points.

Item eight was "lack of empathy." "May start at an early age with violence to animals," Meloy said. Hitler the cat's untimely end came to mind. Two points.

Item nine was "a parasitic lifestyle." I had to think about this for a minute. Harold could be industrious, after all; he didn't live off his wife's money, or his father's. Meloy asked what Harold's primary source of income was. I said he was a loan shark.

"Two points," Meloy said.

Putting aside the question of whether I might have been leading Meloy into an unscientific hollow, he was particularly struck by how overwhelmingly Harold cleared the criminal-versatility bar. That item was itself a checklist of fifteen types of crimes—ranging from obstruction of justice to murder—of which at least six had to have been committed in order to score the full two points. Harold, by our determination, committed fourteen of them (he missed arson). He even met the criteria for crimes against the state, because that category included evasion of income tax.

It took about an hour to run through all twenty criteria. Forty would be a "perfect" score, although anybody who scores thirty or above makes the general cutoff for psychopathy. Harold scored a 35, which put him in the 97th percentile among inmates at maximum-security prisons in North America.

"Wow. I've seen a few people in this range, not many," Meloy said as he recalculated the total. "Ted Bundy would score between 34 and 37."

One of the most confounding things about psychopathy—Harold would call it a miasma of perplexity—is that it has thus far proved all but immune to rehabilitation. Harold's parents, this suggests, were up against a much greater force than they could have grasped. One study published in the journal *Law and Human Behavior* found that psychopaths who underwent therapeutic treatment had a significantly higher violent re-offense rate over time than those who had no therapy.

There is evidence of a biological component to psychopathy. For instance, the findings of several recent studies, including one that made use of brain-imagings, indicate that psychopaths' brains might be abnormally wired, such that they consistently employ irregular speech patterns and process the emotional content of abstract words—such as *grace, power, future*—differently than the rest of us. Furthermore, psychopaths often fail to exhibit the physiological responses most of us have when feeling scared or nervous, such as a quickened heart rate, sweaty palms, or a churning stomach.

And because they lack these basic human responses, they tend to set off warning signals in others. A study that Meloy and his wife, a brain-imaging researcher, published in 2002 found that, of almost six hundred clinicians who had interviewed a patient identified as a psychopath, more than three-quarters had experienced an "autonomic arousal"—typically a skin response on the order of a tingling sensation, goose bumps, or feeling the hair on the back of one's neck stand up. "It's probably an early warning system, a physical defense mechanism responding to the feeling of imminent threat," Meloy told me. "That's why we call psychopaths intraspecies predators."

A line John LeCarré once wrote about his con-artist father—"All the evidence I ever heard suggests he was bent from the day he shook his first rattle"—seemed as applicable to Harold as any piece of information I came across. Indeed, clinical evidence has been inconclusive as to what causes psychopathy, whether a child can be simply born bad or is turned that way by something in his upbringing. Several studies have indicated that psychopaths are neurologically different from the rest of us because the frontal lobes of their brains are abnormal. Dr. Jonathan H. Pincus, a professor of neurology at Georgetown University and the author of *Base Instincts: What Makes Killers Kill,* points to research that found that people who exhibited behavior consistent with psychopathy had frontal lobes 11 percent smaller than those of normal people.

"It could be caused either by a birth defect or trauma," Pincus told me. The frontal lobes are involved in the brain's executive function—what enables a person to plan and to reason. "If there is damage in the frontal lobes, the capacity to make the decisions a person has to in his moral life is diminished," he said. (Although Dr. Pincus is not a believer in the usefulness of the PCL-R, the frontal-lobe theory is not at odds with Hare and Meloy's school of thought, which, in fact, incorporates it.)

What many forensic experts consider the most plausible explanation, in some form or another, is that both genetics and environment come into play, as certain unlucky people are born with a psychopathic predisposition which is then drawn out by their upbringing. A study published in 2002 in *Science* magazine looked at the convergence of two factors, an abusive childhood and an inherited deficiency in a brain enzyme called monoamine oxidase A (MAOA)—which breaks down neurotransmitters like serotonin, dopamine, and noradrenaline—to see if together they were more likely to result in antisocial behavior, including violence.

They were. Of 154 men in the group who had suffered maltreatment as young boys, fifty-five had the genotype for "low-activity" MAOA. Those fifty-five were twice as likely as the men who didn't have the genetic variation to have been convicted of a rape, assault, or robbery by their mid-twenties. They were about four times as likely as the males in the general-study population to be convicted of a violent crime. But genetics alone weren't enough. The boys who were born with the deficiency but not maltreated as children were no more destined for a life of violent crime than the males with the high-activity MAOA genotype.

When I described what I knew about Harold's childhood to Pincus, he said, "The sort of child whose school record is such that he's being held back repeatedly and getting into trouble all the time—whether that's due to environmental factors or something else, such as brain damage—well, those children are a magnet for abuse. Their parents are frustrated with them, they can't understand why one child would be having problems, especially if their other children aren't." Neglect, he added, "could even take the form of a mother not wanting to have the child." I told him Harold was the last of five siblings born over a long time span. Maybe his mother felt she'd already had enough children and regretted his birth? "Sure, entirely plausible," Pincus said.

Typically, when Pincus has examined violent criminals, it has been at the behest of their defense lawyers. He is of the view that most of them have suffered serious maltreatment as children.

Reid Meloy, on the other hand, cited data asserting a "curvilinear" correlation between psychopathy and a child's background. "At a score of zero, you find no abuse and neglect, and then as you look at rising scores in the teens you find increasing abuse—a direct correlation," Meloy said. "But then, when the psychopathy score gets very high, well into the thirties, it likely has very little to do with environmental factors. At that level where your uncle is—well, let's just say there really is evidence that we may be looking at a genotype for the bad seed."

So there was my answer, sort of. I had hoped that by deducing that Harold had been born bent, I absolved my family of any responsibility. But what I was learning meant that either Harold's genes had made him a killer, or else his genes gave him the potential to become a killer, which some sort of childhood mistreatment—quite possibly from his parents—in turn brought to full fruition. Either way, it involved family.

Recently, when I was on the phone with Aunt Beattie, I pressed her about how their parents had treated Harold. Everybody had talked about Mendel hitting him when he got into trouble. Did they mean he hit him the way a lot of fathers spanked their sons?

"No, more than that." Aunt Beattie laughed uncomfortably. "Papa used to really beat him up."

"With an open hand?"

"No, with his fists. But I don't think Papa was the problem. I always said Evil just needed a place to go, and he jumped into Heshy."

I felt protective toward my great-grandfather and toward Beattie's memory of him. I muttered something about how it had probably made no difference. "They say craziness like that could be genetic," I said. "Who knows?"

"You'd better hope not, sweetie," Aunt Beattie said. I'd just told her my wife was pregnant with our first baby.

She was surprised we were giving our child the surname Konigsberg.

"There was a time when I didn't want it," she said.

Part III

A Hard Case

TEN

A Truck Driver

THE WAY HAROLD managed to thwart the Feds time and time again had an action-comics feel to it. No matter how put off I was by his gruesome confessions, no matter how unsettled I was around him, I still found his persistence had been remarkable.

The murder of Anthony Castellito was both Harold's greatest bargaining chit and the killing that eventually came back to haunt him. In its prolonged aftermath, the case involved more betrayals and fluid alliances than Harold could manage by himself.

Castellito had joined Local 560 during the Depression, while working for H. P. Welch, a small trucking company based in Jersey City. He drove Mack chain-drive rigs, which had big wooden steering wheels, turn signals operated by a string that hung from the ceiling, no heat, and no doors on the cab. He was called "Three Fingers" because a childhood accident with a ratchet machine at his parents' bread factory had torn the tips off two fingers on his right hand. Immediately, he was back at work, only to lose his left thumb in the same manner. He learned to button his shirt with his bum hand, his three good fingers moving like a water strider up the placket. He left an extra button undone at the top, the better to show off the tattoo of a baby he'd gotten on his neck after the birth of Anthony Jr.

Castellito had met his wife, Helen, in Hoboken, where she'd been cleaning houses since she was a teenager. She liked his dimples and the way he smiled as he passed her on the street. Castellito was shy and remote. He kissed his wife in front of the kids only on Christmas. Once, years into their marriage, he signed her birthday card "Love, Tony Castellito."

Castellito got involved in a bookmaking ring down by the Hoboken piers. It made him a lot of money, which he couldn't spend, because doing so would have caused his fellow truckers—and tax officials—to wonder where it came from. "It's gotten so I can't move around here," he said to Helen, so they bought the country house in Kerhonkson but rarely spoke of it outside the family. In 1947, Castellito was made a business agent. With the 25 percent salary increase, he was finally able to move his family out of their ground-floor tenement apartment to a double-lot house in New Milford, New Jersey. His first day in the Local 560 office, the union presented him with a Cadillac Fleetwood, since he wouldn't be driving a truck anymore. He went home and took Helen for a ride. "Your father's a businessman," she told the kids proudly. "He wears a suit to work."

Castellito was a devoted advocate of the rank and file. He made his organizer's bones by approaching mothers on Monroe Street and offering to get their teenage sons off the corner. "He gave every kid in Hoboken a union book," Anthony Jr. told me. "He believed in the workingman. He came up at a time when benefits were crap, when a lot of the jobs had just one driver and no helper on the route, no protection from the bosses.

He made it so that if the men had troubles—if they got caught hanging out, cheating on time, drinking, stealing off a truck—they couldn't never get fired."

If Castellito succeeded partly by intimidating the freight-company bosses—threatening a strike, for example, on the occasion that one trucker was ordered by his employer to submit to a lie-detector test—he was also valued by management for his ability to keep truckers in line. After all, the truckers owed him. "These guys were making two hundred dollars a week, getting out of Bayonne and buying homes in Bergen County or down the shore," Anthony Jr. said. "He'd tell them, 'You're gonna give up all this just to steal a load? Think about it.' "

Tony Pro, who was serving at the time as a shop steward at H. P. Welch, first crossed Castellito's path in the 1940s, when Castellito was dispatched by the union to fire him for insubordination. They immediately hit it off, talking for hours, and, instead of giving Tony Pro the sack, Castellito decided to groom him to become a business agent.

"The guy had a fabulous personality, a dynamite smile, a good way with people." Anthony Jr. recalled. Tony Pro was a short and pursy man, muscular and not a little bit pugnacious. Much like himself, Castellito told friends, Tony Pro "came from nowhere"—he was one of six children born to Italian immigrants on the Lower East Side—though he was already well connected to gangsters on both sides of the Hudson River. According to Justice Department records, he had been put in place as a shop steward by a Genovese-family boss in Greenwich Village. "He had no polish on him, no track record, but my dad thought he had potential," Anthony Jr. said. When Anthony Jr. was sixteen and quit school, Castellito procured him a job as a trucker's helper at H. P. Welch, and insisted that Tony Pro serve as his mentor, so Tony Pro taught him to operate a fourteen-wheel tractor-trailer and let him accompany him on his rounds.

Tony Pro rose in stature, from business agent to chapter president (sponsored, behind the scenes, by the Mafia godfather Albert Anastasia) to, in 1960, vice president of the International Brotherhood of Teamsters. Castellito, who was less ambitious than his protégé, agreed to let Tony Pro run for president of the local, and contented himself with the position of secretary-treasurer.

A report by the 1986 Presidential Commission on Organized Crime posited that the Teamsters' relationship with the Mafia dated back to the thirties, when Jimmy Hoffa enlisted gangsters to help out on the union's organizing drives (which, more often than not, took the form of violent revolt against management). Over time, Hoffa encouraged cross-pollination between the leaderships of the Mob and the Teamsters, and by the fifties, the two groups were firmly in cahoots.

The reason the trucking industry was such a gold mine for the Mob, according to the report, was that its structure was essentially a constellation of local barns that enjoyed monopolies in local markets. When the employees of a carrier, for some union-related reason, refused to make a delivery or a pickup, not only was the owner of the trucking outfit financially at risk, but the company on the receiving end of this decision—a construction firm, say, or a manufacturer—was often without another trucking business to call. A trucking strike meant havoc, especially prior to the deregulation of the trucking business, which did not come until the seventies. "Control of the truckers," the members of the commission wrote, "thus provides leverage over thousands of businesses dependent on Teamsters' deliveries."

Neither Tony Pro nor Castellito had much regard for the law. Both, when called to testify in front of Bobby Kennedy and the McClellan Committee, in 1959, cited the Fifth Amendment (Provenzano forty-four times). The owner of a member trucking company testified that both men extorted $17,000 from him between 1953 and 1959, in ex-

change for "labor peace." Still, Castellito claimed to draw a line between the shaking down of freight-company owners and exploiting the
truckers themselves. In 1958, according to *The Teamsters,* a comprehen-
sive history of the union, by Steven Brill, Tony Pro delivered all of the
chapter's votes in the Teamsters' presidential election to Hoffa without
bothering to poll the membership. This was one of the slights that led to
the 1959 formation of the Green Ticket, a faction intent on forcing
Tony Pro and his band of cronies, which included his brothers Sammy
Pro and Nunzie Pro, out of power.

Although Three Fingers Castellito held union office as a member of
Tony Pro's own party, the Local 560 ticket, he was looked upon so well
by the Greens that they did not even field a candidate to oppose him as
secretary-treasurer in the 1959 election. This, of course, did not sit well
with Tony Pro. "There was professional jealousy, let's put it that way,"
Joseph Gallo, a founding member of the Green Ticket, said later.
"Maybe one was more popular with the men than the other."

The flashpoint between the two was Tony Pro's tendency to openly
flaunt his Mob associations, particularly with Harold and Sally Bugs
Briguglio, around union headquarters. It angered Castellito, an F.B.I.
report states, that Tony Pro was "pushing BRIGUGLIO hard for the
position" of business agent, "and CASTELLITO was of the fore-
drawn conclusion that this would open all the Local 560 terminals to
KONIGSBERG'S loan sharking activities through shop stewards
under BRIGUGLIO's control." Castellito told a colleague, "If Tony
Pro was allowed to bring in people like Konigsberg and let them get
control, they would bleed the union dry."

Indeed, as the Feds learned around this time from an informant,
Harold and Tony Pro were planning to build a hospital in Bergen
County and charge every Teamster five cents a day in a required health-
benefits plan. "They estimate that with approximately 300,000 Team-

sters in northern New Jersey, the receipts of the hospital and the hospital plan would be approximately $24,000 a day," an assistant attorney general wrote to J. Edgar Hoover in a memo.

One of Castellito's union confidants told a grand jury that he knew how much Castellito disapproved of Tony Pro's relationship with Harold, and cautioned him to be careful, "or they will bury you." Castellito replied that he had people of his own and could take care of himself.

Anthony Jr. says that his father was planning to retire as soon as he turned fifty, which at the time of his murder was less than a year away. "He'd made enough money on the side from his numbers racket in Hoboken. He was just going to go up to his farm and live out his days."

In the spring of 1961, Tony Pro was indicted for labor extortion. That was when he summoned to his office Harold, Sally Bugs Briguglio, and Big Sal Sinno—the men who, for the past few months, had been plotting the hit on Castellito. Tony Pro told them that he believed the government was going to try to coerce Castellito to testify against him in the case, and the time had come for them to finish the job.

Among Harold's accomplices, the one he knew least was Big Sal Sinno. At the time of the murder, he wasn't even sure of his last name, relationships in the Mob developing as they did on a need-to-know basis. But Big Sal would turn out to be the person whom the government relied on the most to keep Harold in prison forever.

A federal judge once wrote, in his ruling on a racketeering case against "the Provenzano group," that when he first heard Big Sal's life story, "it was obvious that this was the real life version of that cinematic presentation *On the Waterfront*." Tony Pro had first met him in the late forties, when Big Sal, then a trailer-truck driver for the Pilot Freight Company, delivered a shipment of merchandise to First Avenue in Manhattan. When Tony Pro appeared on the scene, Big Sal told authorities later, "He just made himself friendly. We met each other quite a few times after that, and then he approached me as far as giving a load up to him." Big Sal said yes, and, soon after, he relinquished a truck full of 660 cartons of Camel cigarettes to a crew of Tony's Pro's men, who had trailed him to the Lackawana Terminal in Jersey City. Then he called the police to report the load as stolen, and received a $3,000 payoff from Tony Pro.

The relationship went on bearing fruit for both of them, and Big Sal grew entrenched, sharing his proceeds from a gambling ring he ran in exchange for the Mob's permission to operate. Big Sal somehow drew the F.B.I.'s suspicion for giving up a load one time in Newark. He was brought in for questioning, and, according to the F.B.I., an agent attempted to open him up as an organized-crime informant, creating a confidential file with his name on it. "Make me a star, Sal, make me a star," the agent kept pushing. But Big Sal wouldn't tell him anything.

Big Sal began hanging around the rest of the union leadership at the Local 560 building, even befriending Three Fingers Castellito. "Big Sal Sinno would talk to Tony Pro and my father to kill an afternoon," Anthony Castellito Jr. says. "He was teaching me how to play the horses. He used to call me Sonny. He was a good guy, a funny guy."

Big Sal was willing to participate in the murder of his friend Castellito because he depended on Tony Pro for his livelihood. Though presumably he didn't actually want to kill his friend, he was helpless, though in the Mafia the preferred term has always been *loyal*. (As Wilfrid Sheed wrote once in the *New York Review of Books,* "If mafiosi really had the honor and loyalty they profess, they would not need to kill each other half so often.")

Whatever the name of the trait, Tony Pro possessed an extraordinary ability to inspire it. Some twenty years later, following an indictment of the Provenzano group for subjecting Local 560 to gangland rule, one Teamsters officer testified that even if all the charges against Tony Pro, including allegations of murder, were proved to be true, he would still gladly welcome him back to run the union. In fact, the man said, "I would pray for that."

After Harold, Sally Bugs, and Big Sal killed and buried Three Fingers Castellito, it wasn't long before the member trucking companies on his old route—and the attendant stream of payoffs—got handed off to Sally Bugs or Tony Pro. Among them were Wilson Freight, Roadway Express, Super Service, Masters Freight, W. T. Cowan, Ward, TransAmerican, Cooper-Jarrett, Ezor, Miller Transportation, Smith Transport, and New York Central Transport.

At a union meeting on September 14, 1961, Tony Pro announced that he was appointing Sally Bugs a Local 560 business agent. Anthony Jr., who was in the union hall that night, immediately recognized Sally Bugs as one of the two men who'd shown up at his parents' house only a few months earlier, claiming to be F.B.I. men. Shortly after that, his father had vanished.

"Tony Pro calls this guy Sally up to the dais and everybody has to clap," Anthony, Jr. recalled. "And I'm looking at him and I'm upset. I'm sick. I didn't know what to do." Soon afterward, he saw a newspaper photograph of Kayo Konigsberg—whom he recognized as the other so-called F.B.I. agent. He got in touch with federal authorities, who deposed him in front of a grand jury, but he was not encouraged by the experience.

"The F.B.I. gave me the feeling that they didn't care about my father," he said. "They treated his disappearance like it was just gangster-to-gangster." The agents interrogated him about union payoffs and his father's finances. According to a report the agents filed, Anthony Jr. grew irritated and told them that his father rarely discussed business at home. Castellito had earned about three hundred dollars a week, he said, and that was enough for his family to live comfortably at the time. "He never made real big money," he told them. "Do you think if he did I'd still be driving a truck?"

His paranoia wasn't entirely unfounded. Everyone around him took an ambivalent view of Castellito's disappearance. Was he dead or had he run away? Was he a criminal who'd been rubbed out by rival criminals? Were any of his relatives or union friends at risk? Not one union representative ever came by his house or called to ask his wife if she needed anything. Anthony Jr. and his wife confronted their bereavement alone.

In 1965, Anthony Jr. was nominated to run for union trustee by the United Ticket, an opposition party that had incorporated the old Green Ticket and was quickly gaining strength now that Tony Pro was up on extortion charges. "I didn't want to run, but I felt I had to," Anthony Jr. said. "It was the battle of the banners. We had signs up on Route 46, over the George Washington Bridge, on the ramp outside the Lincoln Tunnel. Our motto was Pro's Indicted, Vote United."

As the United Ticket considered itself a reform party, Castellito Sr., by the simple virtues of his disillusionment with Tony Pro and his disappearance, became United's patron saint. A group that called itself the T.C. Club of Teamster Local 560 printed mailers that called for Tony Pro's ouster. One page depicted the jack of spades and the exhortation, "Knock Him Off His Throne—Tony Pro, The One Eye Jack That Acts Like A King."

Fearful that a pro-Castellito bloc could swing the election, Tony Pro offered to give Anthony Jr. a job as a business agent if he didn't run against him. He sent a couple of Anthony Jr.'s friends to his house to try to persuade him.

"Tony, take the job, get a Cadillac and a desk instead of driving a truck," one of them said. "Nobody reads yesterday's newspaper."

When Anthony Jr. drove to Tony Pro's office to decline the offer in person, Tony Pro told him he was stubborn like his father.

The United Ticket didn't win a single position. Tony Pro took the presidential race by a two-to-one margin.

Anthony Jr. ran once more, in 1968, and lost again. Late on election night, when he and his wife, Dorothy, got home, she took his hand and informed him that they were going to spend the weekend down at the shore, where they had a cottage. "We stopped and had breakfast in the middle of the night, got to our house at 3 A.M.," he told me. "We tried to right then and there put it behind us. We said, 'Let them do what they want.'"

He stayed in Local 560 for another six years. He felt stuck there, but driving a truck was the only thing he knew how to do. "It fit my personality—you was a man," he said. "I wasn't going to be a clerk—what, some asshole? I had a mission—to collect my pension. My shit-ass pension, you couldn't buy a pack of cigarettes for it, about $350 a month." It was "spite work," the thought that Tony Pro would be writing him checks for the rest of his life. "I stayed to save face. If I'd have left right away, people would have thought, 'He needs his father to keep his job.'"

Anthony Jr. was forty-two years old when he finally quit. He got his ironworking union book and worked in heavy construction. "They sent me out on a school building that was going up," he said. "I'm a quick learner, and within a year I could do anything—climbing the iron, walking the iron, connect, burn, welding. Then, Atlantic City broke, so we put up the hotels there. Caesar's, the Tropicana, Harrah's, Trump's—I took them all up from the hole. I loved putting the big buildings up—the higher the better. And the best part about it was I was away from all the gangsters, all the hoodlums."

A few times during the 1960s, Anthony Jr. was called on by the F.B.I. to go over the same details about the last days of his father's life. He was unaware that each summons was being brought about by some new wrinkle in Harold Konigsberg's confessions. He didn't even know who was on the government's list of suspects. In 1967, when the Justice Department was secretly struggling over whether to indict Harold in the Castellito murder, agents asked Anthony Jr. to bring them to the farmhouse in Kerhonkson so they could remove carpet samples. He began to suspect that his father had been murdered there, but nobody would tell him a thing.

It wasn't until 1976 that Anthony Jr. heard about the case again. That April, he was subpoenaed by the U.S. Attorney's office in lower Manhattan, and he reluctantly agreed to meet with investigators. "How many times do I have to go through this?" Anthony Jr. said to Dorothy. "How many times does he have to die?" Dorothy agreed to keep him company on the drive in. While he ascended the stone staircase of the federal building at Foley Square, she sat on a park bench and read one of her romance novels.

Just a year earlier, Jimmy Hoffa had gone missing. It was no secret among unionists that a rift had formed between Hoffa and Tony Pro over control of the Teamsters, nor was it unknown to the F.B.I. that in 1967, when both men were at Lewisburg Federal Prison in Pennsylvania on racketeering charges, the two had very nearly come to blows in the cafeteria. "Fat boy, keep something in mind. Your day is coming," Tony Pro threatened Hoffa, according to an F.B.I. interview with an informant who witnessed the scene. "It won't be like me falling down the elevator shaft." In the F.B.I.'s leading scenario, Tony Pro had subsequently hired Sally Bugs and two others to abduct and kill Hoffa outside Detroit.

Anthony Jr. figured that the government's sudden interest in his father was nothing more than an attempt to put pressure on Tony Pro.

"It's only because Jimmy Hoffa vanished that now you're interested in my father?" he asked the investigators as they tried to question him. "Go and find your own case." According to an F.B.I. agent who was in the room, the prosecutor who was leading the interview responded by trying to intimidate Anthony Jr. "Do you know what happens to a man's lungs when he's asphyxiated?" the prosecutor said. "Do you know what the stories are about how your father died?"

The agent suggested a time-out and invited Anthony Jr. to join him for a walk. When they got outside, he reminded Anthony Jr. that they were not there to talk about Jimmy Hoffa. "This has to do with June 6, 1961," he said.

"You have the wrong date," Anthony Jr. said. "The last time anybody saw my dad was on June 5. Why don't you look it up before you make me come up here again?" When they were seated again upstairs, another agent was sent to consult his files and returned to announce that Anthony Jr. was right: the date was Monday, June 5. The mistake, the agent explained, came "because Sal Sinno said June 6."

"Big Sal?" Hearing that name took Anthony Jr. by surprise. There had been rumors that Big Sal was involved in his father's disappearance, but Anthony Jr. was loath to believe them. Big Sal had been his father's friend. Besides, he was supposed to be dead.

Big Sal Sinno, who vanished shortly after taking part in Castellito's murder in 1961, was forgotten but not gone. Big Sal had complained about Tony Pro's failure to reward him for the hit with a cut from the union's rackets. When Big Sal was not seen or heard from after that, most people who knew him assumed he'd been rubbed out by Tony Pro and his gang—just as they'd tried to kill off Harold at the Cabana Club.

In fact, because Big Sal had indeed feared that Tony Pro was going to hunt him down, he had fled New Jersey with a girlfriend in late 1961.

They landed in Milwaukee, had two sons, and eventually, on vacation in Puerto Rico, got married. He worked construction and railroad jobs under aliases, bought property, and built a house on it, but at some point things started to go bad, and his wife turned to prostitution. Naturally, Big Sal later said, this was hard on the family. There were fights.

On December 2, 1975, after Big Sal hit her, she tried to get even. She phoned the police in Hoboken and told them that a "Charles Caputo" living in Fond du Lac, Wisconsin, was actually Big Sal Sinno, who, officers recorded with puzzlement, "is wanted in Hoboken, N.J., for some serious crime." When Big Sal checked out all the New Jersey numbers on his long-distance bill and found out what his wife had done, he hurriedly decamped to Ohio with his kids and tried to make amends with the Provenzanos. From a pay phone, he asked one of Tony Pro's brothers for $25,000 to relocate once again, and requested that it be sent to a P.O. box. Tony Pro offered to give him $5,000 but said that Big Sal had to claim it in person. Big Sal figured he was being set up.

In the meantime, Big Sal's wife was furious at him for taking off with their sons. She called the sheriff's office in Fond du Lac County and again tried to turn him in. This time, she mentioned that he'd been involved with somebody by the name of Anthony "Tony Pro" Provenzano. A sheriff's deputy decided to pass the information to Special Agent John Markey at the F.B.I.'s Green Bay office.

"I don't think this is anything," the deputy said, "but I figured, I might as well."

As it happened, Markey had come across Tony Pro's name just the week before in *Time* magazine. He and Sally "Bugs" Briguglio, *Time* reported, were scheduled to appear before a grand jury in Detroit in the Hoffa case. "I sent a teletype to the Newark office of the F.B.I. and asked for anything they had on Charles Caputo, a.k.a. Sal Sinno," Markey told me recently. "The request went into general, not the organized-crime division, and they ran an indices check with the police departments. They said the only things they had on him were some gambling-warrant violations." He was not made aware that Harold's confessions in the sixties had made Big Sal a suspect in the Castellito murder.

The Newark office did, however, send Markey a photo of Big Sal, on the back of which was a case number. "The case number began with 137," Markey said. "Now, 137 means informant. I figured the bureau was covering something up because he was an informant. I thought it might be a break in the Hoffa case. Otherwise, I wouldn't have done anything." Instead, Markey decided to track down Big Sal. He learned that he had a mistress, so he found her and left his number.

Big Sal was definitely in need of help. After three months in hiding, he found himself broke and unprepared for single-parenthood. The most trying aspect for him was his younger son's asthma, which seemed to act up every time the boy was told he was going to be returned to his mother. "I didn't want to run anymore," Big Sal later explained. So he phoned Markey in the hope of getting himself into the witness-protection program.

They met that night at the Dew Drop Inn on Route 10 in Clinton, Wisconsin. Markey was an unassuming agent, stiff and formal, yet persuasive. He rarely left his house without a jacket and tie. His first words to Big Sal were, "What can you do for me?"

Big Sal put his hand on the table, with two fingers folded underneath, and offered to give the F.B.I. the case of Three Fingers Castellito, which was now fifteen years old. "Every time the beginning of June rolls around, I remember it," he said.

The F.B.I. flew Big Sal to Newark for three weeks to debrief him and see if his story checked out. "It was a unique case for the F.B.I., in that my supervisor didn't know what to do with Sal's kids while he and

I were back east," Markey told me. The boys were ten and thirteen years old, the same age as Markey's two sons, so they ended up staying at his house as his wife looked after them. The boys could double up in the bedrooms, Markey instructed his wife. He told her not to ask questions while he flew back to New Jersey with the boys' father. Big Sal's kids didn't know why they were there, either. "And I wasn't getting a blessing from the Bureau," Markey said. "The Bureau just didn't want to know."

The Markeys' neighbors began to ask about the boys who could be seen playing in their yard all the time and why they weren't in school. "We thought it would be difficult to put them in a new school during the middle of the term, especially if they were going to relocate soon," Markey said. "Everybody got along well. Sal had been raising his kids same as we were. They went to Catholic church and to a public school. Their neighborhood, in Fond du Lac, had been similar to ours, maybe a little nicer, even. It was not a problem with my wife, as far as their manners and cleanliness and that sort of thing."

In Newark, Big Sal was chaperoned by Markey and three other F.B.I. agents. They'd talk all week, then get the weekends off, moving from hotel to hotel every couple of days. It was important not to stay in one place for long—too great a possibility of Big Sal's being recognized on his former home turf. One Friday, just as they were registering at the Betsy Ross, a motel near Red Bank, Big Sal tapped Markey's shoulder and said that he didn't think they should stay there; the piano player advertised in the lounge used to work at one of his clubs. So they drove four hours to North Andover, Massachusetts, and spent the weekend with Markey's parents. They took a day trip into Boston for clams at Durgin Park. They invited Markey's brother and sister-in-law over to play cards.

•　　　•　　　•

When it came time to search for Castellito's corpse, Big Sal fared no better than Harold had. The government quickly realized that the best corroboration of Big Sal's story resided in Harold's 1965 statements to the F.B.I. Both men described the same phony request to hide out the lamster in order to get Castellito alone, the same scenario in which Castellito fought back after being struck on the head, the same venetian-blind cord drawn around his gullet, even the same concatenation of attempts to hide Castellito's body.

And so once again it looked as though the government was going to find itself protecting Harold. William Aronwald, who was in charge of the organized-crime strike force at the U.S. Attorney's office in Manhattan, carted Harold down from Dannemora, and offered to give him a lightened sentence in exchange for testifying against Tony Pro. At that point, Harold was scheduled to be released as early as 1983, when he would become eligible for parole from the extortion sentence.

"I wanted a conviction against Provenzano," Aronwald told me when I visited him at the Westchester office park where he now has a private practice. "Once I told Harold that we had Sinno, he agreed to go along with us. I appreciated that he was a no-bullshit person. He had the *sechel* up here, the smarts. As curious as it sounds, I found him to be a likable guy and in his own way very charming."

The Feds planned to charge the defendants with kidnapping—a federal crime—because a murder charge was a prosecution for state court. But, because Aronwald suspected that they might again have a problem with the statute of limitations for kidnapping, his office teamed up with the district attorney of Ulster County, New York—where the murder had taken place—and issued a joint indictment. The federal charge was kidnapping and the New York State indictment was for murder; both are capital offenses. "We figured that we would probably still get to try it, but just in case it was thrown out of federal court, we knew that, as a backup, the charge would hold in state court," Aronwald said.

When the defense successfully exploited the statute-of-limitations loophole, the federal charge was, indeed, dismissed. Reluctantly, Aronwald's office turned over its case, and years' worth of investigative files, to Ulster County. "I personally was very displeased, because I really wanted to try it," Aronwald recalled. "You're going after Tony Provenzano, Mr. Untouchable. Nobody had been able to lay a hand on him. And you've got this guy Sal Briguglio, who was a goon, and from an organized crime standpoint—I mean, I basically was licking my chops. This was a case that was made in heaven. Of course, once my case went down the tubes, whatever intentions I had to use Konigsberg"—and to cut him some slack—"were certainly not binding to the Ulster County D.A."

And the Ulster County D.A. was not inclined to give Harold any deal at all. He decided to pursue the stiffest possible penalty against Harold as well as the codefendants Tony Pro and Sally Bugs.

As the New York State prosecution moved forward, Aronwald continued to hear from Harold. "He would call me and say he was having problems with the prosecutor and could I help him," he told me. "I had to say at one point, 'There's a conflict here, because I was prosecuting you and now I'm basically giving you advice.' "

Aronwald, a brusque lawyer in C.Y.O.-coach wire-rims, softened at this memory. He asked after Harold and said, "If you see him, tell him I wish him well." He cherished the way that, for years afterward, Harold continued to send his regards on the High Holidays. He said that he would be happy to write a letter on Harold's behalf to the parole board.

"Look, I can't forgive what he did," he went on. "But as far as I'm concerned, if he were released from prison tomorrow, I wouldn't think it would be a mistake. He's done a lot of time."

Such benevolence from Aronwald, of all people, threw me for a loop. Years earlier, he'd had a horrible—and personal—interface with organized crime, when gangsters shot and killed his elderly father at a laundromat in Queens. The government later discovered the killing to have been a botched attempt on the younger Aronwald's life, revenge for his aggressive prosecution of Mob figures. The gunmen had evidently received the order from a Colombo-family boss, along with a slip of paper with one word on it—"Aronwald"—and, looking in the phone book, they settled on the wrong lawyer with that last name. Aronwald's father had worked previously as a judge in parking-ticket cases.

Aronwald vividly recalled his several meetings with Harold—"how he came in, with his blond hair and the meaty arms and barrel chest, you know?" he said. "The only thing he wanted to know when he would come into our office was if we could get him some fried chicken. And the agents would go to Kentucky Fried Chicken and bring him a box and he would devour the whole thing. He was in hog heaven."

ELEVEN

On Trial in Kingston

IN NOVEMBER 1977, Michael Kavanagh, a thirty-three-year-old prosecutor in Ulster County, was elected district attorney, and announced that the trial of Harold, Tony Pro, and Sally Bugs would be his first major case. Kavanagh had arrived in Kingston only three years earlier, following a stint in the complaints bureau of the Manhattan District Attorney. His boss there was Frank Rogers, Harold's onetime nemesis. In 1970, when Rogers had interviewed him for the job, Kavanagh noticed, on a wall near Rogers's desk, a photograph of "a guy in shackles going crazy—the famous *Life* magazine shot of Konigsberg," he recalled. "Frank told me who it was. I remembered reading about Frank and the trial they had, where Konigsberg abused the judge."

A pink-faced man with a brushy mustache and shaggy hair in the style of the day, Kavanagh was ambitious, but he saw the case as less a fulcrum for his career than a million-pointed opportunity to botch it up.

The Feds had relinquished the case to Ulster County the previous year. "The implicit assumption from them was that we weren't up to it," Kavanagh explained. It was not merely the prospect of setting an inexperienced small-town D.A. against some of the biggest names in organized crime but the worry that Ulster County might jettison the case altogether. "It wasn't as if this was our case," Kavanagh admitted. "It didn't involve Ulster County interests. At the time of the indictments, frankly, I never dreamed we'd actually try it. We could have dropped it and nobody around here would have cared or noticed. I was still an assistant D.A., running for D.A. When the ruling came down, I said, 'Oh, my God.' We were in over our heads."

But when the Feds offered to send up a special prosecutor to argue the case on Ulster County's behalf, Kavanagh decided to hold firm. "This was during the middle of my campaign," he said. "I was worried how it would look if I suddenly get some guy in to do this case for us." While the D.A.'s office didn't want to touch the Castellito case before election day (Kavanagh's boss, District Attorney Francis Vogt, was also seeking higher office, as a state judge), "I promised the F.B.I. that if I lost the election, we'd try the case before the new guy came in, which was ridiculous. We'd never have been able to do it."

As he waited for his trial to begin, Harold was housed in the Metropolitan Correctional Center in lower Manhattan. He had the place rigged for reconnaissance. "Nine P.M., I would go into the counselor's office and lock the door from inside," he told me.

"How did you get the keys?"

"Why do you ask stupid questions?"

Harold said he'd phoned around to prisons across the country, "and I asked for the Bureau of Identification. I'd say I was the counselor from the M.C.C., they'd call me back at the M.C.C. office, they'd give me everything," he recalled. "I found out where the informants were. I found out that Big Sal was being hid in Kansas City."

"Did anybody go after him?"

"Well, the decision was decided that we do nothing. And on my own there was not much I could do in the M.C.C., was there?"

Ulster County is small—Kingston's population was twenty thousand at the time—and even in simple matters of logistics the trial tested its manpower and resources. Of particular concern was whether its police force could protect the jury and witness pools from tampering. Toward the end of jury selection, for instance, a prospective juror approached Tony Pro's nephew in the courthouse lobby and slipped him a business card with the message "If you want, we can do business" written on the back. When they met up later, the man offered to deliver a not-guilty verdict in exchange for $20,000. The nephew reported the incident to local authorities. They outfitted him with a tape recorder, which he used to capture a repeat offer. But this chain of events led nowhere. Three weeks later, the would-be juror died mysteriously in an airplane crash in Westerly, Rhode Island. (State police found no evidence of foul play.)

The government struggled even to safeguard the defendants and to keep an eye on their lawyers. In March 1978, about two months before the trial began, Sally Bugs was shot and killed by two unidentified men in Little Italy. Tony Pro was believed to have ordered the hit. He was simultaneously facing racketeering charges in Manhattan and feared that Sally Bugs was on the verge of cooperating with the government in that case. This left Harold and Tony Pro as the only two defendants.

Then, on May 15, 1978, less than an hour before opening arguments were to be heard against Harold and Tony Pro, Tony Pro's seventy-two-year-old lawyer, Murray Edelbaum, excused himself, claiming an indeterminate "medical problem," and fled the courthouse for the coronary-care unit of a local hospital. Refusing to declare a mistrial, Judge John J. Clyne adjourned the case for two weeks. He had the jurors bused to the Kingston Holiday Inn and informed Tony Pro of his options: God willing, he said, Edelbaum would be his lawyer on May 31. If not, he could find another lawyer, or else he was free to mount his own defense. But Clyne would be hearing the case on May 31. Edelbaum, lo and behold, enjoyed a miraculous recovery in Boca Raton, where he and Tony Pro had repaired.

As the costs to the county mounted, Kavanagh called down to Washington and secured $40,000 in supplemental funding for law enforcement. Ironically, a portion of this went toward protecting the alleged hit man. Because an intelligence report from the state police described a contract on Harold's life that dated to 1966 and was worth $250,000, the government had to employ no fewer than fifty men to look after him, between the courthouse—where he spent business hours—and his holding cell, at the nearby state prison in Napanoch. One day, as Harold was getting ferried into town, the Kingston *Daily Freeman* reported, the sight of all the trooper cars on the freeway exit sent him into such a fugue state that he dove to the floor and wrapped his hands tightly around his head.

The increased security transformed Kingston's lovingly designated Historic Business District overnight. "This place was Mulberry Street," Kavanagh recalled. "You've got guys right out of *The Godfather* pulling up in limousines." Sharpshooters lined up on the roof of the jewelry store that faced the courthouse. "Those people had never seen anything like it," Ivan Fisher, whom Harold had hired as his lawyer, said. "We're talking canines who could smell gunpowder."

Fisher, a highly able protégé of one of Harold's former lawyers, began to worry that he'd made a mistake in taking Harold's case as soon as he found himself wondering how to handle the juror-bribery attempt. He'd learned of it from a member of Tony Pro's camp—it was essentially offered to both defendants as a package deal—and, instead of immediately reporting it to the judge, he went to tell Harold about the entreaty. "It was a big violation of ethical responsibility, particularly given who my client was," he told me. "I mean, I really had no ethical choice but to go to the judge first thing."

Fisher is a dapper man of tremendous girth, a self-described "born-again Orthodox" Jew, and a lifelong collector of seamy criminal clients. He represented Jack Henry Abbot and one of the defendants in the French Connection case. Not long ago, we met for dinner at a kosher steakhouse on the Upper East Side to discuss the Kingston trial. A knit *kipah* perched obediently on his head. He wore a bespoke suit (this I know because he told me), a Ferragamo tie, and dainty black cap-toed shoes. At length, Fisher assured me that he never would have taken part in the bribe, but he also knew that bringing the information to Harold was opening the door for him. "If Harold wanted to take them up on the bribery offer, he wouldn't have told me. He'd have just gone ahead with it," he said. "The only conceivable thing for me to do was to reject it outright and not even let Harold know. You know, ironically, I'd gone to Harold first because I wanted to impress him."

He was quiet long enough to unburden his fork of a large morsel of the T-bone special. "Imagine, wanting to prove your moral purity to Harold Konigsberg!"

Fisher took the case for a mere $2,500 in expenses, but still Harold managed to obtain what they needed. "During our lunch breaks, he ordered in four-pound buckets of shrimp, with fresh tartar sauce, fresh cocktail sauce," Fisher recalled abashedly. "It was before I was kosher."

While Harold moved through the courthouse lobby pretending that nobody noticed him, hiding his face with a straw hat, Tony Pro—free on bail—chatted up the daily throng of reporters and court buffs. The *Freeman* took note of his "tanned chest"; the way the "gold inlays in his teeth shine through the white porcelain"; how "his navy blue jacket with baby blue lining hangs impeccably." A townsperson said, "Tony Pro was a hit in Kingston. He'd go order a shrimp cocktail and leave a hundred dollars."

While they shared a preference for pre-murder-trial shrimp cocktail, Harold and Tony Pro refused to speak to each other. This was despite each man's knowledge that his own best hope resided in a joint acquittal. Tony Pro was aware that Harold had been willing to rat him out to the F.B.I. on this very case. Harold, for his part, was still waiting for his take from the Local 560 rackets—and had even tried to squeeze the money from Tony Pro with a lawsuit, claiming that he was owed for his work as "a union negotiator, consultant, and advisor."

The trial began on May 31, 1978. The prosecution's case turned largely on testimony from Big Sal and John Nadratowski, the neighbor of Castellito's who had seen Harold on the victim's property on the day of the murder. Kavanagh also made use of a convicted loan shark and racketeer named Ralph (Little Ralphie) Picardo, who emerged from the witness-relocation program to testify that Tony Pro had once bragged to him about the murder over lunch at a coffee shop in Hudson County.

It wasn't an easy case for the prosecution—no body, the only eyewitness rendered less than sympathetic by virtue of having participated in the murder—but the defense team also carried a heavy oar. The best it could do to suggest reasonable doubt was to accuse the government of wanting Harold and Tony Pro too badly. "You don't believe the United States is prepared to give immunity to Salvatore Sinno merely for his confession, do you?" Fisher asked the court, adding later, "The truth shouldn't cost that much."

As is often the case with Mafia prosecutions, the D.A.'s toughest challenge was getting the members of the jury to identify with the victim. "This kind of case could come across to jurors as very cold, but Kavanagh did an excellent job by calling Castellito's son as his last witness," said Albert Sproul, the F.B.I. agent who secured Anthony Castellito Jr.'s participation and kept him company throughout the trial. During questioning, Kavanagh got Anthony Jr. talking about the day he realized his father wasn't coming home, and let it emerge that Anthony Jr. had been about to get married at the time. Kavanagh told me that drawing out the tragedy of the case had required some manipulation.

"We got away with murder with Castellito—the son's testimony in particular," he said, with no apparent irony. "Look, after all, Castellito was ready to hide out a guy who's on the lam from the law. There was a shadowy part to him that the defense never fully developed. And fortunately we were able to create another impression—of him as a union savior who was going to come in and undo the terrible harms that Provenzano had done to that union, of a solid Italian gentleman, a family man who was home every night for his wife. The man was obviously not the saint that we portrayed him to be."

Harold and Tony Pro were both found guilty.

Judge Clyne permitted Harold to speak at the sentencing hearing. Harold thanked his lawyer, offered that he held only one other judge in higher regard ("and that's not to be disrespectful"), and praised the U.S. Constitution, the Hon. Adam Clayton Powell Jr., and the late Supreme Court Justice Hugo Black.

"Mr. Konigsberg, please," Judge Clyne said. "I am trying to be liberal. We all know what the sentence is going to be." Judge Clyne sentenced Harold and Tony Pro to life in prison, with the earliest possibility for parole set at twenty-six years and eight months.

Anthony Jr. left the courthouse excited. "It was my happy day," he said. "Parking was a dollar. I gave the attendant a five and said, 'Do me a favor. I don't drink. Go buy somebody a drink on me.' I drove three hours home, no stops, whistling up the highway. I came in and said to my wife, 'It's all over.'"

But it wasn't. In 1981, after a series of appeals, the state of New York affirmed Tony Pro's conviction but ruled, by a three-to-two vote, to overturn Harold's.

Harold had pulled yet another Houdini act. Back when he was working the phones over his shrimp-bucket lunches with Ivan Fisher, he'd learned somehow that the New York secretary of state possessed a sealed file on John Nadratowski, Castellito's neighbor. Nadratowski was the D.A.'s only non-accomplice witness who could put Harold at the scene of the crime. According to a report inside the file, New York State had sanctioned Nadratowski for writing five bogus checks between 1965 and 1968, and as a result had suspended his real-estate license. One of these transactions had involved depositing payment for a piece of property he did not own; another had resulted in his arrest.

"They were the cheating kind of misdeeds, the kind that call into question a witness's believability," Fisher said. "It said the witness was a crook, a thief, in his own county. Forget gold, it was platinum." But when Fisher had tried to cross-examine the witness on these grounds, Kavanagh objected and was sustained; the judge considered the material on Nadratowski irrelevant to the case. Big mistake, wrote the appellate court:

[T]he limitations placed upon the cross-examination of witness Nadratowski with respect to prior bad acts were so gross as to constitute an abuse of discretion by the trial court requiring re-

versal of Konigsberg's conviction since there is no evidence corroborating the testimony of accomplice Sinno as to Konigsberg's
guilt other than the testimony of Nadratowski.

Fisher admitted that the entire appeal had been built on Harold's investigation. "Not even the prosecution had a copy of that file, but
Harold somehow heard about it and then got someone to go into it and
read the contents to him," he said. "We were like two kids doing a fra-
ternity prank on the phone."

Kavanagh considered dropping the charges against Harold. To have
put away Tony Pro was a grand victory in itself. But when Kavanagh
was informed that dismissing the case against Harold could make him
eligible for parole in 1983—only two years down the road—he instructed his staff to get ready for a retrial.

TWELVE

The Thunder Stuff at the End

HAROLD'S OLDER DAUGHTER, who was seventeen, had shown up in Kingston every day for the trial and sat in the front row. She sobbed when Big Sal, the prosecution linchpin, described the details of Castellito's murder. "He left me when I was one year old and now I'll never see him again," the *Freeman* quoted her as telling a fellow spectator.

The proceedings were likely a big revelation to Harold's girls, who'd been very young at the time of his last trial, in Manhattan. I wonder if, as they grew up with their father in prison, their mother ever told them about the gravity of the accusations against him. By the time of the retrial, both daughters were in college, and Harold told them not to come because he didn't want to impose. In any case, trying to look like a family man hadn't done him any good thus far, so this time around he wanted to be sure the jury saw him as pitiable and lonely.

While he was happy to have his wife's and daughters' sympathy, it could also upset him when they observed him in a position of weakness. For a time, during the last year of her life, Harold even forbade his wife from coming to see him at Auburn. He'd lost his temper with the prison staff during a recent visit, when she'd tried to bring him a thirty-pound fruit basket and a guard had dismantled it to check for contraband.

He told me about this one morning, over a breakfast of corn chips and Pepsi.

"The cocksuckers put the whole basket back together wrong," he said. "They put the Spanish fruits—the mangoes—on top. It squashed the grapes and plums and the nectarines, all of them was ruined. It made her sad. I didn't think she should be put through that."

Sometime in 1968, Harold began filling his legal correspondence with references to "G-d" and eventually he got on the Department of Corrections kosher meal plan (which, at Auburn, is superior to what the rest of the inmates eat). "Services Wednesday I never miss," he said. But, those perquisites aside, he no longer enjoys the privileged existence he once did in prison. He wanted to be sure I understood this. "I'm in the fucking Philistines in here."

He slid his fingers into the bag of chips, plucking out a few remaining fragments.

"I figure I don't have more than another year or two left on this earth," he added, and for this reason in particular he was intent on getting paroled. "As soon as I get myself out of this place, the first thing I'm gonna do is make sure my grandson gets a bar mitzvah." One of his daughters' boys had quit Hebrew school, and the burden of imparting a proper education was now on his shoulders.

His other goal was to father a son with a Jewish mother. "I'm gonna save my seed," he said. "I'm gonna find an Orthodox girl and pay her to have my son. Do you know you, me, your father, and your brother are the only ones left in my father's line named Konigsberg? We're the last of the *Kohens*."

Many Jews with names deriving from Cohen—Cohn, Kahn, Katz, Kaplan—count themselves as *Kohanim*, the exalted priest tribe of Israel. They are believed to be descendants of Moses' older brother, Aaron, the first Jewish high priest. The *Kohanim* are the first group called to read from the Torah in synagogue, and were historically governed by special restrictions, particularly regarding marriage—a *Kohen* who married a divorced woman, a convert, or a Gentile was required to relinquish his priesthood—and contact with the dead. There are laws that forbid entering a cemetery except to bury a family member, and being in the same room as a dead person.

As far as I had ever heard, Mendel was the last member of the Konigsberg family for whom the *Kohen* birthright held any significance. My father said that Mendel had arrived in this country with some sort of verification on paper, of which he was very proud, but the honor was lost on Grandpa Leo, and interest faded ever more with subsequent generations.

"I want a *Kohen*," Harold said, pausing to chew. "Yeah, I would like that, to honor my father. I would like that very much."

Harold awoke before dawn on April 23, 1981, and rode from Napanoch into Kingston for a new hearing. He had on a yellow hopsack sports jacket that his wife had bought for him, a handkerchief in the breast pocket. It had been nearly three years since the first murder trial, and he was about to spring a new scheme on the government.

Alone at the defense table, he informed the court that he and Ivan Fisher had ended their relationship and he would now be acting as his own lawyer. The picture in the next day's paper showed a relieved smile on Fisher's face as he repaired to his Mercedes limousine and left Kingston for good.

That afternoon, Harold demanded that the county allot him a
$100,000 defense fund, to pay for a fully outfitted office and a staff of
secretaries and researchers. This was denied, though he was given a
room in the courthouse with his own phone line. He asked for a change
of venue, claiming that Kavanagh's comments to the Ulster County
press about his criminal record—he offered a stack of clippings and
radio transcripts—would be prejudicial. He was told to make this request in the form of a written motion. He requested a gag order on all parties. This was granted. He requested bail, but Judge Clyne, with visible
sarcasm, told him that was highly unlikely.

"It's not funny," Harold said.

Clyne tried repeatedly to talk Harold out of his *pro se* strategy, prop-
ping up his glasses on his forehead and patiently extolling the option of
a public defender. He promised to treat Harold to a shrimp dinner if
he'd acquiesce. "I don't want spies in my camp," Harold said, but
weeks later he did agree to take on Joshua Koplowitz, a prominent attorney from nearby Woodstock, as his court-appointed "legal adviser."

"The county offered me twenty-five dollars," Koplowitz recalled. "I
said, 'Absolutely.' I went to meet Harold in his cell and tried to lay
down the ground rules. I said, 'Don't test my limits.' We got into some
kind of an argument over negotiating the size of the table in his office."

At one of their first hearings together, Harold asked Judge Clyne
where his shrimp dinner was. "All right," Clyne said. "That was with
two types of sauce?" The details of Harold's eating preferences during
the first trial had circulated widely among black robes in central New
York State.

"I make that sauce myself," Harold said. "I will be happy to make a
gallon for you, if you want. Just give me the stuff. It only needs refrig-
eration."

"All that sauce was your own during the trial?"

"Sure," Harold said, claiming he'd learned the recipe from "a fine Chinese man" when he served as a ship's second cook in the merchant marine. And then, as if anybody believed this, he added, "Chung Woo was his name."

Koplowitz had arrived in Ulster County by way of a clerkship in Oregon, Legal Aid work in Manhattan, a string of civil-rights cases, and a high-profile trial representing a man who faced the death penalty. He has long served as counsel to the Ulster County Democratic Party. When I met him, he revealed himself to be, like every lawyer who ever worked for Harold, proud of the rogue connection yet very glad to have it far behind him.

"I found him stimulating," Koplowitz said. "He wanted to impress upon me that he could make things happen. He said, 'Do you like Broadway shows? I'm gonna fix you and your wife up with some tickets to *Sugar Babies*'—that was the big musical at the time. My wife couldn't go, so I brought my fourteen-year-old daughter. Afterward, a car and driver took us to the restaurant his cousin owned in Kew Gardens"—in Queens. "There were ten people waiting for us at a table, including Harold's wife and daughters, and one of them was dating Lee Mazzilli from the Mets. At some point, the phone rang. Harold was calling from Napanoch. He insisted on talking to every person there."

Eventually, of course, the bloom came off the rose. "After the trial was over, I don't know if it was ten letters from him I had to not respond to or twelve," Koplowitz said. "He kept wanting me to represent him on a million things. *Dayenu*, you know?"

Harold's first priority for the retrial was securing a new judge—Judge Clyne's nickname was Maximum John—and in July he got his wish, when state officials pulled Clyne off the case. The reason they gave was that Clyne's services were needed in his hometown of Albany, beset as the courts there were with "a heavy backlog" of cases. But, according to people on both sides of Harold's case, Clyne's removal had more to do with a reimbursement request submitted to the court by a private investigator whom Harold had hired. The voucher demanded $14,250.20 from the court and was accompanied by an affidavit from one of the private eyes detailing a weeklong surveillance of Judge Clyne. According to the document, the judge "was quite active with members of Mr. Kavanagh's staff," particularly the D.A.'s secretary, Katherine Whalen:

> [O]n more occasions than the ordinary court business would indicate Kay Whalen would drive to the Howard Johnson's Restaurant located on Route 28, Kingston, New York, and park her vehicle in the rear of the building.... Surveillance showed that shortly after, Whalen entered the Judge's vehicle and they would then depart for their rendezvous, whose only purpose we would have to assume involved Mr. Konigsberg, since Judge Clyne would be conscious of the effect upon the trial if it were known that he were working with the prosecutor's office without the knowledge of the defendant.

Not included with the expense report, but, instead, sent directly to Clyne's chambers, were photographs of the judge meeting Whalen in the parking lot. "I rented a motel room in the Howard Johnson's and waited," the photographer who took the pictures for the investigator told me. "Never for very long, though, because I had instructions what time of day they met. Harold knew about the affair somehow. He had a great antenna."

"The crazy thing about it was that the judge himself authorized and paid for the investigation," recalled Marvin Newberg, a clerk for the judge who replaced Clyne. "The county gave Konigsberg fifteen thousand dollars for discovery, and this was where it went. It was quite an embarrassment."

Harold was elated to learn the name of Clyne's replacement: Louis B. Scheinman. "He thought there would be some kind of ethnic bonding with a Jewish judge," Koplowitz said. "It's normal to look for anything to play up, but Harold wasn't so subtle. He started using Yiddish words in court. And poor Judge Scheinman! He died so young." That became the joke around town after Scheinman's death, just two years later, at sixty-one, that Harold's behavior had taken a decade or two off his life. "Lou would walk into the court so beaten down," Kavanagh said. "You could see him aging before your very eyes."

During the period between the trial, in 1978, and the retrial, in 1982, Harold earned his G.E.D. and took correspondence courses through Ulster County Community College. According to a probation officer's report from this time, he was one semester shy of receiving his A.A. degree. Meanwhile, he filed a $4.9 million civil-rights lawsuit against Ulster County, alleging that several county officials, including Kavanagh and Judge Clyne, had conspired to limit his prison privileges as he prepared his defense. He tried to subpoena the whole lot of them, and when they ignored his requests he obtained a court order from a judge to depose Kavanagh.

"I had to drive to Napanoch and sit there in front of him for four hours while he exercised his right to interview me," Kavanagh recalled. "Oh, it was awful! The fact that he'd persuaded a federal judge to make me submit to an interrogation from him, to participate in his accusing the hell out of me." By that point, Harold had addressed Kavanagh in court as "a transvestite," "a fraud," and the illegitimate son of the previous D.A., and characterized his time in office as "a reign of terror."

Harold's delay tactics ensured the county a full year of pregame warm-up before the trial actually began. Almost every day, he had at least an hour's worth of new applications to hold more hearings, at which Kavanagh eventually waived his right to be present. "I worried my appearance wouldn't look so good," he explained. Harold made hundreds of preliminary motions—motions to remove Kavanagh as prosecutor, to remove Scheinman as judge, to rule as inadmissible various pieces of witness testimony that had been heard in the first trial (and in many cases had already been challenged unsuccessfully by the defense). There was Harold's motion requesting $12,000 from the court to finance a poll that would determine whether Ulster County was fit to provide Harold a fair trial. Scheinman shot it down immediately. "We can't keep going on like this forever," he cautioned Harold. During one hearing, he threw up his hands, told Harold to submit all subsequent motions in writing, and walked out of the courtroom.

While Harold and the judge were going back and forth, Harold's old statements to the F.B.I. made their way into the case. In 1976, when Kavanagh was preparing for the first trial and came upon the interview reports, "I imagined I was hearing the confessions of Luca Brasi—the number of people he was claiming responsibility for killing was astonishing," he told me. He had planned to introduce them in the original trial as evidence, but discovered that for technical reasons this would be feasible only if he tried Harold and Tony Pro separately. "And I didn't think we could hold this case together up here for any longer than one trial," he said.

But because he was retrying only Harold this time, Kavanagh figured he was free to bring the confessions into court. On August 11, 1982, two agents who from 1965 to 1967 had conducted the bulk of the interviews were brought to Kingston for a closed hearing. Kavanagh's goal as he questioned the agents was to establish the veracity of the reports, which he did quickly. The F.B.I. men said that Harold had confessed to the murder of Anthony Castellito, and if they were called to testify in his trial they could swear to it again.

Harold protested. He said he'd been given immunity by the F.B.I. at the time, in exchange for his statements. He said the F.B.I. would back him on this. He said he'd subpoena J. Edgar Hoover if that was what it took.

Though neither the prosecution team nor the judge believed Harold, the hearing took a surprising turn during cross-examination, when one of the agents, Frank Donnelley, said that despite Harold's failure to produce Castellito's body—the explicitly named condition for immunity—"we fully expected Harold Konigsberg to get immunity." The F.B.I. had never actually *granted* it, Donnelley explained. In fact, he recalled having consistently advised Harold that anything he said could be used against him in court. "But we told him we would . . . send his request to Washington," he said.

Donnelley's partner, Paul Durkin, supported this. "I think that was understood from the beginning," he testified, speaking to Harold, "that everything you did furnish us would be kept in a confidential vein."

Kavanagh was confused despite the agents' understanding. There was nothing in the documents to suggest immunity, and, in fact, each report led off with the statement that Harold had been advised of his rights and that anything he said was subject to prosecution. "You give me something that says they cannot be used and I won't use them," Kavanagh told the agents. But they couldn't.

"They kept dancing around it," Kavanagh recalled. "To a person they were all of the view that by using them I would be giving Harold the shaft, that it was unfair to him! It was mind-boggling."

Although Kavanagh protested, Scheinman ruled the confessions inadmissible. "I tell you, I was a little surprised at some of the things I heard in this hearing," Scheinman said. "I thought it would be an ordinary and standard hearing, where the police officers would come in and say that no promises were made, and I learned differently."

"Thank God for that," Harold said, and praised the judge for his virtue. "I know you are a good Jew, period, and I know you care and you are not ashamed to stand up and say, 'I'm a Jew.'"

Kavanagh had never tried a *pro se* defendant before. "Notwithstanding the fact that this guy was the consummate jailhouse lawyer, *pro se* cases are difficult in the best of circumstances," he told me. "Any time you get one up there, they're honored in the breach. They're helped more than they're hurt by the inequality. They use the lawyer's role to make their case without having to take the stand. They can effectively testify but can't be cross-examined."

Also, whatever edge the prosecutor possesses in legal knowledge can work against him. "Here I am as a prosecutor, and there are certain things I could do to take advantage, things I could exploit, but I'd better not," Kavanagh said, "because if a defense lawyer had been there they wouldn't have happened." Kavanagh worried that Harold's lack of legal expertise might well serve as the basis for a later appeal. "And I didn't want to be up there trying this case a third time," he said.

For the same reasons, the judge gave Harold the run of the place. "Lou Scheinman's charitableness was extraordinary," Joshua Koplowitz said. "He allowed as much evidence to go in as he possibly could." Harold marked a total of 274 exhibits for identification or as evidence, while Kavanagh marked 21. The transcript of the retrial is 5,211 pages, more than twice as long as the first trial.

Jury selection—eight days, 1,573 pages—was Harold's finest hour. "He was like Milton Berle onstage," Koplowitz said. "He was Mr. Charm." Pacing to and fro between defense table and judge's seat and pausing midsentence for effect, Harold would cock his head, fold his soup-bone arms, and ask the potential jurors if they understood what it meant for a defendant to be "clothed in the right of the presumption of innocence." He told one prospective juror that he could see that she was an extremely intelligent woman, and told a man who mentioned a two-year-old granddaughter that he didn't look old enough to have one. He told a butcher that, when the trial was over, he'd appreciate his advice on how to wrap and tie a roast. To a man who said he had two daughters: "You will have problems in due time. Hope you earn a lot of money." To a candidate whom he observed clipping coupons: "Everybody does it with the prices the way things are. I wish I could help you."

The question Harold asked most frequently of prospective jurors was whether they had a prejudice against any kind of religious group. "I am of the Jewish faith, and I believe deeply in my God, my one God and only God," he said. "I have learned from reading newspapers in Ulster County that there are various . . . antireligious groups, and there also is an American Nazi Party group, and there also is Ku Klux Klan groups in Ulster County. I don't wish to embarrass anybody, and I don't wish to create a problem with anybody. All I say is, will any one of you who have these problems, whether subconsciously or consciously, bring it to the court's attention privately and we can discuss it in chambers without anybody knowing the better or the worse of the situation?"

He inquired of the jury pool whether the terms "Mob" or "organized crime" evoked any negative associations. "You don't like Mob people?" he asked one man. He asked another if he'd ever heard a maxim that would likely have biased him, "An attorney who has himself for a client has a fool for a client." When the man said no, Harold told him, "Well, you have today." Another man was excused after he admitted that, although he had no prior knowledge of the case, he was very familiar with the name Kayo Konigsberg, as he'd heard of him often while growing up in New York City.

Don Williams, one of Kavanagh's assistant D.A.'s, was assigned to handle the voir dire and had specific instructions to try to needle Harold, "so that the jury candidates would hopefully see the volatile side of Harold Konigsberg," he said. "You know, not the charismatic and human side, the articulate man with a sense of humor. He had such a good delivery with the jurors, I was told to do something to get on his nerves and hope that he'd go off the deep end."

During a break on a day when Harold had been especially light on his feet, both counsels convened with the judge for an off-the-record discussion, and Harold basked in the glow of his own performance. "Konigsberg said he was always very gracious to the women," Williams, who had also sat in on the supression hearing with the F.B.I. agents, recalled. "I reminded him that had not always been the case. I brought up the fact that one of his victims in the murder confessions was a woman. As I remember it, he had a violent outburst and the judge had to end the jury selection early that day."

Scheinman let Harold remain in his courthouse office late into the night and on weekends as he worked on his defense, and allowed him to choose which deputies guarded him. He insisted that no mention was made before the jury of Harold's prior convictions, nor that he had already been tried once for Castellito's murder. Harold appreciated all of this. "I love you as a human being," he told Scheinman. "If everybody in this room knew what I knew about you, they would love you, too."

Harold said he intended to have Tony Pro delivered from prison to testify on his behalf. "You know, if you call him, you run a great danger of having stuff come out that you don't want," Scheinman warned him. "Tony Pro can hurt you real bad." Nonetheless, he protected Harold's right to do so, and firmly instructed Kavanagh not to ask potential jurors how likely they might be to trust a witness if they knew the witness had been convicted of murder. That, he explained in a private conference with both counsels, carried a suggestion of the prior trial. From the transcript:

> THE COURT: Just say "committed a murder." If you want to talk about "convicted of drugs" or something else which is not involved in this case here, you can say "convicted of drugs." I just don't want you to say anything which indicates that there was a conviction in connection with this particular case.
>
> KONIGSBERG: If he asks about "conviction of drugs" and there is no conviction of drugs, I will move for a mistrial.
>
> THE COURT: Of course. I said I don't know if there was any conviction.
>
> KONIGSBERG: I'm frightened to death of drugs.
>
> THE COURT: I have no idea what Mr. Provenzano has been convicted of. Maybe he has been convicted of buggery, I don't know.
>
> KONIGSBERG: What is buggery?
>
> THE COURT: I don't know really.
>
> (Whereupon, the proceedings were reconvened in the courtroom.)

After they interviewed more than 120 candidates, counselors from both sides agreed on their jury. Harold was upbeat. "I will turn out to be Clarence Darrow before it's all through," he said.

On the first Tuesday in October 1982, in his opening statement, Harold promised to demonstrate how he was being framed by a "corrupt" D.A., a man whose witnesses were guilty of "perjuries, swindles, and frauds upon innocent, hardworking people out of their monies and properties." It was a heavy-handed gambit. Rather than merely trying to cast doubt on all kinds of small but significant aspects of the government witnesses' recollections, Harold was hoping to persuade jurors of his own moral superiority to everybody involved in the prosecution's case.

As for Big Sal Sinno, Harold was pleased to inform the jury that he'd once made money off of an illegal card game (Harold had done more than his share of similar things); that he had been able to operate this card game by paying off public officials (Harold had done this, too); that he had taken part in the hijacking of a commercial truck (also this); that he had once been arrested for robbery and, in the course of this crime, pistol-whipped his mark, and also made use of a phony Social Security number and a false identity (ibid., ibid., ibid.). Harold called Big Sal "an admitted liar," "a thief," "a common gambler," "a philanderer," and "a man who lies at the drop of a hat."

He began his cross-examination of Big Sal by asking him to list all the aliases he'd used in the past, and offered that if Big Sal couldn't even be straight about his real name, then even his assertion of having ever personally known Harold was questionable. (For this reason, it particularly irked Harold each time Big Sal addressed him by his first name. "At this point, Mr. Sinno, I'm Harold *Konigsberg*," he said, adding that Big Sal could go by whichever of his assumed identities he preferred.)

Harold asked Big Sal to describe the first time they ever met, and Big Sal responded that he was once sent by the Mafia to see Harold in the Hudson County Jail. "We had demitasse, and we had Italian pastry in the warden's office."

"In the warden's office?" Harold said. "Was I the warden, Mr. Sinno?"

"No. You were a prisoner," Big Sal said. Harold accused him of bringing in prejudicial information and requested a mistrial.

Harold cross-examined Big Sal for three days, eleven courtroom hours altogether. "Mr. Sinno, did you ever socialize with me?" he asked. "Have you ever been to my home, with my family?"

"No. You have been in my home, though," Big Sal said. "You had a woman you wanted to bring there. I gave you the okay, remember?" They had a long exchange about the location of the apartment, the name of the landlord, whether Harold had told Big Sal that he liked the apartment so much he actually wanted to buy it, whether this fact meant he had money, who this woman was, the year of the alleged tryst (whether it was during Harold's marriage), whether Big Sal actually saw her, and whether upon his return Big Sal had noticed that his bed had been "upset."

"Let's get off this," Scheinman finally told Harold.

"I'm pretty insulted, Judge," Harold said. "It's out of my league."

Big Sal stood up well to Harold, knowing that the government was behind him. As he neared the end of his testimony, his voice was hoarse and he looked bored on the stand, resting his head in the crook of his arm or wiping his glasses meticulously. "You're repeating questions," he told Harold. "You're not making much sense." Harold spent nearly an hour making Big Sal describe his fellow accomplices. When they got to Harold himself, Big Sal said, "You were about . . . a third of the size you are now. In other words, you looked good in them days. You looked real good."

Harold said, "You mean like I'm a little lopsided now?"

"Yes. You are a barrel."

"I agree."

"You are a barrel. That's true."

"Let's get down to business," Harold said.

Big Sal was still agreeing. "You are," he said. "I will give you a description of you. Do you want it? All the way or what?" He estimated that in 1961, Harold had weighed about 190. "How many pounds are you now, about four hundred?"

Everybody in the courtroom laughed. Harold turned to the judge.

"I'm not asking you to strike it, Your Honor," he said. "I know I'm lop-sided. I want to get my weight down."

Big Sal fondly remembered a ring Harold had worn, with large dia-monds in the shape of a horseshoe, and he couldn't help but marvel at Harold's hair. "You had blondish hair, straight blondish—you looked a lot better," he said. "Straight back you wore it."

John Nadratowski, Castellito's neighbor, took the stand and recalled his reaction upon encountering Harold, Big Sal, and Sally Bugs in Ker-honkson on the day Castellito disappeared: "I said to my wife, you know, 'Hon, these guys look like hoodlums to me. . . . I'm going to stop at the state police.'"

"Tell us," Harold asked, "when was it that you decided the people looked like hoodlums that you claim were there?"

"Well, when they behaved in the manner you did," Nadratowski replied, adding that Big Sal and Sally Bugs "seemed to be subservient to you in some manner. And seemed to make me feel suspicious because they didn't talk very much. It was a hush-hush thing." He went on, "The fact that there is a strange car parked on that piece of property. I blow the horn. I hear some digging. The digging stops—or shoveling, or whatever you want to call it. No one comes to answer the call, though. I turn around, looking for people. You come flying up the hill in this Cadillac, flash some kind of identification. I don't know what to tell you, you know what I mean? It makes me suspicious."

Since Harold had won the right to a retrial in the first place by ex-ploiting Nadratowski's history of bad checks, he tried a dozen different ways to trap him into contradicting himself. He also focused on a dis-crepancy between the description that Nadratowski gave police of Harold's height—six feet or more—and Harold's actual height of five feet nine. "The relative proportions is something he could not have missed with a missing machine," one of Harold's lawyers had once claimed of Nadratowski's errant characterization. In fact, it was hardly the only time somebody mistakenly inflated Harold's physical stature. Even Big Sal, who'd spent several days in Harold's presence—and was sitting right in front of him—testified that he was six feet even.

Later, I had another look at Peter Maas's description of Harold's fictitious double, King Kong Karpstein, which had been written years before the trial. "Most people," the narrator said, "experienced such an immediate rush of terror in his presence that they invariably ascribed several additional inches to his height and fifty or so pounds to his heft. Indeed, he had acquired basic law enforcement statistics of six feet five and two hundred ninety pounds after his initial booking for assault and battery"—at which six cops, after failing in their attempt to subdue him for a mug shot, "finally resorted to estimating his proportions."

It occurs to me that when I recall our visits now, I, too, picture Harold as much larger than he really is.

There was a pattern to Harold's interrogations. He would either use his cross-examination to pose the very same questions that Kavanagh already had—over and over with slight nuances of phrasing, hoping to trip witnesses into some kind of verbal inconsistency—or he would ask if the witness was getting paid by the government in exchange for testimony (which, of course, Harold himself had tried to do back when he offered to flip). He demanded to know if Big Sal had let the U.S. Marshals treat him to Chinese food during lunch recess one day.

"He was a genius at looking stuff up in the legal precedents and mastering them," the private investigator he had hired, Walter Byer, said. "A number of times, he even straightened out Josh Koplowitz on them." As Harold's court-appointed legal adviser, Koplowitz said, his suggestions for how to "gently deconstruct" the prosecution's witnesses were put to use at first, but he came to see himself increasingly as a babysitter. "There were certain things he would focus on and keep hammering," Koplowitz told me. "Certain things he kept"—he shook his hands as if wringing a doll's neck—"obsessing over. A lot of my energy was spent trying to convince him that he was barking up the wrong tree. After a while, I said, 'Fuck it—it's his gig.' He's not somebody you can talk out of something."

He began to move for a mistrial at the slightest prompting—small talk among witnesses, for example, or on the occasion that Kavanagh misheard something Scheinman said and then apologized, explaining that he was tired. (It reflected poorly on his cross-examination, Harold averred, to have the D.A. on the record declaring fatigue right in the middle of it.)

Cracks in Harold's composure began to show through as he increasingly allowed the jury to see him making the trial into a personal matter between himself and the prosecution team. One day, according to a newspaper account, when he accused Kavanagh of "corruption, dishonesty, and suppression of evidence," he swung his fists in the air. Two sheriff's deputies rose to their feet behind him, decided that he didn't need restraining, then sat back down. Some people in the courtroom chuckled each time he referred to Kavanagh's chief assistant D.A., a man named Holly Carnright, as "that handsome young man" at the government's table. But observers were put decidedly on edge by the way Harold would, during a break, offhandedly mention by name the wives and children of the prosecution team's attorneys, or their home addresses, or, in one case, where and when an assistant D.A.'s mother got her hair done every week.

When he began his interrogation of Anthony Castellito Jr., Harold approached the stand and introduced himself, a quite unnecessary act of showmanship. "The nerve of this man, the guy who killed my father, interrogating me like I'm the one who shouldn't be trusted," Anthony Jr. recalled. "The nerve. The whole way through I'm just looking at him without looking at him."

Harold tried to exploit contradictory statements Anthony Jr. had given about the condition in which he'd found the country house when he first went there after his father disappeared. In 1966, Anthony Jr. had told the F.B.I. that he'd seen no sign of an intruder. But in 1961, during one of his initial interviews with the F.B.I.—and also now in his testimony—he said he noticed a door had been thrown open with such force that the doorknob left an imprint in the adjacent wall and caused plaster to flake off.

"We don't operate like that in our house," Anthony Jr. said to Harold. When he had asked his mother if she'd noticed the damage beforehand, she told him she hadn't, and besides, she never would have left the wall banged up the way it was. "She is not a dirty woman. That is what this is coming down to?"

"That is your explanation?" Harold said.

"That is my explanation," Anthony Jr. said.

It was at this point in my reading of the retrial transcript that I realized I'd come to root for Harold's humiliation. I didn't want to allow myself to be in any way charmed by him, like all those people who'd encountered him without the benefit of knowledge. I spent several weeks in Kingston combing through the D.A.'s old files from the case. I knew it was superstitious, but, as I was taking notes, I wouldn't refer to Harold by his initials because they're the same as my father's. I enjoyed seeing a letter that Kavanagh had written to the state parole board, requesting the chance to weigh in whenever Harold's name came up for review, because he would certainly have a few things to say.

The odd documents that I had previously found funny and charming—such as an invoice a court stenographer sent to Harold, post-scripted with an update on his son's Little League season—left me cold now. In a show-cause order he submitted, he'd taken the opportunity to accuse correctional officers of unfairly confiscating drugs that had been prescribed for his high blood pressure and other purported ailments. He was also upset with the New York Department of Corrections, he wrote, for not delivering on its promise of weekly access to Jewish services. "Your deponent claims that the Rabbi must be with the pills because I have seen neither."

I could recognize the handiwork of his typewriter a mile away—the ranting legal submissions, in ALL CAPS, sloppily Xeroxed and amended in pen, full of righteous accusation. I pictured Harold alone in his cell, feverishly composing long into the night, summoning outrage again and again.

I caught myself laughing at a detective's memo that referred to Harold as "Gorilla." I found a news clipping onto which somebody in the D.A.'s office had drawn a halo above Kavanagh's head and horns springing from Harold's, and, for a moment, before I realized the significance of the horns, I laughed at that, too.

George (the Greek) Vangelakos, gray and slovenly in a workman's shirt, was the first of Harold's defense witnesses. Although George the Greek was alleged to have been a participant in Castellito's abduction—he was the man who dug the grave in Kerhonkson and among those who did away with Castellito's car, according to the government—he had escaped prosecution because of insufficient corroborating evidence. A longtime Teamster and hoodlum who had done God knows what to still wear the yoke of Harold's beast of burden, George the Greek testified that he had never been asked by the defendant to go dig a hole anyplace, that he had never been to Kerhonkson, that he had not buried

Anthony Castellito, that he had never committed a crime with Big Sal, and that neither Harold nor Sally Bugs had ever brought him a 1961 gold Cadillac and asked him to cut it up.

Harold also called as a witness a private investigator he'd commissioned to have a look at the old Castellito house. The private investigator said that there didn't appear to be adequate space behind the door for somebody to hide, "not readily."

He called on a real-estate man from Hudson County to testify that the location of the Local 560 headquarters, an intersection Big Sal called "Five Corners," went by no such name. The only Five Corners the agent knew of was in Jersey City.

One day, Harold even lugged into the courtroom two huge pieces of lead-filled rubber hose—one weighed forty-seven pounds and one weighed twenty-four pounds—and tried unsuccessfully to offer them as evidence. He said they matched the length and width of the weapon Big Sal had described attacking Castellito with, and that at such dimensions they would be far too heavy to use as a cudgel. After the jury was excused, Kavanagh picked up one of the hoses out of curiosity. "Why don't you hit somebody on the head with that, Mike?" Harold asked him.

"I've got a prime candidate, but I don't think it would do any good," Kavanagh said.

"You're right, because I'd defend myself to the maximum," Harold said. "You'd need more than that."

The morning the jurors were planning to begin their deliberations, seven of them arrived early in order to meet with Judge Scheinman. Each reported getting a strange telephone call over the weekend.

Juror No. 4, Phyllis Howland: "A man was on the phone and he said, 'Phyllis?' and I thought, My first name, my goodness. I didn't recognize the voice, and he said, 'I'm a corrections officer from Napanoch. We need your help to convict Harold.' I hung up. . . . That was it."

Juror No. 5, John Grube: "He said, 'We got a little problem. I want you to help us out with it. . . .' He says, 'Well, Mr. Konigsberg,' he says, 'he's a bad person, and we want you to convict him.' "

Alternate Juror No. 2, Marianna Ferrari: "My husband answered the phone at about 9:25 . . . and a gentleman got on and asked for me. My husband said, 'Well, she is indisposed presently. May I take a message for her?' And he said he was a correctional officer and suggested that if I wanted to remain up here to be sure to convict Konigsberg."

Nobody had any doubt about what was going on. "The only person who would have anything to gain by this would be the defendant if Your Honor had seen fit to declare mistrial," Kavanagh told Judge Scheinman in his chambers. He added that in such an event it would be "extremely difficult if not impossible" to retry the case. He turned to Harold and said, "There isn't any question in my mind, Mr. Konigsberg, that you are responsible."

Harold, of course, denied any involvement. "I hope the bastards get caught," he told Scheinman, who managed to keep the trial moving forward and instructed both counsels to have their summations ready to go when they got back from lunch.

Harold's was five hours long. Striding proudly to the well of the courtroom like a teenage congregant making his first *aliyah*, Harold posited that Anthony Castellito was not even dead and was still hiding out somewhere. "He disappeared for his own reasons, whatever they are," he said. He called Anthony Jr. "a little bit of a liar," for furnishing the government with "dirty evidence." He said that Anthony Jr.'s motivation was that he disliked Tony Pro for never making him a business agent.

At 5:50 P.M., Judge Scheinman asked if he would be willing to adjourn for the evening. "I would appreciate that, because I recognize now that I would like to finish with the thunder stuff at the end," Harold said. "Right now I'm just warming up."

The next morning, Harold vowed to the ladies and gentlemen of the jury that he could identify "a hundred holes" in the D.A.'s argument. "I am now going to start crumbling the case," he said. With that, he reached into a sleeve of Saltines on the defense table and crushed one in his hand. Every time he made a point, he'd crumble a cracker. By the time he was done, there was a pile of crumbs on the floor big enough to feed half the pigeons in Central Park, and Harold was ready to trust the jurors with his fate.

"I feel right now like I was born in my mother's arms, may she rest in peace, God bless her soul," he told them. "That is how safe I feel."

When Kavanagh stood up in the well, he warned the jury in advance that he might get worked up. "I must tell you that I guess because of my Irish background, I tend to become somewhat emotional," he said. "I must also tell you that there is no way that I can adequately express to you the rage . . . I feel because of the charges, the allegations, the insinuations that have been made in this courtroom. . . . Let's take the kid gloves off. I have been accused by this defendant by the way in which I conducted this case of manufacturing evidence, of suborning perjury. You name it, that charge has been made about me and my integrity."

Kavanagh said he spoke for the family of Anthony Castellito, particularly Anthony Jr., in expressing outrage at Harold's tactics. "This man is not satisfied with killing his father, he has branded him a liar. He has accused him of committing a serious crime on the witness stand. . . . Anthony Castellito—that poor kid—we are talking about his father, and he gets in here in this courtroom, and he has to confront and be questioned by the man who killed his father. Can you imagine what went through his heart and his mind as he is on that stand?"

He pointed to Harold, sitting calmly at the defense table. "That is not the real Harold Konigsberg," he said. "The person that you saw in this courtroom, who is concerned about his religion and his family, is not the Harold Konigsberg of 1961. Harold Konigsberg is a hired killer."

As soon as Kavanagh was through, Harold moved for a mistrial. He took issue with what he called the D.A.'s "cute little maneuvers—you know, '*the real Harold*.'"

"Would the real Harold please stand up?" Scheinman said.

"Yes, sir." Harold stood.

"All right. Your application is denied."

It took the jury less than three hours to pronounce Harold guilty. "We had no trouble agreeing on that," Juror No. 3, Frank Cordero, told me. "The evidence was so strong against him. I never got a sense anybody of us was especially sympathetic to Konigsberg. They say if you're a layman, don't take a professional's job."

Michael Kavanagh is now a State Supreme Court judge in Ulster County. On a hot spring morning, I found him in his chambers with his penny loafers on his desk, his legs crossed at the ankles. Having just let a jury out to deliberate in a medical malpractice trial, he was now in the middle of the *Times* crossword puzzle. For all his law-and-order fomentation as a trial lawyer, Kavanagh was self-effacingly forthright, offering that he was impatient for a verdict that day because he had an 11:30 tee time. He made broad predictions about the case in front of him—how the defense "might have blown it by letting that loose cannon on the jury." And after his clerk came in and got his signature for a subpoena, he joked that he had no idea what it was. "I sign whatever she puts in front of me," he said, laughing boisterously. His face turned red and he clapped his hands. "I probably shouldn't have signed it."

Although even by Kavanagh's own admission his career as a jurist and a public servant had been nothing special, I wanted to see him as a heroic figure. He told me he had not been "some kind of achiever" in high school and only continued his education (Merrimack College, "a pretty mediocre school and I was mediocre there, too, a C-plus student") under pressure from his mother—whom he jokingly remembered as "a very tough bitch," clapping and blushing again. Unsure what to do next, he enrolled at Villanova's law school. "I found that I liked it," he said. "Not the working hard, but I liked the legal concepts." After he won convictions in a couple of hotly contested cases, the Republican Party in New York drafted him as a sacrificial candidate for lieutenant governor in 1984 (running with Andy O'Rourke, who was trying to unseat Mario Cuomo). Later, his appointment to a federal judgeship collapsed when, speaking at a legal secretaries' banquet, he told an offensive joke about a recent rape case.

One day, when I was standing in front of the Kingston courthouse and phoning for a taxi to bring me to the train station, Kavanagh happened to roar by in his Buick and offer me a lift. I'd enjoyed getting to know him, and having the opportunity to show him the vast difference between Harold and the rest of the Konigsbergs. I'd faulted my father and his relatives for their efforts to distance themselves from Harold, but now I realized I was doing the same thing.

Both lawyers involved in Harold's defense, Ivan Fisher and Joshua Koplowitz, had raved to me, unsolicited, about Kavanagh's righteously envenomed approach in the trials. "He gave a brilliant summation, very impassioned and powerful, very personal," Koplowitz said. "That was his thing—he's a good guy and he believed. He believed Harold was a bad guy. He didn't have to work something up." I also recalled a passage, toward the end of the retrial, where Harold had asked the judge to censure the D.A. "based on Mr. Kavanagh's conduct," he said, "making personal issues, his feelings and crying in front of the jury."

"Were you crying?" Judge Scheinman inquired of Kavanagh.

"I was close, Judge. I was close," Kavanagh said.

But although just hearing Kavanagh's name sent Harold into paroxysms, Kavanagh didn't return the intensity of feeling, beyond, perhaps, his lingering irritation over Harold's ability to get his dander up in court.

In his car, I asked Kavanagh how much thought he ever gave to the atrociousness of Harold's crimes.

"Not much," he said. "I had a case to try. I certainly didn't see it in terms of what was right and what was wrong, as avenging the death of Castellito. Most prosecutors would tell you they get beyond that."

A moment later, he said, "I'll tell you one thing about the trial. The government arranged to give me a dummy license plate, so nobody could get into the D.M.V. records and track down my car. If cops pulled me over for speeding and ran the plate through their computer, it would come back as not registered to any human being, but they can tell it's some special government plate and they're not allowed to ticket me. I tend to drive too fast, so the thing was a godsend."

He laughed heartily and slapped the steering wheel. "They gave me an ugly car, but I kept that license plate for twenty years. I tried to use it as a judge, but they wouldn't let me."

When I combed through Kavanagh's files from the case, I discovered a dozen or so tablets of yellow foolscap filled with square, simple handwriting—the notes he'd taken during the two trials. There were crib sheets for his opening and closing statements which, though he had barely glanced at them in court, matched up nearly word for word with the actual transcripts. I figured that if there was something more to plumb in Kavanagh's feelings about the case, it would be documented in the notebooks, and I pored over each page. There were doodlings, in thick black felt-tip—geometric shapes, single block-lettered words with arrows and rays emanating from each letter, words that, in no way profound, apparently held prominence in his mind at the moment he was writing them: "SALVATORE Sinno"; "Briguglio." In letters running diagonally down one page: "BE Calm." And in another trial pad, in gigantic, shadowed lettering: "VICTORY," "BEACH HOUSE," "REPETITIOUS," "U.S. Rep." Also, I noticed, he had begun listing all fifty states but stopped at thirty-seven.

Harold was back in Judge Scheinman's court for a sentencing hearing on November 24, 1982. Invited to make his plea for leniency, he presented more than forty motions to set aside his verdict. Scheinman reminded him that they'd convened to establish his punishment.

"I'm sentencing Mr. Kavanagh," Harold said. "You know, we may not be in Nazi Germany, but Goebbels lives in the heart of Kavanagh.... Whatever you know about me, what you think you know about me, there is no man in this world that has more courage than me; maybe as much. I faced death many, many times, and I never walked from it. I am not a coward. Mr. Kavanagh—can he address himself as such?... When he started his campaign of lies and manipulations through the press, what did he want me to do? Stand still? He wanted me to let him kick me in the balls and I will say, 'Thank you.' I don't say 'Thank you' to people who kick me—"

Scheinman interjected and told Harold to watch his language.

"You must remember that I didn't do it intentionally," Harold said. "I just say it as it rolls."

Harold lamented the preponderance of "ambitious persons in government who are willing to build their careers on the lives of innocent people," though he allowed that this had moved him to a good deal of introspection:

I think about all the people who utilized and abused me over life and got all the benefits of life, and here I am today unjustly, and I say to myself, "These twenty years of punishment that I have been subjected to by the authorized representatives of our government has been beyond reason or logic.... Why have you reached the point where you are no longer interested in retribution, retaliation, and are only thinking of good works and only thinking of how to better society? ... Maybe it's better one goes to his maker than live in a society that is so corrupt and dishonest, prejudiced, and biased as I have witnessed. Whatever I was yesterday in my lifetime, those acts that were illegal or wrong, even though they did not travel to innocent people, even though they did not work against people that were outside of my realm, I faced the reality of them [and] I even regret those.

The judge was not moved by Harold's logic. "It would indeed be an uncivilized society," he said, that did not adequately punish a man who committed a murder for hire. "Consequently, the fact that life has not been a bed of roses is something that you cannot blame society for." Scheinman added that, although the death penalty had been in effect when Harold killed Castellito, there was, regrettably, no death penalty in New York as the two of them sat there now. "The only sentence that the court can impose at this time is a sentence of life imprisonment."

Then, to Harold's surprise, Scheinman ordered the sentence to run consecutive to—not concurrently with—his thirty- to forty-four-year term for the extortion of Fat Joe Cannistraci.

This meant he would not become eligible for parole any earlier than 1998.

"The police always said if they ever lock him up they're going to throw away the key," his sister Ruthie told me once, giggling.

But in the courtroom, Harold said nothing. He simply stared at the judge. The judge stared back.

•   •   •

Tony Pro died in Lompoc, California, in 1988, having been succeeded as president of Local 560 first by his brother Nunzie Pro, then by Sammy Pro, and finally by his own daughter, Josephine Provenzano ("Josie Pro," one may assume). The government trusteeship of Local 560, a regulatory action that stemmed from the Castellito case, lasted from 1986 to 1999.

Big Sal Sinno and his sons entered Witness Relocation with new identities—and three different last names—and under the terms of the program were required to report regularly to the U.S. Marshals Service. "I know he was out in California at one point," Kavanagh said. "Periodically Sal would get arrested for speeding and he'd call me to fix the ticket. I'd have to call a prosecutor and say, 'You got a guy out there, and I know this is an extraordinary request I'm making, and I can't tell you why you've got to dismiss these charges, but it would be very important, so please accept my assurance.'"

Perquisites aside, Big Sal found government oversight stifling and quit the program. John Markey, his F.B.I. chaperone from Wisconsin, said, "The last time he called me he'd been about to be married the following weekend but his bride-to-be had died. His older boy was a blue-chip football prospect in college, a 305-pound offensive lineman. They thought Oakland was going to draft him but he blew out his knee his senior year. He became a social worker and married very well. I sent a present."

In 1988, when he was sixty-one, Big Sal got arrested on an East Village corner in broad daylight, minutes after fatally shooting an acquaintance in a personal dispute. A police detective quoted the next day in the *Times* described the killing as "very professionally done."

•   •   •

"These district attorneys, they built their careers on me," Harold told me. He seemed to resent their benefiting from his reputation even more than he did his life sentence. "They framed me on little nothing charges. They gave me maximum sentences and for that they make a career? Do you know what their story is?" Here he gave his best attempt at the singsongy Irish cadences of a Fordham Law alumnus. *"Well, he got away with so many things!"* To Harold, they were "frauds and opportunists" who'd improved their lot in life by changing the rules on him.

He spoke of his plan to track down Kavanagh once his release from prison was mandated—whether by appeal or parole hearing—"and I will choke him with that verdict," he said. He made a throttling gesture. "I will let him suck wind through his asshole."

"How can you say that?"

He shrugged. "I'm a very expressionable guy." He was serene again, adjusting his prison-issued bifocals.

Part IV

The Champion of All Losses

THIRTEEN

A Final Trip to Auburn

THE ARC FOR most people who let Harold into their lives had a similar progression. People viewed him first with curiosity—for some, this amounted to fascination; others even felt there was something to gain from the acquaintance. After that came the realization of awful entanglement. And then, finally, revulsion and fear, though by that point one might already have wandered too deep into the loblolly to find a way out.

The revulsion as I experienced it had something to do with self-reproach for thinking I wasn't getting myself entangled when, of course, I was. I regretted forging as much of a relationship as I had, and providing him with a way back into our family. And I found it dispiriting to be thinking about him every day.

The funny thing about blood is, you can't control how you feel about your relatives. Even after I had seen what Harold had done to others, I was unable to hate him quite as deeply as I wanted to, or even as much as I felt I should. And yet I was a lot less capable of wishing him any possibility of redemption than I'd have been if given the chance to forgive a stranger for the same sins. The thing about blood is that you can't undo what fundamentally connects you to somebody else.

I was unable, then, to see Harold for what he was. His dangerousness didn't seem entirely real. He was a very old seventy-three and out of touch with modernity, impotent to bring significant harm on anybody but himself. I couldn't see him as anything but an apparition of Kayo Konigsberg.

Until, that is, the last time I went to see him. Now when I recall the anxieties he had instilled in me during the years preceding that visit, they seem positively quaint.

Although at first my visits took as much time as the prison would allow, from 9 A.M. to 3:30, eventually I found myself doing things to make the day at Auburn a little shorter: eating a leisurely breakfast in Syracuse, say, and deciding to read every box score and batting statistic in the *USA Today* sports section (I don't even like baseball); running errands on the way over to the prison (such as stopping by the Cornell campus—an hour's drive in another direction—to purchase my brother a T-shirt); flying up from New York City on the morning of a visit, rather than arriving upstate the night before.

When Harold would send me to buy him Doritos, I began to wonder if feeding him junk food could kill him. I started averaging the ages of the people in the *Times* obituaries every day to see if the odds were against him yet. Though, at the same time, I registered a certain pleasure that a person in my family was indestructible—the history of personal risk and bad eating habits be damned. We were made of good stock.

After nine visits, I considered the possibility that I'd heard everything I could from Harold and that there was no further reason to see him. Of course, there were still questions I wanted answered, but his responses were all sounding the same. And there was plenty of him left to explore outside that visiting room at Auburn. Without explicitly letting him know I was doing so, I broke off contact.

Soon, he wrote to ask me where I was and to note that, although he didn't expect me to care, he was not feeling so well and needed to lie down for a while. I expected him to persist—"Just because I'm mad at someone doesn't mean I don't write them," he'd said once—but for two years I heard nothing. I fretted that he had something up his sleeve, that one night my doorbell would ring and somebody would serve me with a subpoena to testify to the *durance vile* he'd endured in prison, or to make me into an unwitting accomplice in some would-be scam.

I might never have seen him again, and, in fact, I wish I hadn't. But in the summer of 2001 I went back to Auburn. My objectives that day, in order of lengthening tether on reality, were: to do him the courtesy of letting him know that *The New Yorker* would soon be publishing my story on him; to share what I'd learned about him from our family and from some of the participants in the cases that had come to trial, and to give him the opportunity to respond; to make a final plea for a more robust approval of the project than he'd thus far given me; and to ask him to cooperate with the magazine's fact-checking department. I was anxious about confronting Harold, but reassured myself that the worst that could happen was that he would be furious and before long I'd be out of there. I didn't need his blessing. I was simply gathering and passing on a set of facts that pertained to him and there was nothing he could do about it.

And so, without bothering with a heads-up note, I boarded a flight from LaGuardia, checked into the Sheraton on the edge of the Syracuse campus, slept badly, went to Starbucks for coffee, returned to my room to check my e-mail, walked back out to by a newspaper, read it in the lobby, drove to McDonald's for breakfast, and, finally, made my way to Auburn.

I parked in the loose-gravel lot in front of the prison. A deliveryman from the local grinder house had arrived with lunch orders for the desk officers even though it was only ten-thirty (days begin and end early in prison). After I signed in quite deliberately as a normal visitor, without "paralegal" privileges, word of my arrival was sent down to Harold's cell. I recognized all three of the guards manning the visitors' center and shook their hands. I wanted them to think of me as somebody who was on their side, not Harold's. I hoped it might intimidate Harold to see us acting chummy.

They assigned me to a table in a far corner of the room, but I asked to be switched to someplace near the guards' station. I explained that he wasn't expecting me. "The surprise might make him temperamental."

I was nervous, so I tried to make conversation, asking the screws how Harold had been. I asked if both daughters had been coming to visit or just one. They said they weren't sure. I asked what other well-known criminals were currently at Auburn. Robert Chambers, they said. I asked how Chambers got along with the inmate population. Fine, they said, from what they saw.

I remembered one of the guards as the man who'd worn the enamel Puerto Rico pin, and recalled how my recognizing the flag had won me points with Harold. When the guard got a call telling him his lunch had arrived and went on his break, I took this as cause for worry. I demanded assurance that it was okay for the correctional staff to be left a man down. Impatient to be rid of me, perhaps, one of them phoned down to Harold's wing to find out what was taking so long.

"Evidently, he's not in a good mood," the guard reported with amusement. Cause for more worry. I asked why the guards didn't carry guns. What if there were some kind of riot? An Officer Eggersdorf provided a long disquisition on techniques in riot control, but added, "Fights aren't real common in the visitors' room. They tend to behave different with their families around." He reminded me that I was free to take a seat. Then I glanced toward the prisoners' entrance and saw Harold coming across the floor.

He looked no older than I'd left him, although I decided there was something less sinister to him now. His pants were rolled into big cuffs, like hand-me-downs a child hasn't yet grown into. His hair still shone majestic and dull, like a field of frost-thickened stalks, but was long overdue for a trim. It suggested carelessness, eccentricity, whimsy. It was almost ladylike.

This time he offered no kiss or handshake.

"Go and get me a Dr Pepper," he said.

Harold had nothing but complaints for me. Why were we seated so close to the guards? Why hadn't I given him notice that I was coming? Where had I been the past two years? "Last thing I heard from you was you'll be in touch soon," he said. "How soon do you call this?" He asked about the unveiling of a relative's headstone that was scheduled for the coming week. He'd given his daughters firm orders to attend. When I said I wouldn't be able to make it and pointed out that not even my grandmother or my grandaunts were going because they found it too hard to take, he looked at me disdainfully. "I ain't interested in that wishy-washy bullshit of yours," he said.

I was not off to a good start.

"So what are you gonna tell me is it that brings you here?" he said. I'd been rehearsing for this for months. I told him I had "a lot of impatient editors" on my hands. The magazine story was going to press the following week.

Harold spent a moment processing my words as he took off his reading glasses.

"The day something that has my name in it and your name on it hits the street, you are dead," he said. "I'm going to kill you. I'm going to chop you up a hundred different ways. And you can put that in your fucking magazine. They'll know who did it."

I didn't know what to say. It occurred to me that I should have seen this coming.

"The kind of person that would disgrace his family that way, that would disgrace my beloved brother's name like this, you forfeit your blood connection," he said. "I can't believe you come from the same line as my father. And to think, you're a *Kohen*."

I believe I managed something to the effect of "Calm down" as my gaze drifted to the guards' station.

He made a claw with his thumb and two fingers. "I only need this to kill you," he said. "I'll go right through your eye and rip your brain out of your fucking head. You'd be dead before the guards get here." He chuckled. "I'll bet you whimper like a baby when I kill you, a cock-sucker like you."

Harold hated not being in charge. "Since you was last here I didn't have a fucking thing to do with you, no calls, no visits, nothing." He said he hadn't "authorized" his sisters or my grandmother to speak with me.

I said I was sure my grandmother would prefer that I not write about him, but she'd spoken to me about him anyway. And so had Aunt Ruthie and Aunt Beattie. Again, I wanted him to feel outflanked.

"Your grandmother can't stop me from killing you," Harold said. "God can't stop me, so how's your fucking grandmother going to stop me?"

He relaxed his posture, stretching his legs in a leisurely manner. "What did my sisters say about me?"

I said they remembered him as a beautiful baby. "Beattie's still got the curls from your first haircut."

His eyes welled up.

"You're no good, kid," he said. "I been in here thirty-eight years. What makes you think you can kill me in here like that? You wouldn't last thirty-eight minutes in this place."

But I wasn't the one killing him, I said. I told him I had nothing to do with the acts he committed, acts that had made him a public figure.

"That kind of double-talk, it's worthy of torture," Harold said, jerking upright. "I should take a meat cleaver to you and cut off your arms and legs first. Whatever I done my whole life, I never done it wishy-washy like you. I only know one way—straight through." He pushed his hand forward smoothly across the tabletop. "I go straight. I've always done the honorable thing."

"You mean like killing people?"

"Sure, killing people is perfectly honorable." He smirked at me. "Killing people is perfectly honorable when they dishonor their own."

I said that a lot of what I learned about him came from testimony, court records, government documents. And I told him I knew about his confessions to the F.B.I.

"And how many people did they put away because of what I supposedly told the F.B.I.?" he said. "Court records! You ain't even any good as a reporter. A real journalist gets the secrets."

He sucked down his Dr Pepper. The taking of nourishment seemed to calm him. "Go make me some of that popcorn from the machines," he said. "And get me orange soda."

At the microwave, I noticed that I was sweating through the sports jacket I had worn out of deference to Harold. I walked back to our table, opened the popcorn bag, and spread it before him.

"You're trying to buy me off—this popcorn," he said. I laughed a little, wondering if he liked me enough to let me live. He asked how much money I had in the bank. "I want to see if I can borrow fifty thousand dollars off you. Get myself a lawyer and get the hell out of here."

He was shifting gears. Soon, he issued the familiar inquiries about all my cousins and their careers. He'd been informed, somehow, that I'd left my old magazine job and had spent the previous summer in Montana—"where your father owns a piece of property."

I didn't like that he knew so much. When he asked about my brother, who had just finished medical school, I resisted the urge to brag that he was going into orthopedic surgery and that his wife was trying to decide between a future in endocrinology or oncology. Instead, I simply said they were doing "medical residencies."

"Basic medicine," Harold said dismissively. "So they can treat colds, basically."

"That's right," I said.

There is something about having to withstand interrogation from a con man that actually makes the squirrelly act of lying feel somehow strong and defiant, a wily act of self-preservation. If I was lowering myself to his level, it was because it was the only way to play him. He started quizzing me about how much money I made, what else I'd been writing about, if I still lived at the same address, how old I was now. I offered minimal answers. When he asked what my birthday was, I lied and said November 18.

Harold blinked. "What?"

November 18 is his birthday. Mine is later in the month.

I said I was surprised that he wasn't aware we shared a birthday. I must have lied because I wanted him to worry that his powers were going dull. Also, I hoped to present some grounds for kinship, because our actual kinship was obviously not protection enough.

He shook his head. "You were born under a curse," he said.

Our visit lasted two hours. I asked if there was anything I could do to make him more amenable to the fact that my story was about to be published, and he went back to listing all the ways he was going to kill me: by strangling me with his bootlaces, by shoving a soda bottle up my ass and lighting a firecracker in it. He said my grandmother could visit me at my grave and the thought of that would give him pleasure for the rest of his life.

When I gave up, I pushed my chair away from the table and told him he'd be getting a letter from a fact checker.

"I'll make both of you suck my prick and then I'll kill you both," Harold said.

At the exit, I thought, I can't let him end the visit like this. I walked back into the room. A guard was escorting Harold toward a side door that led to the cell blocks. "You know I mean you no harm," I called out.

He looked at me and nodded his head. "I mean you harm!" he shouted. It was the only time he raised his voice all day.

I returned home that afternoon dumbfounded. I wondered if Harold was bluffing. I had gotten his back up, and this was probably the only way he knew how to negotiate. On the other hand, it wasn't idle threats that had got him a life sentence. I began running an odds chart in my mind, wondering if Harold could actually arrange to have me hurt if he wanted to, and whether he really wanted to. The answers were maybe not and probably, or else the other way around.

I couldn't recall ever before having had a serious problem on my hands that I was afraid to share with my parents. I decided not to call them, but by evening they found me, phoning from their country house in Montana. I had told them that I was going up to Auburn, and they were anxious to hear about it. I tried to downplay the severity of Harold's threat with my father, but it all tumbled out. "Well, you're not going to hold off on publishing the story," he said right away. "You didn't become a writer so that you could take orders from some villain."

This was a lovely sentiment. But I was scared that Harold was going to kill me.

"Call Grandma," Dad said. "Everybody listens to her."

So, in a moment of tension, this was the default fourth-down call.

We devised a plan to have Grandma Frieda get Harold on the phone—she wouldn't want to speak to him, but she would do it—via one of his daughters and talk some sense into him. She was at Aunt Ruthie's house for dinner, and when I phoned there, I got a round of I told you sos.

"You said you wanted to write about him," Ruthie said. "Heshy's a lot of hot air."

Ruthie's daughter Mendy said, "You made your bed, now you've got to lie in it."

But there was also some reassurance. "I wish you hadn't gone and done this," Frieda said. "But nobody threatens my grandson." She said she would take care of it.

I called a friend and told her what my day had brought. "So Granny's going to call off the hit?" my friend said. I had to admit the whole thing had about it the ring of farce. Even so, I was almost relieved that Harold had snapped like this. In doing so, he was relinquishing whatever benefit of the doubt his family still gave him. Everybody would finally have to acknowledge him for what he was: deranged, vindictive, and homicidal.

Wouldn't they?

Because Harold knew my address, I decided to go to a hotel for the night just to be on the safe side. When I got to my room, I checked my messages at home and found that my grandmother had already called. She was reporting back from her conversation with Harold's daughter.

"The guards heard Heshy lose his temper when you surprised him today," she said, sounding hysterical. "Eric, they're going to punish him by putting him into a place where he doesn't get to leave or see anybody or talk to his daughters for the next two years." She was in tears. "Eric, Uncle Heshy's going to die in solitary."

I couldn't believe this. She felt sorry for him. She was taking his side.

Somebody—either Harold or his daughter—was feeding Frieda a line. He wasn't going into solitary confinement, and he was not getting slapped with two years of any punishment. As I was leaving Auburn, a couple of the guards—who had indeed been witness when Harold "lost his temper"—had asked if I wanted to file an account of the threat with the warden. I told them I did. They said that the most likely punishment would be keeplock, a "solitary-like" arrangement with no phone or library privileges, for a mere thirty to sixty days.

Regardless, my father made a flurry of phone calls—to Grandma Frieda, to Harold's daughter, and to me. He reported that Harold's daughter had said that she resigned herself to my writing whatever I was going to write, and her father would have to as well. "He does whatever my sister and I tell him," she explained. "We're all he has now." She also assured my father that the death threat was bogus: "You'd lose your temper, too, if you were in prison for thirty-eight years."

However, my father informed me, she wanted me to contact the warden at Auburn and put in writing that, after talking with other family members, I did not fear for my safety anymore. Except I wasn't supposed to use the word *anymore*.

I asked how it made sense for me to write a letter on behalf of somebody who was threatening my life.

"I, for one, would feel a lot better," my father said, adding that the bargain could have been worse. At first, he said, Harold's daughter had wanted me to write that "while voices were raised, my uncle and I had a pleasant visit," and that, whatever the guards thought they'd witnessed, they were mistaken.

I offered to call her myself to work out the details. "Just let me handle it," my dad said. "If I put two hotheads on the phone with each other, you'll start calling each other names and undo everything I've just done."

My mother took the phone from him and went out on the porch where my dad couldn't hear her. "When I say your father is white as a sheet, I mean he's white as a sheet," she told me. "He's pacing all over the house. You're forcing him to talk to some crazy cousin he doesn't even know."

He'd been made uncomfortable enough a few days earlier, when I had entreated him to spend a couple of hours on the phone with a fact checker from the magazine, to help her vet my article. The checker told me that it had gone faster than expected, because my father simply answered yes to every matter in question. "Well, I didn't want to get in the way and cause anybody more work," he explained to me. "Anyway, you know I don't know much about Heshy."

Now, my mother said, he was standing at the refrigerator asking her opinion on the hypothetical likelihood that some inmate to whom Harold might have given legal advice could repay the favor by enlisting a bunch of thugs in the Bronx to come and rough me up.

"In case you aren't aware, this is not the sort of problem Dad and I are used to dealing with," she said. "Don't you understand? Dad feels responsible. He didn't want to tell you what you could or couldn't do. Then he not only gave you a wide berth, he took so much grief from his mother! And now, to see him worried that something he did might have endangered you, to see him afraid like this—"

She didn't have to finish the sentence. Everyone had asked me to let stand the Konigsbergs' unfortunate secret, but now I had my father in a panic, wondering whether the word of a hit man's daughter was reliable when she said I wasn't at risk. I'd never seen my father afraid before.

I faxed a letter to the prison warden, worded in a way that I was comfortable with. When somebody from Auburn called to offer me the opportunity to testify to the threat in a prison hearing, I never returned the call. The warden sentenced Harold to thirty days in keeplock, which was then downgraded to fifteen days. And because, by the time of the ruling, more than fifteen days had passed since the infraction, the punishment was somehow suspended altogether.

I never heard from Harold after that, and I sure as hell wasn't going to initiate further contact. When a few weeks passed, then months, and I continued to walk the earth, I came to think that if Harold was really going to kill me he'd have done it already. Which is not to say that the thought of him doesn't still scare the hell out of me.

FOURTEEN

Punta Gorda

"YOU PROBABLY don't know the kind of guy my father was," Anthony Castellito Jr. said. "My father was a tough guy. If Kayo was so tough, why'd he have to have a bunch of other guys helping him? I didn't hear how it happened until after the trial. The agents told me, 'Your father hurt somebody in that fight. Somebody got hit hard.' I didn't hear them no more. I was just thinking, 'Four guys ambush him and hit him with a pipe and he's putting up a struggle!' That made me feel good a little."

Since 1989, Anthony Jr. has lived on the west coast of Florida, where my letter reached him. Somebody with access to the Local 560 pension fund's mailing list had been kind enough to give me his address. "I can't believe at this time in my life that I would be talking to a Konigsberg," he'd said when we first spoke. "When I saw the name on the envelope, I thought it was Kayo. I thought, What, is he saying, 'I'm sorry'? There's been a lot of heartaches because of him. My kid sister, God, if I say any-thing about what happened to our father, she loses it. She cries. She's got a swimming pool, a beautiful family. They have parties. Sometimes I tell her, 'I know somebody up there who'd be very proud of you right now.'"

In March 2002, Anthony Jr. met me at the golf club at his retirement community in Punta Gorda. He has a sandkicker's physique and a silver mustache, and with canvas Top-Siders and green Bermuda shorts, he looked more like a retired navy captain enjoying his golden years on the consultancy circuit than the hard-luck laborer I'd pictured. His wife, Dorothy, greeted me with a hug and led us out to the patio, which had a view of Charlotte Harbor. She, too, cut an appealing figure, in jeans, a tai-lored dress shirt, and big sunglasses with etched gold hinges. On a picnic table were a stack of teacups and saucers and a box of Mallomars still cold from the freezer.

"I always say to her, 'I wonder how much happier our life would have been if what happened didn't happen,'" Anthony Jr. said. "I would have been a business agent. I would have made more money. Being rich—you can't get no richer than where we live now. We always had the prettiest houses in the best neighborhoods, we have no debts on our credit cards. But still, everybody in our family's been getting mad at each other ever since. You tell your uncle he didn't just kill this guy, he destroyed a whole family."

The first problem was that after the abduction Castellito's brother Mandy, who was also in Local 560, volunteered to nominate Tony Pro for president one night at the union hall. Anthony Jr. stood up at that meeting and called his uncle "Judas." In private, Anthony Jr. recalled, "I told him, 'I think this guy had something to do with Dad's disappear-ance, and you're up his ass.'"

"Sonny, your father used to take care of me, and now he's gone,"

Mandy replied. He said that Tony Pro had offered to help him make a down payment on a house.

Anthony Jr.'s mother refused to testify in the trial over her husband's murder. She said he'd been missing for so many years that by now she'd moved on. And that wasn't what bothered Anthony Jr. the most. "The only thing she did wrong was all of a sudden she realized that all his money was hers," he said.

Dorothy, who had been sitting quietly with us, watching the cabin cruisers drift in and out of the marina, chimed in. "And she and her other kids wasted it on better houses, better cars," she said. "Everybody in the family changed instantly, and their thinking was, Don't tell Tony. One of his sisters bought a condo and a time-share down here in Florida without letting us know."

"We were up in New Jersey and decided to stop by my mother's," Anthony Jr. said. "I'm ringing the bell and walking around the house. The woman next door comes out and says, 'Sonny, what are you doing here? Your mother's in Florida with your sister.' I'm so embarrassed. We look like a family of hillbillies."

Dorothy brought out a pack of Tourney cigarettes and a large mailing envelope that served as her scrapbook. Anthony Jr. wordlessly lit two Tourney cigarettes, and handed one to her. I opened a United Ticket pamphlet from the 1965 campaign—the one Anthony Jr. had run in—and saw all the ads placed in memory of his father. "Tony Castellito is missed by hundreds of thousands of Teamster friends throughout the country," one read. "We would like to salute you, Mr. 560, wherever you are."

When we came upon a snapshot of Anthony Jr. at a construction site in Atlantic City, wearing a hard hat and a tank top, he quickly flipped it over. "What are we looking at these for?" he said.

"You're shy," Dorothy said. After a moment, he glanced back at her and winked.

Anthony Jr. talked about the trial in Kingston. Hearing Michael Kavanagh's name elicited a smile. "When he found out my father's traitor brother Mandy might be testifying as a character witness on behalf of Tony Pro, Kavanagh promised me he'd tear him a new one," Anthony Jr. said. "He said, 'I'm waiting for him.' I told Kavanagh to run for governor. He was a great guy. If he would have had me for a friend, I'd have liked to be his friend. I used to tell all the lawyers, 'If it wasn't for this trial, you wouldn't even be talking to me.' "

I went inside for a glass of water. The Castellitos' condo had white-tiled floors and beige love seats brocaded with palm trees. The TV was tuned to a closed-circuit channel that played Muzak and listed the weather and the daily schedule at their retirement community. "Let me tell you something, marriage is the greatest life in the world," Anthony Jr. said. "This girl and I, we been together since we were eighteen. We paid twenty-seven dollars to hire a justice of the peace and we eloped. Afterward, we stopped at a restaurant near Kerhonkson and had dinner like two little kids. Outside it was fancy, all colored lights. We went inside, it was a dive. Dorothy had on a dress and a corsage. We had sandwiches and a drink and we drove home. She saved my life. I might've wound up stuck in Hoboken."

Dorothy put up their life savings to open an apparel store called the Clothes Tree in Rockland County, New York. "In five years, we didn't know where to put the money, she'd done so well," he said. "That gave us the kick in the ass that we needed to get up to a certain bracket of life. So now we had two homes, I drove a Cadillac, she drove a Ford, we bought a sailboat." He took up golf and just in the past year they started going to church, which they hadn't done since they were newlyweds.

"I was down on everybody. I only believed in me and her," Anthony

Jr. said. "I won't go to Catholic church. It just doesn't speak to me no more. The Presbyterian minister here I like, but I haven't spoken to him about my father. In fact, nobody down here knows nothing about my business, and that's how I want it. If I say, 'My father was in the union and they murdered him,' what can anybody say? Why would they be interested?"

Dorothy was checking the caller I.D. on their telephone throughout the day to see if their daughter, a nurse who lives in Pennsylvania, had tried to reach them. "We talk to our little girl twice a day; she's all we have," she said. "*Our little girl*—she's fifty. She's our only child and Tony spoils her, but she grew up to be a fine lady. He bought her a car on her seventeenth birthday. She didn't know how to drive. A year later she wanted a Mercedes and he wanted to buy it for her. I told him in private it was out of the question."

"I wanted her to marry someone like you," Anthony Jr. said, pointing at me. "You know, a professional man. My motto was, the more I spoil her, the more she's gonna be looking for somebody who can give her that. And it turned out just the opposite. She married somebody like me. She was going to school to be a doctor, and the guy was so jealous. He quit his job so she had to work nights to support him.

"And then for fourteen years we begged her, 'Throw him out. We'll throw him out—I'll throw him out,'" he went on. "It got to the point where she gave him fifty dollars and a suitcase and told him, 'Go home to your mother.' Then she met this nice Irish fellow. They got married. They can't have kids because when she was about twenty-two she had cancer of the ovaries. And that was the end of grandkids, which was sad, because we couldn't wait."

They wanted grandchildren so much that they'd tried to adopt their son-in-law's niece and nephew during a custody dispute. "We wanted to bring someone up in peace," Dorothy said. "Not having to raise a kid the way we did when Tony's father died, with all the crying and the questions."

It was getting on toward four o'clock and we hadn't eaten lunch yet, so we had a bite at the retirement-community cantina. Dorothy talked about real estate values on the Gulf Coast and about their social obligations for the rest of the week. They were going to visit a friend of Anthony Jr.'s in the hospital, and that was about it. The way that she seemed to have command of their schedule and finances reminded me a bit of Frieda's stewardship of Leo. In fact, there was a lot about the Castellitos' relationship that mirrored my grandparents'—that us-against-the-world closeness, the fortress built partially on a mistrust of others. Dorothy did her best to modulate her husband's spirits and protect him from stress. She fielded my calls for weeks before she let him know I was coming to meet them, because, she said, she didn't want him thinking about it until he had to.

We returned to the Castellitos' patio. The harbor was silent, save for some night herons and the scuttle of a gecko attempting to crawl up the drainpipe. A spotlight on the roof clicked on to illuminate a yucca tree in a large planter. I told them all about Grandpa Leo, what scant contact he'd had with Harold, how he'd given a little grocer the bulk rate on a single ham.

"When you think of your grandfather, you think of my father," Anthony Jr. said. "Because when it came to the workingman, he believed that he's got to get a break someplace in life. Your family was probably nice people. And then they had the other element."

Dorothy asked if I'd ever considered changing my last name. They seemed to be taking pity on me.

"We're like the same people, you and I are," Anthony Jr. said. "Except you've got a better job, a better education."

"You're a nice young man," Dorothy said.

"He's a nice young man," Tony said, turning to his wife. "But if it weren't for what happened, would he be talking to me?"

•   •   •

When I got back to my motel, I sat outside by the swimming pool and watched the cars rush over the causeway in the dark. The pool lights were off, but two sets of young parents and children were still splashing around, families on spring break.

It occurred to me that Harold had had no relationship to Anthony Castellito. The two had only met in passing before he tore that blind cord off the wall. Anthony Jr.'s biggest grudge was against Tony Pro, the person who'd conceived of the murder and had profited most from it. If Tony Pro had decided to deputize a different hit man, the end result would have been the same. And it was just as possible, depending on Harold's schedule or which Mob boss also happened to need a piece of work done at the time, that somebody other than Castellito could have been Harold's victim that day. It was a deliberate, carefully plotted act, but it wasn't personal. Yet the Castellitos and I wanted to forge a personal relationship because of it. They had received my visit with openness and friendship.

"Maybe I want to see a psychiatrist now," Anthony Jr. said. This was the next morning, over breakfast. Dorothy was in the kitchen. He was withdrawn and skittish, hungover from permitting himself to talk so much the day before. "You ever turn the light out at night and you start thinking?" he said. "Things go okay for a while, and then, when everything is nice and quiet, I'll remember something's always there for me to be sad about. I go to bed around quarter to one, then I'm up at three o'clock and I go outside—on the front porch, out back. I watch television until I'm so sick of it that I go sit in the bathroom and smoke my two cigarettes." I'd noticed that he stowed a few cigarettes and ashtrays in locations all over the house—among the leaves of a plant, for instance, in the guest bathroom.

"Sometimes I see somebody who walks like my father—he has a

nice gait, he maybe rocks from side to side," he said. "It reminds me. I walk in a store down here and there's a guy who's smoking a cigar. I says, Parodis? I smelled my father's Italian cigar. You put it in the book: it doesn't go away. It never will go away. You just walk with it, if that's the terminology they use—you walk alongside it."

Anthony Jr. remembered Harold dropping by the union headquarters, the only time his father had met him. "My dad threw him the hell out and went to see Tony Pro. He told him, 'If you're going to meet this Jew bastard'—I'm sorry to say it—'you meet him outside.' My father didn't like it that Tony Pro let his Mafia guys hang around. And then to think that what brought them there was to plot his death right under his nose! He should have known there was a nigger in the woodpile.

"By the way, Kayo, when he wanted to be in the Mafia, the Italians laughed at him. I heard they chased him out of a place on Mulberry Street. He had money showing through his shirt pocket, a thin white shirt, it was so cheap. They said, 'Go back to Jersey. When we need you, we'll call.'

"The bottom line is this. You took my father, I'm hurting by it. They made a big mistake when they killed Anthony Castellito. The man they killed was a good man. If you talk to your uncle, could you please ask him where my father is, I mean the body? My mother just passed away at eighty-four, multiple heart attacks. It's a shame to die not knowing where your husband is. My sisters and I told her, 'Ma, he never even knew what happened, it was so fast.' I can't tell her he fought for his life, that he died in his kitchen."

FIFTEEN

Unmarked Graves

IN SOME SENSE, Anthony Jr. was the most fortunate of the people Harold's victims had left behind. He at least knew what his father's fate had been, and he was also granted the dignity of seeing Harold and Tony Pro sent up for good. But Harold had told the F.B.I. about twenty murders, deaths, and disappearances, and so, after the convictions in the Castellito case, that still left nineteen other sets of unanswered questions—nineteen dead ends, botched investigations, and lives cut short.

I felt much worse for these people than for my family. Ultimately, despite all he put them through, Harold didn't destroy any of the Konigsbergs, not in the way he ended and upended many other lives, a point underscored, if not made, by my trip to Punta Gorda. But the information on these other cases was scarce. In late 2003, four and a half years after I'd filed a Freedom of Information Act request—and a subsequent lawsuit—a district-court judge in Washington, D.C., finally ordered the

F.B.I. to release to me 18,000 pages on Harold. Three large boxes arrived at my door, each bundled neatly into reams with thick rubber bands, but it didn't take long to see that my lawsuit was a bust. The Bureau had me sent thousands upon thousands of blank or nearly blank pages. Except for some newspaper clippings, almost everything had been vigorously whited out.

And so, armed by now with no small antipathy toward Harold, I went back to my initial cache of confidential F.B.I. reports. Some of these files pertained to the cold cases and were more detailed than I'd realized. There was documentation that several of the killings had yielded follow-up investigations before they were abandoned. Even so, as I went about revisiting some of them, the indignation with which I started was quickly undercut by a feeling of futility. These were homicides that nobody, it appeared, had cared to solve. It should have been no wonder, then, that despite whatever material data I eventually scraped together, I couldn't solve or resolve them, either. Still, these cases presented another way to measure the ripples Harold had sent through the world.

The case that had held the most promise for the F.B.I. involved three victims. Two, Kenneth Later and Barbara Delmar, had disappeared in the spring of 1963, and their remains, per Harold's directions, had been found in the boneyard at Mafia Memorial Park. The corpse of the third, a man named Alfred Betts, was discovered on May 23, 1963, in an abandoned car in the Bronx, and the cause of death was determined to be a homicidal injection of narcotics.

In 1965, when Harold began talking to the F.B.I., he said that he and a Mafia figure named Joe Stassi had been responsible for the killings. By this time, J. Edgar Hoover had already named Stassi among the targets of the F.B.I.'s Top Hoodlum Program.

Based on what I was able to piece together, the fated relationship that the three victims—Betts, Delmar, and Later—had to Harold and Stassi went like this:

Al Betts and Barbara Delmar's husband were partners in a pornographic film operation financed by Harold and Stassi.

According to confidential F.B.I. informants, Betts and Kenneth Later were also drug runners in a major heroin-smuggling ring that Stassi operated out of Mexico.

When Delmar's husband went to jail for violating parole from an old obscenity charge, she began receiving his share of the proceeds from the pornography business. A friend of hers described this to the F.B.I. as a ritual in which Barbara would check into a hotel room in midtown and wait for a phone call summoning her to the lobby, where she would receive an envelope from "this monster Harold."

On March 19, 1963, a federal grand jury in Texas indicted Joe Stassi on heroin-running charges. He posted bail and became a fugitive.

Catherine D'Unger, a private investigator in Texas whom Stassi had hired as part of his legal-defense effort, told me that Kenneth Later was about to be named as a witness against Stassi at the time. Harold told the F.B.I. that Stassi wanted Later dead because Later was weak; he was sure the government was going to twist his arm and make him testify.

Harold confessed that he and Stassi planned the murder of Kenneth Later together and carried it out on March 29 in northern New Jersey. He said that he watched as Stassi shot Later, and then, while Later was still alive, the two of them lowered his body into a steel drum and poured "about twenty" gallons of acid over him.

It appears that the other two murders also had to do with suspicions that the targets might testify against Harold and Stassi. Al Betts was killed two months later, and Barbara Delmar disappeared about a month after that, on June 21. The day before she vanished, her niece told the F.B.I., the two of them had been in the middle of dinner at

Delmar's home in Danbury, Connecticut, when Delmar excused herself to take a "very important" telephone call "from Harold." In the morning, she packed a weekend bag with three dresses, a stole, and a nightgown, then boarded a bus for Manhattan.

The 302s and Justice Department memorandums that I've seen are short on details of the Betts and Delmar murders. "KONIGSBERG, when mentioning anything concerning ALFRED BETTS or BARBARA DELMAR, became emotionally upset," an F.B.I. report dated June 3, 1965, reads. "He did offer the information that the reasons BETTS and DELMAR were killed were very flimsy and involved a pornography operation several years ago."

After Stassi turned up in Miami in January 1966, prosecutors managed to put him away for narcotics trafficking but decided not to bother with a case against him or Harold for any of the three killings. Harold's confessions, on their own, were insufficient. "The fact that Konigsberg did lead the Government to the gravesite makes it clear that Konigsberg was somehow involved," reads an internal Justice Department memo about the Kenneth Later murder, noting that corroboration beyond that "is minimal."

"It was a disappointing effort, because the witnesses who might have corroborated his statements were either gone or they didn't remember," Special Agent John Wilgus told me. "We worked on it for a year at least. There comes a time when you have to move on."

I studied the photos that the tabloids had run of the victims when their bodies were discovered. Barbara Delmar had dirty-blond hair and farouche, awkward features. In one shot, she was poolside, ungracefully tugging up the top of her Esther Williams bathing suit. Kenneth Later looked like Hoss Cartwright on *Bonanza*. Against the background of lurid newspaper copy, the pictures of this man and woman who'd got themselves into the sort of trouble they wouldn't live to tell about seemed to point up a bathetic quality in their smiles, as if anyone could have seen, just by looking at these people, the lack of self-control that had led them to their fall. I sensed this disdain also in a Justice Department memo from 1967 that discussed how to proceed with Harold's statements, and ultimately advised against trying to pursue any of these cases in favor of the Castellito disappearance. The latter was a more viable case, the memo explained, in part because the victim had held "a significant union position." I interpreted the memo to mean that these other victims were insignificant—both to the Mob and to the law.

Their loved ones, when I sought out some of them, were surprised to learn that the F.B.I. knew so much about the unprosecuted killings. None had even been told of Harold's confessions.

Kenneth Later was a former theatrical agent who, according to his bio in *Variety*, enjoyed a fat stretch in the forties and fifties ("inked Sophie Tucker to a deal at the old Hurricane"), but had all but given up on showbiz by the time of his disappearance. He made the acquaintance of Joe Stassi, a regular at El Morocco, and the two of them invested together in a casino in Havana. When he vanished, Kenneth Later had been engaged to marry a young divorced mother from Cuba named Daisy Carmenalte. She is now in her sixties, happily married and living in Buenos Aires. I called on her at her son's house in Connecticut, where she had come to visit and play with her grandchildren.

Daisy had a genteel manner and cinnamon-streaked hair. She sat in a wing chair and hugged her knees like an adolescent. She told me, "The day Ken disappear, he said he was going to Aqueduct to see the races. I go over to his apartment. Everything was still there. You know, like, the thing you put all the cosmetics in, and his toothbrush? So I know something happen. I wait, I wait, but nobody calls to tell me anything. Ken always say to me he didn't have any family. I called the superintendent of his building, and he say a lot of things were missing from Ken's apartment.

The lawyers, the friends, they were taking things. I called the lawyer and he say to come by the apartment if I wanted something."

The name Harold Konigsberg was unfamiliar to her, and when I showed her his photo from around the time she might have met him, she said, much to my chagrin, that he looked a bit like me, "only *corpulento*."

Daisy exhibited no strong reaction upon learning the identities of her fiancé's killers, nor to the fact that the messenger of this news was related to one of them. All that mattered to her was the person she'd lost.

I wasn't in any position to apologize on Harold's behalf, but visiting with the survivors of his victims and hearing about the awfulness of what they'd gone through was gratifying for me in a way that went beyond the satisfaction of fact-finding. I felt, symbolically anyway, as if I was acting as the Konigsbergs' goodwill emissary.

"Ken was a gentleman," Daisy said. "He bought me pearls. He took my son and me to beach and carried him over his shoulder. He called me Daisicita. He sang the song, 'Daisy, Daisy, give me your answer, do. Because I'm so crazy, crazy in love for you.' I remember about two months before he died, he was lying on the bed and he say, 'I have the blues.' I had never heard that expression, 'the blues.' But I understood what he meant, because I never seen him sad like that before.

"Four years after he disappear, the F.B.I. knock on my door," Daisy told me. "They said Ken have some not good friends who are in the Mafia, and that's maybe the reason Ken disappear. They ask if I remember what Ken wear from the dentist in his mouth. And did he wear something because he had a hernia. I told them, yes, he wear it all the time, and, yes, the dental plates. The F.B.I. said, 'That's him.' They found him under the chicken shed. Oh my God, oh my God ..."

Barbara Delmar's story struck me as the most plaintive, an irrefragable case of collateral damage. She had come to New York from tiny Nauvoo, Alabama, ten years earlier to seek her fortune as an actress. Before she met her husband, she had dated his cousin, Kenny Delmar, the actor who played Senator Cleghorn on *The Fred Allen Show* in the late forties. (His character inspired the cartoon chicken Foghorn Leghorn.) When that didn't pan out, she'd become "involved," according to the F.B.I., in her husband's "French film" business. (Some people described her as a "showgirl.") She left several immediate survivors, including both parents and a sister back home in Alabama. I phoned a relative of hers who'd grown up with her, introduced myself, and explained that my grand-uncle had claimed responsibility for her murder.

"That was a long time ago," the relative said. She was skeptical of the information I had to offer. "Her parents spent their life savings on a private detective trying to find what happened to her after she disappeared," she said. "They never could find out a single thing. It broke their hearts."

Delmar's parents, Minnie and William, were subsistence farmers who sold vegetables off a wagon. "She came back down here one time after she'd moved away," the relative recalled. "She pulled into the service station on Highway 5 in a fur coat and the man she was with was driving a Cadillac. I thought she just married well. Not many people from Nauvoo leaving and going anywhere, and not many of them come back with a fur coat. She was smiling and laughing, talking a streak. Oh, she was happy."

At one point after Harold's confessions, agents had shown up at the home of Al Betts's widow and children and told her what they had on the killing.

"The F.B.I. said your uncle was the one who did it," Alfred Betts Jr. told me. "Obviously, there was no indictment in the works. They never explained to us why not."

I was at Al Jr.'s house in Cliffside Park, New Jersey. We sat on the rear deck, built on stilts and looking across the Hudson River to the Bronx. One of his sons was lying on a couch inside, watching the Mets game.

"I'm trying to remember, did I tell my kids about this?" Al Jr. said. "I don't know if it ever really came up. I probably told them something like, 'Stay straight and narrow, because my own dad didn't.' I guess he wanted to be a two-bit criminal his whole life."

Al Jr. was three years old when he lost his father. As soon as it happened, his family moved from Long Island to New Jersey, to be near his mother's family. "She was scared that your uncle might come after her, too. My mother didn't even bother to sell the house. As a homeowner, I still don't know how she could just up and leave a house like that. We went on welfare afterward, but I didn't like it. They'd give us these vouchers for lunch, but I wouldn't use them. I got a little too much pride in me. I just wouldn't eat sometimes. No big deal.

"I know about what my father was doing. My mother told me. Pornographic movies—he was selling them. Drugs—I remember when I got older hearing about how he'd gone down to Mexico."

Though he had no warm feelings for his father, Al Jr. wanted to know what had led to his murder. "When I was young, I was a little, you know, revengeful," he said. "I kept notes, but then after a while I made myself stop thinking about it. There was a time when your uncle was in the basement with my father. My mother said he was a pretty scary guy."

I filed another Freedom of Information Act request with the F.B.I.— this one pertaining to Betts's father—and helped him make his own request under separate cover, in case, as a relative, he would receive preferential treatment. Eight months later, each of us received a manila envelope containing newly released material from the F.B.I. Although the file was ninety-six pages long, the only unredacted view it gave of Alfred Betts's life was his arrest record—"for smut (misdemeanor)"—and a list of the 225 reels of films that agents seized from his office, among them, *The Casting Couch, Virgin Bride, The Efficient Maid, Hot Hotel*, AKA "*Detective One Hung Low of the Hotel Cherry*," and *Kutie Kut Ups*, AKA "*Three Lesbians.*"

If what Harold told the F.B.I. about the Betts, Later, and Delmar murders was true, the only other person with firsthand knowledge was his alleged accomplice, Joe Stassi. I figured he was dead—he was some twenty years older than Harold. But before I tried to confirm the assumption, I got a call from a man named Richard Stratton, a convicted drug dealer turned filmmaker, who was shooting a documentary on "an old gangster" he'd met long ago in prison: Joe Stassi. It turned out that Stassi was still alive, among the general population, and ninety-five or ninety-six years old (he had claimed two different birth years, "for Social Security purposes"). The night I telephoned Stassi's house in Florida, his live-in nurse told me that she'd just then decided to relieve herself of her duties and called Stassi's only living brother, Giacomino (a.k.a. Little Jakey), in Arizona. She told him she had booked Stassi a one-way ticket to Tucson and was putting him on a plane in the morning.

When I arrived in Tucson later in the week, Little Jakey's common-law wife, Joanie, informed me that Joe was now an inpatient at the Tucson Heart Hospital. On his second night in Arizona, Joanie said, she'd noticed the edema in his toes, shiny and swollen "like big blue jelly beans." They rushed Joe to the emergency room, where doctors pumped "four pounds of water" out of his legs and expressed astonishment that he was still alive. Somehow, he'd survived a cardiac arrest and was already feeling enough like himself to attack two nurses with scissors as they tried to stop him from cutting his own hair.

The drive to the hospital cut through hills of sagebrush and saguaro cactus. Stassi had been told that I was coming to visit. He sat up in bed when I walked into his room. "Would you mind getting me some orange juice?" he said.

Stassi was tiny, five feet six and weightless. He had neatly combed charcoal hair, a suntan, the beginnings of a mustache (the nurses had given in to him on that), and a huge Tom-and-Jerry-style bandage tied around one of his shins. He was wearing a pajama top and a diaper. And, with my help, he was now holding a Styrofoam cup of juice.

He squeezed the sides to make a spout, puckered long before it was to his face, then drank gingerly, using his left hand to steady his right.

"You know, I used to like a good sandwich," he said. He spoke in a whimper, struggling to push out every word. "Now I've lost my taste for food. I don't know what the hell I'm still here for."

I asked Stassi what he remembered about my granduncle.

"No one knew Kayo as well as I did," he said.

He found a flexi-straw and had another go at his juice.

He said that the last time he'd seen him, Harold had been about to meet with New York City detectives who'd demanded his presence at department headquarters. Though Harold had told Stassi he could talk his way out of whatever trouble he was in, they'd booked him on extortion charges as soon as he arrived.

"I told him don't go," Stassi said.

So why did he?

Stassi shut his eyes, then opened them slowly. "You've seen him," he said. "Oh, Kayo, he thought he was a genius." Stassi belittled Harold and whatever danger he posed in much the same way that my family had. He told me about how, a few days before the arrest, the F.B.I. had come to Harold's office to question him. Harold cursed at the agents and accused them of taking $30,000 from his safe, then got two of his henchmen to sign a false affidavit supporting the allegation. "Kayo was just full of those scams. He wouldn't let nothing get away from him. He was a mug. That means I'm saying he was an embarrassment to all of us."

I told Stassi that I knew the F.B.I. had investigated him and Harold for the murders of Kenneth Later, Barbara Delmar, and Alfred Betts. I told him I knew that Harold had implicated them both. I'd anticipated a showdown and agonized over how to present the question, but Stassi simply inhaled and took my forearm.

"I don't know," he said as loudly as he could. He took another deep breath and let my arm go.

But Harold told the F.B.I. the two of them were involved in the killings, I said, though the statement came out more as a question. I was losing my accusatory gumption, but I tried one more time. "Did you and Harold kill these people?"

"I don't want to talk about that. Kayo's abusing me. He's lying."

I asked if Stassi had ever known Kenneth Later.

"Kenny Later," Stassi said wearily. "He was an acquaintance. He hung out in the Stage Deli."

"So how did he die?"

"How the hell should I know?"

Stassi said he'd long suspected Harold of furnishing information about him to the F.B.I. "There was nothing on me," he said. "If there was any proof, I would have been arrested in one minute. But because of you there's plenty of proof that Kayo's a rat, and you know it and now I know it. Anyone that was half decent would dislike Kayo. He took every advantage of everybody."

He started wheezing, and a nurse who was in the room to take his vitals spun around to ask if he was all right. He drank a cup of water and stared out the window. His room had a view of the Santa Rita Mountains. It was quickly sinking in that I'd been unrealistic in hoping to hear a Mob boss, even on his deathbed (he died seven months later), give himself up on a series of unprosecuted murders. What could I offer in return? Peace of mind? "Closure"?

What Stassi was interested in talking about—like Harold and probably like every elderly gangster assessing life through a rearview mirror—was seeing himself memorialized in a feature film (in addition to the documentary already in the works). "I want to see a picture made, *Joseph Stassi: No Witnesses*," he said. "What I did was what I did. I'm Joe Stassi. The entire time, one of the most important people in New York, there was no witnesses. The story of my life—Joe Stassi!"

"But wasn't Harold a witness?" I said.

"Oh, I don't know," he snapped. "I gave you all the answers I'm gonna give. It's a waste of time."

Stassi's brother Jakey appeared shortly in the corridor with Joanie. Jakey was petite and thumb-shaped, a youthful eighty-five. Joanie walked with a cane and had accessorized herself like a Sedona schoolmarm—ponytail, enormous Lucite eyeglasses, and copper beads. She had said over the phone that Jakey had worked for Joe for much of his life and spent a couple of terms in prison for arms dealing and involvement in a floating abortion clinic. "Jakey was the sweet one—he never should have gone into the business," she said. "He was the one—'Jake, hold the gun while we go inside.' Joe was never any good to Jakey, but he used to help him out financially and Jakey is terrified of him." (From an F.B.I. report on Joe Stassi: "His brother, JAKE, has cost him a considerable amount of money.")

"Don't tell Joe we're here," Jakey whispered. "He'll get agitation."

All day, the two of them had put off breaking the news to Joe that they were committing him to a nursing home. Meanwhile, the old man refused to sign a will. And though he was unlikely ever to be ambulatory again, doctors were saying that he might have bought himself another year or two on earth. "It's the rest of us who may not make it," Joanie said. She said that the next time this happened, she was taking Joe to Tucson Heart Hospital by way of Phoenix.

This, I reasoned, is what Harold would be putting somebody through if our family hadn't written him off. As it is, he can probably look forward to winding down his life in a prison hospital.

Jakey waved a nurse into the room to do his dirty work for him while he remained in the hallway. "You're going to a new home, Joe," the nurse said. "It's a nursing home."

"Tell them to book me on a flight to New York tomorrow," Stassi said.

The nurse had her hair in a chignon and wore a floral lab coat. "Who's going to take care of you?" she said gently.

"Oh, I know thousands of people," he said. "I haven't seen anybody for thirteen, fourteen years, but I could run into somebody. Somebody could always buy me dinner."

"And then where are you going to live, Joe?"

Stassi turned to me. "What sort of place have you got?"

Jakey and Joanie finally came in. "Joe, you got to go to the nursing home so's the doctors can give you the medication you need."

"Jakey, I'm gonna tell you what I told the doctors, which is take their medications and shove them up their ass," Stassi said.

Soon, he and I were alone again. He looked at me quizzically. "What are you thinking?" he said.

I was thinking about how I might extricate myself from the hospital. My parents, as it happened, were also within the environs of Tucson. They had come to Canyon Ranch for my mother's birthday and I had plans to meet up with them for dinner. If I hurried, we could eat in time to go back to their casita and watch the Knicks on TV.

Stassi noticed me staring at his wrist. He had a handsome tank watch from Tiffany. "I've had some of the most beautiful collections of watches," he said, visibly flattered. "I had an Alexander—that's a Russian diamond that's impossible to find. I put it on a ring for myself. When you see one, whoever's got it can ask whatever price they want."

"How did you get one?"

"How did I get one? I put a gun to a guy's head."

I tried to find out what had become of the original investigations of the three killings. But none of the local authorities could locate the records. Captain Ray Ferrari, of the N.Y.P.D.'s cold-case squad, told me, "Files get lost. Files are moved. These cases are what, forty years old? To be honest with you, we got a lot of stuff that's more pressing right now."

As for some of the other homicides on which Harold had given statements to the F.B.I., I got similar responses from police and prosecutors in Jersey City, Hoboken, and Paterson, and in Hudson, Essex, and Passaic counties. Even to me, the particulars of the cases were all sounding the same by now.

In the summer of 2002, when all seemed lost, my request to the Bergen County prosecutor's office generated an excited response. This concerned the murder of John Joseph Scanlon, an Irish gangster who had operated on the west side of Manhattan. On the morning of October 1, 1958, just after Scanlon dropped off four of his five children at their suburban school—John Jr. was home with a rash—his car was run off the road in Bergen County, New Jersey, by a pale-colored Lincoln. At the moment of impact, according to the coroner's report, a man in the back seat of the Lincoln fired the fatal shots to Scanlon's head. Although eight teams of detectives were put to work, the case languished.

In his 1965 interviews with the Bureau, Harold confessed to carrying out the hit, with the assistance of another hoodlum who was with him in the Lincoln. Following up, the F.B.I. located an original eyewitness to the crime, who identified a photograph of Harold's accomplice as the driver of the Lincoln—which would indicate that Harold was the shooter (though in one conversation he told agents that the accomplice—his old colleague Sally Bugs Briguglio—was the shooter). Also, Harold's description of the stolen car and the license plates they'd used matched with those the police had found abandoned near the shooting.

As soon as I explained my curiosity to the Bergen County Attorney's office and faxed over Harold's confession reports, I got a call from a police detective named Robert Anzilotti. "This is probably going to surprise you," he said, "but I went and looked this case up, and it was never closed. And there's absolutely no mention of your uncle, and no mention that the F.B.I. ever contacted us after they got these confessions."

Hoping to resolve the case, the Bergen County prosecutor's office began a reinvestigation in late 2002. A section chief there had recently had success opening and prosecuting two other cold cases. But when Anzilotti asked the F.B.I. to forward more information about the Bureau's findings, he was told that the files couldn't be found.

I arranged to meet Anzilotti and a colleague of his in a coffee shop. "You'll recognize me as a cop right away," he said. Anzilotti, who is in his midthirties, had on a square-shouldered suit. He had a sharply angled beard and was built along the lines of a loving cup. He told me that their office had several ways of pursuing Harold's confessions, but that all would be better served if he were willing to re-admit to the killing today. "We're obviously not looking to use what's in these F.B.I. pages to track down ten peripheral people and make a case," Anzilotti said.

I told Anzilotti that I couldn't imagine Harold willingly absorbing another conviction, and the officers couldn't give him anything that would be meaningful to him, short of letting him out. Even if they offered a concurrent sentence on this, he'd never allow prosecutors to hang another murder on him, or at least not without making their lives miserable first.

In the spring of 2003, Anzilotti sent two detectives to Auburn. I had made him promise that nobody would tell Harold that I was the one responsible for bringing the case to their attention, although part of me wished they would. The question was moot, however, because Harold refused to come out of his cell, yelling profanities at the detectives from down the hall. "He didn't even want to hear why they wanted to talk to him," Anzilotti wrote me in an e-mail. "He did, however, ask for their business cards." The following winter, Detective Anzilotti told me that, while he was considering flying the detectives to Auburn again, "I'm still sort of expecting him to reach out to us."

In early 2004, he said that he still hadn't forgotten about the case but was swamped with other homicide investigations. "We'll have to see how the next year plays out," he said. "I'd like to give it a shot someday, but I've got a lot on my plate at the moment."

In 2005, Anzilotti told me that the Scanlon homicide was "on the back burner for now, but I'm definitely interested in it. Let me know if you hear anything more about it, will you?"

Shortly before Scanlon was killed, he'd moved his family from Hell's Kitchen to a suburb outside the city. I found a phone number for his youngest daughter, who was still living there.

"Oh my God, oh my God. I never had any idea who killed him," she said. In fact, until four or five years ago, she was under the impression that her father had died "in a strange car accident." Her son had been assigned a school project that brought them both to the county library's microfiche collection. She was helping him cull through headlines in the local paper from 1958 when she came across a report of her father's fate, "gunned down in gangland fashion." The Manhattan District Attorney had called Scanlon "the most vicious goon on the waterfront." He had once been charged with opening fire on a Greenwich Village stoop after a girlfriend dumped him, killing a sixty-six-year-old woman and a teenage boy.

"When I saw the newspaper, I was purely disgusted," she said. "My image of my father was always this wonderful man, good father, good husband. My mother talks about a soul mate. I cried all the way home. I told my husband and he said, 'There was always rumors about your dad and I didn't mention it.'"

Scanlon's daughter had never heard of Harold either, and had no interest in learning more about her father's death. "I don't care if the case is ever solved," she said. "It's over, it's in the past, but they should hook him into a chair and electrocute him. I'm sorry. I want to meet the man and spit in his face."

She was, by turns, impassive, sarcastic, grieving, irritable, and above all ambivalent, even about the loss of her father. "Maybe we'd have been worse off if my father had lived with his criminal activities and not been killed," she said. "I think my mother thanks God that they didn't do it at the house. She raised five children with good values. There's been no arrests or troubles with the law."

She wanted to know the "nationality" of the name Konigsberg. I told her.

"He was Jewish in the Mafia?" she said. "How many people did he kill again? I'll tell you, in my religion, he's not going to heaven with that on his record."

Most recently, I was contacted by Jerry Wolkoff, a man with a surname I immediately recognized. The protracted strangulation of Samuel Wolkoff, his father, was one of the murders Harold had boasted of to the F.B.I.

Jerry's ordeal was no less excruciating than that of the other survivors. He was ten years old when he lost his father, in 1958. When his father's sister heard about it on her kitchen radio, she collapsed from a fatal heart attack, and the family ended up holding a joint funeral. "I became a husband and a father and I became a social worker, but I have a hard time getting close to people," Jerry said. "I been cut open. My kids are angry with me. They say I taught them how to take when somebody pays you a compliment never to believe them. Well, how do you relate to people when your upbringing was such that when you were a boy your father was tied up like a pig and killed?"

About ten years ago, Jerry began to look into the case, filing requests "with every law-enforcement office from here to Guam," and hiring a private eye. Through these efforts, he was able to glean that the prime suspect had been Harold Konigsberg—a detective let him know surreptitiously that Harold's name, which he had never heard before, was all over a heavily redacted case file—but that all of the government's investigations had been subsequently left to rot. Eventually, his was, too. "I gave up because after a while none of the authorities would return my messages," Jerry said. "Somebody got killed and nobody cared."

And though Jerry had called me looking for answers and I was able to share some with him in the form of Harold's F.B.I. statements, he still couldn't see the point in holding out any hope for resolution. "It's useless," he said when I visited his house on Long Island. "It's not going to give me back the past forty-seven years with my father."

In his dining room, Jerry took a picture frame from the credenza and thrust it at me. It held a faded photograph of his parents at their wedding. "Look at this," he said. "Samuel Wolkoff was a person. *He lived.*"

SIXTEEN

Peace and Quiet

HAROLD'S LATEST parole hearing was in April 2004, when he was seventy-six. An Auburn correctional officer led him into a sterile conference room, where three commissioners of the state parole board sat waiting.

"Your name, for the record, please?" Commissioner George Johnson asked him.

"Harold Konigsberg, 71A-0224."

"You're making a reappearance before the board, is that correct?"

"This is the fourth time," Harold said, according to a transcript. Every even-numbered year, beginning in 1998, he has come up for, and been denied, conditional release.

The commissioners ran through the heaviest convictions on Harold's record, noting that it dated all the way back to 1946. They asked if he had taken part in any rehabilitative programs, such as Aggression Replacement Training therapy. Harold told them he hadn't. They took out his disci-

plinary record, which listed more than sixty infractions since 1979, including five significant violations: for bribery, for possession of
weapons, for "unauthorized exchange," for harassment, and a Tier III
charge in 2001 for "threats"—to me, of course.

If Harold should obtain a release, Commissioner Johnson asked,
how was he planning to live? He answered that he would draw income
from Social Security. "I been paying since 1972," he said. He reminded
the officers that he'd been locked up forty-one years straight. By now,
he added, he didn't have much hope for parole but was going through
the motions for his children and grandchildren. He showed the members of the parole board a photograph of his departed wife.

"What is your point?" Commissioner Johnson said.

"My point is, I ain't going to live two years," Harold said. "That's
what—"

"Okay, thank you. Commissioners, any further questions?"

Commissioner William Crowe wanted to know one thing. "You sit
before us convicted of a brutal—"

"Say that slow," Harold said. He claimed not to hear well anymore.

"You sit before us convicted of a brutal, vicious, and violent crime.
What is your position with regard to those crimes today?"

"What can I say?"

"Did you commit the crimes?"

"I got convicted twice."

The parole commissioner asked him again. He was giving him the
opportunity to admit his guilt.

"I'm not going to go into that," Harold said. In reference to one of
the others in the room, he added, "He said earlier that I didn't have to."

Parole was denied and a new hearing set for 2006.

●　　　●　　　●

Just recently, I saw the report the witnessing guards had written up on the day Harold threatened me. One thing they heard him say—"I broke his neck and I'll break yours"—I don't even remember.

I believe Harold meant business that day. Most of our family still turns a blind eye to Harold's record, but my grandmother's response was so swift and forceful as to suggest that perhaps she knew full well what he could do. She put out the fire, all the while dismissing the incident as mere nuisance and using it as an occasion to reprimand Harold and me both for mutual encroachment.

Shortly after Harold vowed to kill me, he sent my grandmother a note, accompanied by a copy of the complaint I'd filed immediately at the prison (which Auburn officials had sworn they would keep in confidence). He wrote that to bring such shame as I had on his beloved father's family rendered me somebody who "isn't even a person." I can't say more about his letter, because to this day my grandmother refuses to show it to me. Whenever I ask, she says she can't remember where she put it, and recalls instead the "beautiful" condolence note he sent her after my aunt died, and how he used to cheat at cards when he was nine years old.

"When he wrote that letter about you, he was mad at me," my grandmother said recently. We were out at my parents' ranch in Montana where she was finally visiting us, seven years after they'd bought the land. The stuffed heads of an elk and a buffalo stared down at the kitchen island. "He thought I approved of what you're doing."

"He said he was going to kill me."

"Well, he doesn't like you," she said. "If somebody wrote a life story about me, how would it be if they just picked out the bad things?"

"Mother!" my dad cut in. "He's a *murderer*."

I was heartened that at least some information had been processed.

"Really?" she said. "Come on, how can they say he killed someone if nobody ever found the body?"

She related a tale from her childhood, about the time a teacher had mistakenly declared her the winner of a school-yard footrace, although she had seen a little black girl's leg cross the finish line ahead of hers. "And I lied and accepted the prize," she said. "But that's not the best thing I did. So now I would want somebody telling that story about me?"

If I hadn't been so frightened that last day at Auburn, it might have been possible to feel a sort of sympathy for Harold. He was alone and bereft, unable to exert control over even his brother's grandson.

"My dear nephew, I been betrayed by everybody," he had said one afternoon during one of my first visits to Auburn. He shuffled into the visitors' room, combing back the wings of his hair. Beside us, another inmate and his female visitor were laying out a plastic chess set. "I'll tell you something. Since I been incarcerated, none of my family ..." He had to think of how he wanted to put it. "Have any of them ever visited me? How many of my family ever write me a letter? How many ever asked my wife how I was doing?"

A minute or so earlier, I'd asked whether he ever thought about how he ended up the way he did. I imagined he hadn't heard me, because he got up and announced that he was taking a piss. He told me to get him two Dr Peppers and two bagels.

Sitting back down at our table now, he said, "I came from good people—everybody honest. Nobody else in the family did what I did. Let me ask you, does your father work hard? Did your grandfather work hard? So, I don't know where I came from."

The guards were rounding up everybody; visiting hours were almost over. I asked Harold if he wanted me to come back the next day.

"Well, I could use another bagel," he said. He peered at me and chuckled.

He wanted to know whether I'd had a bar mitzvah or knew any Yiddish. He said it was too bad that none of his siblings or their children were observant any longer. "The Bible I have here was given to me by my

Uncle Ernest, on my mother's side," he said. "I say the *shema* every morning and every night. I wish all my loved ones and those I care about to remain healthy and don't ask for nothing for myself. You know that my parents worked every day of their lives until four-thirty on Friday, and then nothing until sundown on Saturday?"

He took a long pull of his soda. He started crying.

"Good God, my parents," he said, "I let them down in every way."

For a moment, I thought he was actually acknowledging the shame he had brought his family. I put my hand on his, but he recoiled and groaned. "Aw, you're like a salesman now," he said. "I separated myself a hundred different ways from my family. What are you expecting to understand?"

In the Konigsberg family's view of itself, there was no place for Harold. My relatives pretended not to have any emotional stake in him, and now it is not so hard for me to see the wisdom of their defensive formations. Especially my grandfather, who in keeping his head down and doing what his wife expected of him was nothing more than average, and nothing less than heroic. I explored Harold's life story because I wanted to hold the truth in my hands. But perhaps my grandfather already had.

I have looked at him for as long as I could, from a hundred different perspectives, and from every point the answer is the same. There were no wrongs done to him or by him that I could right. That my grandparents emerged from the crucible with no more damages than a tendency toward excessive rosiness and a gritted-teeth sense of entitlement impresses me all the more. They willed themselves along and all of us are lucky for that.

•　　　•　　　•

My grandfather is buried at King Solomon Cemetery in Clifton, New Jersey, on a well-maintained site shaded by red oak trees. My grandmother visits his grave often. A few years ago, she and Aunt Ruthie drove out together, sitting for a while on the marble bench Frieda had installed on an adjacent plot and marking their presence by setting small rocks on Leo's headstone. On the way home, conversation turned to their own eventual places of rest.

My grandmother informed her sister-in-law that before his death, she and Grandpa Leo, always with one eye on the future, had purchased eight plots at the cemetery, in case other relatives wanted to be near them. Aunt Ruthie, however, planned to be buried with her parents and her late husband, at an older cemetery in Staten Island. As they ticked off the names in the family, they realized that though Leo and Frieda still had several extra places, all the others had already secured their own. All of them, that was, but Harold.

"How would you like to have Heshy buried in one of your plots?" Aunt Ruthie said. My grandmother swatted the air dismissively.

"I want to lie in peace and quiet," she said.

Source Notes and Acknowledgments

I N RESEARCHING THIS BOOK, I conducted more than one hundred interviews and read in excess of 20,000 pages of court testimony. I also made use of thousands of pages of government documents—confidential F.B.I. surveillance reports and interview reports, correspondence among officials in the U.S. Department of Justice, police and detectives' records, and legal motions. In addition, I benefited from the several hundred news accounts pertaining to Harold and various cases in which he was involved.

In places where I have quoted conversations between people, the words come directly from one or more of the following (a) transcripts of courtroom sessions or wiretappings; (b) documents compiled by the government or motions introduced in court; (c) recollections recounted to me by a participant in the conversation I describe; or in a few instances, (d) from newspaper accounts published at the time.

For their help, I am indebted to the following: Laurie Staiger and the staff of the Ulster County District Attorney's office; the Bayonne Police Department; Guy Gregory in the Hudson County Prosecutor's Office;

Sgt. John Becker of the Kearny, New Jersey, Police Department; Lt. Kevin Smith and Det. Patrick Bellotti of the Nassau County Police Department; James Santulli in the Bergen County Prosecutor's Office; Kenneth Cobb and the New York Municpal Archives; David Boddiger and the New York City Department of Records; Crystal Wardlaw and the U.S. District Court archives in Philadelphia; Anne Crowell and Robyn Bennett at the New York State Division of Parole; John Celardo and the National Archives and Records Administration.

I am grateful for the reporting done by the *Kingston* (New York) *Freeman* (the work of Lynn Mulvaney and Matt Spireng in particular), the Middletown *Times-Herald-Record* (Peter C. Kutschera and Jeff Muise in particular), the *New York Times* (Jack Roth and Sidney Zion in particular), the New York *Daily News* (Maggie Bartel and Henry Lee in particular), the *New York Post* (Joseph Fleurey in particular), the New York *Herald-Tribune*, the *New York Journal-American*, *New York Newsday*, the Nyack (New York) *Journal-News*, the *Jersey Journal*, the *Hudson Dispatch*, the Bayonne *Times*, the Bergen County *Record*, the *Newark Star-Ledger*, the *Philadelphia Inquirer*, the Philadelphia *Daily News*, and the Springfield (Missouri) *News-Leader*, among others. Thanks also to the staffs of the Jersey City Public Library, the New York Public Library, and the Bayonne Public Library.

Special thanks to Anthony Castellito Jr. and Dorothy Castellito, the Hon. Michael Kavanagh, Jerry Wolkoff, Alfred Betts Jr., Daisy Carmenalte, Frieda Konigsberg, Rochelle Henriques, Ruth Eckhaus, Beattie Herskovitz, Harold Konigsberg (son of Zelig Konigsberg), Ruthie Greenfield, Marlene Altschuler, Faygie Grossman, Faye Berlin, Ivan Fisher, Frank Lopez, Ray Brown, Joshua Koplowitz, Walter Byer, Arnold Stone, Joe Coffey, Dave Satz, William Aronwald, Edwin Stier, Albert Sproul, John Markey, Jack Bonami, Bill Bonanno, Michael Hardy, Joe Jaffe, Don Horowitz, John Connors, Kenneth Hackmann,

John Wilgus, Hoyt Peavy, Leonard Newman, the Hon. Allan Broomer, Murray Gross, Bob Nicholson, Eddie Wright, William Lynch, Shane Creamer, Sybil Landau, Ramsey Clark, Ronald Goldfarb, Marvin Newberg, Don Williams, Holley Carnright, Robert Scheinman, Det. Robert Anzilotti, Capt. Ray Ferrari, Andy Rosenzweig, Frankie Polera, Don Hockstein, Det. Teddy Stein, Al Stein, Milton Polevoy, Hy Rappoport, Sandy Haft, Anthony Cortellessa, Florence Shapiro Winnick, Bernie Rosenberg, Rep. Neil Gallagher, Rep. Barney Frank, Steve Roberts, Edward L. Wolf, Dr. Reid Meloy, Dr. Jonathan Pincus, Dr. Michael Weissberg, Dr. Glen Gabbard, Leon Wieseltier, Alex Star, Jenna Weisman Joselit, Joshua Michael Zeitz, Michael Aaron Rockland, Edward S. Shapiro, Helene Stapinski, Albert Fried, Deborah Dash Moore, Robert Silverman, Sidney Zion, Peter Maas, Denny Walsh, Russell Sackett, Anthony Summers, Becky Hayutin, Alan Zavod, Kenneth Delmar, Berta Townsend, Eleanore Barbito, Ivan Fail, Leonard Melnick, Earl Humphreys, Richie Roberts, Sari Leon, Michael Steinhardt, Richard Stratton, Joan Brundage, Giacomino Stassi, Blair Zwillman, Richard Boiardo, Catherine D'Unger, Bob Whisnant, and other sources quoted in the book.

Thanks to Ed Klaris, Michael Reynolds, Jim Lesar, and Julie Hilden for their wise counsel, and to Toma Ovici and Paul Feinberg for their thoughtfulness. To Boris Bencic for the book jacket inspiration. To Gillian Linden, Anne Stringfield, Austin Kelly, and most extensively Sasha Smith for valuable research assistance.

Thanks to Henry Finder, David Remnick, Mary Norris, David Hirshey, the excellent Nick Trautwein, Sloan Harris, Katharine Cluverius, and Shauna Lyon—the ace up my sleeve—for their editorial judgment and support. Thanks to Maisie Kirn for the many hours of beseating she put into this project. Thanks also to Yaddo, the Freedom Forum, the Writers Room, Big Timber Ranch, 113 East Callendar Street, Casa

Nica, and the Sackett household for providing me with space to work.

Special thanks to Beau Konigsberg, Sarah Boos Konigsberg, Kate Boo, Bill Finnegan, Mike Crowley, Tara Smith, Leo Kropywiansky, Lis Harris, Nick Paumgarten, Josh Shenk, John Bowe, Michael Agger, Nathaniel Wice, Bliss Broyard, and Anne Landsman, each of whom read parts or all of the manuscript, and whose effort, friendship, and love improved it immensely.

Special thanks to my wife, Ruth Davis Konigsberg, who also happens to be the best editor in town and who has truly been my collaborator on every page of this book.

For the unending, unconditional, unequaled love that my parents, Marilyn and Harvey Konigsberg, have given me, the extent of my gratitude cannot be fully expressed in words.

Bibliography

Anonymous. *Bayonne Centennial Historical Revue*. Bayonne, N.J.: 1961 (Collection of Bayonne Public Library).

———. "Jewish Prisoners in Penal Institutions of the State of New York." Files of The American Jewish Committee, Statistical Department. January 2, 1930 (Center for Jewish History, American Jewish Historical Society archive).

Ard, Patricia M., and Michael Aaron Rockland. *The Jews of New Jersey: A Pictorial History*. New Brunswick: Rutgers University Press, 2002.

Ardrey, Richard. *The Territorial Imperative*. New York: Atheneum, 1966.

Astor, Mary. *The Incredible Charlie Carewe*. New York: Dell Publishing Co., 1960.

Bingham, Theodore A. "Foreign Criminals in New York." *North American Review*, September 1908.

Birmingham, Stephen. *"Our Crowd": The Great Jewish Families of New York*. New York: Harper & Row, 1967.

Breines, Paul. *Tough Jews: Politics, Fantasies, and the Moral Dilemma of American Jewry*. New York: Basic Books, 1990.

Brill, Steven. *The Teamsters*. New York: Simon & Schuster, 1978.

Cahan, Abraham. *The Rise of David Levinsky*. New York: Harper & Brothers, 1917.

Carey, Benedict. "For the Worst of Us, the Diagnosis May Be 'Evil.'" *New York Times*, February 8, 2005.

Caspi, Avshalom, et. al. "Role of Genotype in the Cycle of Violence in Maltreated Children." *Science*, August 2, 2002.

Clark, Ramsey. *Crime in America*. New York: Simon & Schuster, 1970.

Cleckley, Hervey, M.D. *The Mask of Sanity*. 5th ed. Augusta, Ga.: Emily S. Cleckley, 1988.

Clemenceau, Georges. *At the Foot of Sinai*. New York: Bernard G. Richards Company, 1922.

Coffey, Joseph J., and Jerry Schmetterer. *The Coffey Files: One Cop's War Against the Mob*. New York: St. Martin's Press, 1992.

Criminal Law Reporter staff. *The Criminal Law Revolution and Its Aftermath 1960–1972*. Washington, D.C.: Bureau of National Affairs, 1973.

DeLoach, Cartha D. *Hoover's F.B.I.: The Inside Story by Hoover's Trusted Lieutenant*. Washington, D.C.: Regnery Publishing, 1995.

DePalma, Anthony. "Exodus." *New Jersey Monthly*, September 1985.

Diagnostic and Statistical Manual of Mental Disorders: DSM-IV. Washington, D.C.: American Psychiatric Association, 1994.

Espenshade, Thomas J., ed. *A Stone's Throw from Ellis Island: Economic Implications of Immigration to New Jersey*. Lanham, Md.: University Press of America, 1994.

Farmer, Frank. "The Medical Center: A Look Past the Gates." Springfield *News-Leader*, December 10, 1972.

Fleming, Thomas. "There Is No Mafia in Jersey City." *Scanlan's Monthly*, April 1970.

Fried, Albert. *The Rise and Fall of the Jewish Gangster in America*. Rev. ed. New York: Columbia University Press, 1993.

Fried, Joseph P. "Following Up: Fourteen Years After Slaying, Theories, Not Answers." *New York Times*, July 29, 2001.

Gabbard, Glen O., M.D. *The Psychology of "The Sopranos."* New York: Basic Books, 2002.

Gallagher, Robert S., and Ronald Semple. "The Life and Times of Tony Pro." *The Reporter*, September 12, 1963.

Gamm, Gerald. *Urban Exodus: Why the Jews Left Boston and the Catholics Stayed*. Cambridge: Harvard University Press, 1999.

Gage, Nicholas. *The Mafia Is Not an Equal Opportunity Employer*. New York: McGraw-Hill, 1971.

————, ed. *Mafia, U.S.A*. New York: The Playboy Press, 1972.

Gilman, Sander L. *Smart Jews: The Construction of the Image of Jewish Superior Intelligence*. Lincoln: University of Nebraska Press, 1996.

Glazer, Nathan. "Why Jews Stay Sober." *Commentary*, February 1952.

Goldfarb, Ronald. *Perfect Villains, Imperfect Heroes: Robert F. Kennedy's War Against Organized Crime*. New York: Random House, 1995.

Gordon, Albert I. *Jews in Suburbia*. Boston: Beacon Press, 1959.

Guthman, Edwin O., and Jeffrey Shulman, eds. *Robert Kennedy in His Own Words:*

The Unpublished Recollections of the Kennedy Years. New York: Bantam Books, 1988.

Hare, Robert D., PhD. *Without Conscience: The Disturbing World of Psychopaths Among Us*. New York: Guilford Publications, 1993.

————, David J. Cooke, and Stephen D. Hart. "Psychopathic and Sadistic Personality Disorder." in *The Oxford Textbook of Psychopathology*, edited by Theodore Millon, Paul H. Blarney, and Roger D. Davis. Oxford: Oxford University Press, 1999.

Helmreich, William B. *The Enduring Community: The Jews of Newark and Metrowest*. New Brunswick, N.J.: Transaction Publishers, 1999.

Hoffman, William, and Lake Headley. *Contract Killer*. New York: Thunder's Mouth Press, 1992.

Howe, Irving. *World of Our Fathers: The Journey of the East European Jews to America and the Life They Found and Made*. New York: Pantheon Books, 1976.

Jackson, Kenneth T., ed. *The Encyclopedia of New York City*. New Haven: Yale University Press, 1995.

Joselit, Jenna Weissman. *Our Gang: Jewish Crime and the New York Jewish Community, 1900–1940*. Bloomington: Indiana University Press, 1983.

Kefauver, Estes. *Crime in America*. Garden City, N.Y.: Doubleday & Company, 1951.

Kennedy, Robert F. *The Enemy Within*. New York: Popular Library, 1960.

Kocieniewski, David. "Decline and Fall of an Empire." *New York Times*, January 17, 1999.

Kwitney, Jonathan. *Vicious Circles: The Mafia in the Marketplace*. New York: W. W. Norton & Company, 1979.

Levine, Hillel, and Lawrence Harmon. *The Death of an American Jewish Community: A Tragedy of Good Intentions*. New York: The Free Press, 1992.

Linfield, H.S. Correspondence, as Director of Jewish Statistical Bureau, with Cyrus Adler, 1934 (Center for Jewish History, American Jewish Historical Society archive).

Maas, Peter. *Made in America*. New York: The Viking Press, 1979.

————. *The Valachi Papers*. New York: G. P. Putnam's Sons, 1968.

Maclean, Don. *Pictorial History of the Mafia*. New York: Galahad Books, 1974.

March, William. *The Bad Seed*. New York: Holt, Rinehart & Winston, 1954.

Maurer, David W. *The Big Con: The Story of the Confidence Man*. Indianapolis: Bobbs-Merrill, 1940.

Meloy, J. Reid. *The Psychopathic Mind: Origins, Dynamics, and Treatment*. Northvale, N.J.: Jason Aronson, 2002.

————. *Violence Risk and Threat Assessment: A Practical Guide for Mental Health and Criminal Justice Professionals*. San Diego: Special Training Services, 2000.

Melville, Herman. *The Confidence-Man.* New York: Dix & Edwards, 1857.

Moldea, Dan E. *The Hoffa Wars: Teamsters, Rebels, Politicians, and the Mob.* New York: Paddington Press, 1978.

Moore, Deborah Dash. *At Home in America: Second Generation New York Jews.* New York: Columbia University Press, 1981.

Moore, William Howard. *The Kefauver Committee and the Politics of Crime 1950–1952.* Columbia: University of Missouri Press, 1974.

Moscow, Warren. *The Last of the Big-Time Bosses: The Life and Times of Carmine DeSapio and the Decline and Fall of Tammany Hall.* New York: Stein and Day, 1971.

Nelli, Humbert S. *The Business of Crime: Italians and Syndicate Crime in the United States.* Chicago: University of Chicago Press, 1976.

Nesbit, Frederick, M.D. *Sweet Auburn: Recollections of a Prison Psychiatrist.* Atlantic Beach, N.C.: Frederick Nesbit, 1999.

Pincus, Jonathan H., M.D. *Base Instincts: What Makes Killers Kill.* New York: W. W. Norton & Company, 2001.

Plate, Thomas. *Crime Pays!* New York: Simon & Schuster, 1975.

President's Commission on Organized Crime, Hon. Irving R. Kaufman, chair. *Report to the President and the Attorney General.* Washington, D.C.: 1986.

Radin, Adolph M. *Work Among Jewish Prisoners: First Monthly Report to the Jewish Ministers' Association of New York.* New York: Press of Philip Cowen, 1891.

Riis, Jacob. *How the Other Half Lives.* New York: Charles Scribner's Sons, 1890.

Roberts, Steven V. "Old Fashioned at 27." *The New York Times Magazine,* December 6, 1970.

Rockaway, Robert A. *But—He Was Good to His Mother: The Lives and Crimes of Jewish Criminals.* Jerusalem: Gefen Publishing House, 1993.

Roth, Philip. *American Pastoral.* New York: Houghton Mifflin, 1997.

———. *The Counterlife.* New York: Farrar, Straus and Giroux, 1986.

———. *The Facts: A Novelist's Autobiography.* New York: Farrar, Straus and Giroux, 1988.

———. *Goodbye, Columbus.* New York: Houghton-Mifflin, 1959.

Sabsovich, Katharine. *Adventures in Idealism: A Personal Record of the Life of Professor Sabsovich.* New York: privately printed for the author, 1922.

Schnitzer, Henry R. *As They Were: Bayonne and Jersey City.* New York: Vantage Press, 1973.

———. *Thy Goodly Tent: The Past Fifty Years at Temple Emanu-el, Bayonne, N.J.* Bayonne: Temple Emanu-El, 1961.

Schwartz, Joel, and Daniel Prosser, eds. *Cities of the Garden State: Essays in the Urban and Suburban History of New Jersey.* Dubuque, Iowa: Kendall/Hunt Publishing Company, 1977.

Shapiro, Edward S. "The Jews of New Jersey." In *The New Jersey Ethnic Experience*, edited by Barbara Cunningham. Union City, N.J.: Wm. H. Wise & Co., 1976.

Shaw, Douglas V. *Immigration and Ethnicity in New Jersey History.* Trenton: New Jersey Historical Commission, Department of State, 1994.

Sheed, Wilfrid. *Three Mobs: Labor, Church, and Mafia.* New York: Sheed and Ward, 1974.

Shengold, Leonard, M.D. *Soul Murder: The Effects of Childhood Abuse and Deprivation.* New York: Ballantine Books, 1989.

Shpall, Leo, ed. "Korolenko's Letters on the Woodbine Colony." *Proceedings of the New Jersey Historical Society: A Magazine of New Jersey History,* April 1965.

Silverman, Robert A. "Criminality Among Jews, an Overview." *Issues in Criminality,* Summer 1971.

Sklare, Marshall, ed. *The Jews: Social Patterns of an American Group.* New York: The Free Press, 1958.

————, and Joseph Greenblum. *Jewish Identity on the Suburban Frontier.* Chicago: University of Chicago Press, 1967.

Smith, Sandy. "The Congressman and the Hoodlum." *Life,* August 9, 1968.

Stapinski, Helene. *Five-Finger Discount: A Crooked Family History.* New York: Random House, 2001.

Stuart, Mark A. *Gangster #2: Longy Zwillman, the Man Who Invented Organized Crime.* Secaucus, N.J.: Lyle Stuart, 1985.

Steinberg, Alfred. *The Bosses.* New York: The Macmillan Company, 1972.

Stratton, Richard. "The Man Who Killed Dutch Schultz." *GQ,* September 2001.

Summers, Anthony. *Official and Confidential: The Secret Life of J. Edgar Hoover.* New York: G. P. Putnam's Sons, 1993.

Talese, Gay. *Honor Thy Father.* New York: World Publishing, 1971.

Trilling, Lionel. *The Moral Obligation to Be Intelligent: Selected Essays.* New York: Farrar, Straus and Giroux, 2000.

Turkus, Burton B., and Sid Feder. *Murder, Inc.: The Story of "the Syndicate."* New York: Farrar, Straus and Young, 1951.

Villano, Anthony, with Gerald Astor. *Brick Agent.* New York: Ballantine Books, 1977.

Von Hoffman, Nicholas. *Citizen Cohn.* Garden City, N.Y.: Doubleday, 1988.

Walsh, Denny. "The Gorilla Cowed His Keepers." *Life,* January 25, 1971.

Weissberg, Michael, M.D. *The First Sin of Ross Michael Carlson: A Psychiatrist's Personal Account of Murder, Multiple Personality Disorder, and Modern Justice.* New York: Delacorte Press, 1992.

Werb, Morris R. *Jewish Suburbia: A Historical and Comparative Study of Jewish Communities in Three New Jersey Suburbs.* Unpublished Ph.D. dissertation, New York University, 1959.

Whitcomb, Royden Page. *History of Bayonne, New Jersey.* Bayonne: R. P. Whitcomb, 1904.

Zeitz, Joshua Michael. *"White Ethnic" New York: Religion, Ethnicity, and Political Culture, 1945–1970.* Manuscript in preparation.

Zion, Sidney. "Bar Tales." In *Read All About It! The Collected Adventures of a Maverick Reporter.* New York: Summit Books, 1982.

———. "Aspects of a Modern Hero." *Harper's,* August 1974.